Pelican Books
Fact and Fiction in Psychology

Dr H. J. Eysenck, who was born in 1916, obtained his
Ph.D and D.Sc. degrees in psychology at London
University after school and university experience in
Germany, France, and England. Having worked as a
psychologist at the war-time Mill Hill Emergency
Hospital, he was appointed Professor of Psychology in
the University of London, and Director of the
Psychological Department at the Institute of
Psychiatry (Maudsley and Bethlem Royal Hospitals).
He has lectured in many countries, and been Visiting
Professor at the Universities of Pennsylvania and of
California. Known mainly through his experimental
researches in the field of personality, he has written
some three hundred articles in technical journals, as
well as several books including *Dimensions of Personality*,
The Scientific Study of Personality, *The Psychology of
Politics*, *The Dynamics of Anxiety and Hysteria*, *Uses and
Abuses of Psychology*, *Sense and Nonsense in Psychology*,
Know Your Own I.Q., and *Check Your Own I.Q.* Among
his more recent publications are *The Biological Basis of
Personality* and *Description and Measurement of Personality*.
He has edited a *Handbook of Abnormal Psychology*,
two volumes of *Experiments in Personality*, *Experiments
with Drugs*, and *Behaviour Therapy and the Neuroses*. He is
Editor-in-Chief of the journal *Behaviour Research and
Therapy*. He advocates the highest degree of scientific
rigour in the design of psychological experiments and
is very critical of much loose thinking current at
present under the guise of 'psychology'.

H. J. Eysenck

Fact and Fiction in Psychology

Penguin Books

Penguin Books Ltd, Harmondsworth,
Middlesex, England
Penguin Books Inc., 7110 Ambassador Road,
Baltimore, Maryland 21207, U.S.A.
Penguin Books Australia Ltd, Ringwood,
Victoria, Australia

First published 1965
Reprinted 1966, 1968, 1970, 1972
Copyright © H. J. Eysenck, 1965

Made and printed in Great Britain by
C. Nicholls & Company Ltd
Set in Monotype Baskerville

Contents

RP 17-29
52-94
chp 1

Theories are not true or false;
they are fertile or sterile.
CLAUDE BERNARD

Editorial Foreword

The author of this book has written an Introduction as good as any Editorial Foreword could hope to be. A point or two may perhaps be added by way of guidance to the naïve, but more especially the suspicious reader. All writers on Psychology are exposed to suspicion (on grounds themselves of psychological interest) but Professor Eysenck is under special suspicion as a 'controversial figure' in contemporary psychology – a description he accepts not without a measure of satisfaction. On this he has things to say himself in his Introduction. His writings are of course 'controversial' in that he writes with skill and gusto on controversial subjects. There is, however, nothing controversial in the fundamental thesis that runs through all his writings. This is the thesis (paradoxical perhaps) that controversial issues can be taken out of controversy by being made subjects of strict scientific inquiry, or – to put it otherwise – *any explanatory theory must be supported by scientific evidence*. This, so far from being controversial, is accepted by all scientific psychologists, even by many who differ from him in some of his detailed applications of the principle.

This is the third volume in a distinguished trilogy. *Uses and Abuses of Psychology* was published in 1953. *Sense and Nonsense in Psychology* followed in 1957. Now comes *Fact and Fiction in Psychology*. The author would prefer that these books were read in the order of their publication, but agrees that each is self-contained. Indeed Chapter 1 of this volume, on a 'Visit to a Psychological Laboratory', could have been an introduction to the whole series. Time was, and perhaps still is, when many people, including many otherwise well-informed people, found the idea of a psychological laboratory quite surprising. After reading this chapter there should be no ground for such perplexity. The point is not that psychologists use instruments. More important is the fact that psychologists use scientific method and that instruments are often aids in research. Psychology, in short, is today one of the natural sciences. The impression that psychologists in general and Professor Eysenck in particular are controversial writers arises from the rapid extension of scientific methods to the study of controversial subjects.

Those who read this trilogy in the order of publication will gain much insight into the ways in which the scientific approach to disputations which have arisen has been extended in the middle years of this century. The case for intelligence tests discussed in *Uses and Abuses* is now almost past history. Interest in opinion polls has been boiling up through the decade covered by the Trilogy. So, too, has interest in the Borderlands of Knowledge explored in *Sense and Nonsense*. *Fact and Fiction* extends further the application of the principles of the scientific approach to controversial issues in the theory of personality and the practice of therapy for personality disorders.

Those who read the three volumes of this trilogy in reverse may recall that Bernard Shaw published his three novels in the reverse order of writing, and that he records that he enjoyed his reviewers' comments on the 'development of his style'. Those who read Professor Eysenck's three 'entertainments' in reverse may miss the subtler features in the development of his style but they will appreciate both the range of his erudition and the consistent integrity of his approach to current problems in psychology.

C. A. Mace

Introduction

This is the third of these 'entertainments', to borrow a term from Graham Greene to describe this trilogy of popularizations of modern psychology. Like *Uses and Abuses of Psychology* and *Sense and Nonsense in Psychology*, the present book may be read on its own, but the reader may find that reading them in sequence will give him a better understanding of the subjects discussed here. What I have dealt with in the present book are mainly topics relating to personality, its nature and measurement, and also to the way in which personality is implicated in neuroses, in accidents, in criminal behaviour, and in other social interactions. I have tried to simplify what is, in essence, a very complex and difficult topic, and no doubt to some I will seem to have oversimplified. I have tried occasionally to insert a warning, when I felt I could not do justice to a topic for lack of space, but to some degree, of course, it is inevitable that in a book of this kind many important points should be left out which the writer would have liked to have included. More detailed treatments will be found in the books mentioned at the end of this volume, under the heading 'Suggested Readings'.

The two predecessors of this book have often been called 'controversial', and indeed the writer has become so used to this term that he feels almost a sense of deprivation when the chairman at a meeting, in introducing him, forgets to use this descriptive term. However, the word 'controversial' has two meanings, and it is important to discriminate between them. You may say that an issue is controversial because people are in fact arguing about it, and are having a controversy. In this sense, the flatness or rotundity of the earth is controversial; there are still flat-earthers who believe that all the demonstrations of the last three hundred years are quite false and that they have right on their side.

From their point of view, therefore, we might say that the shape of the earth is still a controversial matter. However, from the scientific point of view, I do not think one would agree that this is so; all those people who are qualified to judge are agreed that in fact the earth has a certain shape and it is not flat. From the scientific point of view, there is no controversy on this point, and, therefore, it is not 'controversial' any longer.

To say this is not to say that some of the points made in this book are not in fact controversial. The stress which I have laid on personality, for instance, is one which to many experimental psychologists may seem quite exaggerated. They often feel that psychology, like other sciences, essentially traces the functional dependence of one variable on another and that this can be done without postulating notions such as those of personality, temperament, and so forth. I believe that this simple analogue of psychology to the physical sciences is quite mistaken. In so far as one individual differs from another his individuality must come into the equation and upset the simple, routine reliance on functional relations. Individuals do differ, partly by heredity, partly by upbringing, and it seems to me that psychology will never advance very far without a recognition of the complexities which are produced by this fact of personality. I am unrepentant therefore, but at the same time conscious of the fact that some psychologists whose work I admire and whose opinions I feel must be considered very seriously, nevertheless disagree with me on this point, and so far, then, it may justly be said that the opinions voiced in this book are indeed controversial.

Probably equally controversial is the view which pervades the pages of this book, namely that personality can be studied scientifically by means of laboratory experiments. Human beings are much too complex, many critics say, to make possible any investigation along these lines, and any attempt to do so is doomed to failure. This may, of course, be true; only the attempt will show whether it is in fact feasible or not. I see no reason to depart, in these investigations, from the well-proven methods of science; as Clark

Maxwell put it so well, 'In the study of any complex object, we must fix our attention on those elements of it which we are able to observe and to cause to vary, and ignore those which we can neither observe nor cause to vary.' Again, I may be wrong in believing that this advice is as valuable in psychology as it is in physics, but the evidence to date suggests that we can go a long way towards our aim by following Maxwell's advice.

I have been controversial in one more way. The popularizer in science usually plays it safe and deals only with those phenomena and theories which are very widely accepted and fully documented. I have gone beyond this and have tried to suggest to the reader the possibilities which are inherent in a scientific psychology. In doing so, I have, of necessity, speculated rather freely, and have gone well beyond facts ascertained by careful and patient research. As far as possible, I have always tried to make clear what the facts are and where imagination has taken over. The reader may feel that I have gone too far in this direction and that I would have done better had I stuck closely to the facts. However, as T. H. Huxley put it, 'Those who refuse to go beyond fact seldom get as far as fact,' and I have made a particular point of trying to show the reader why certain facts are important and why laboratory investigations of certain types are being carried out. This cannot be done without giving them a wider setting than that of the laboratory itself.

These, then, are the points on which this book is controversial, and the reader has been warned. I shall consider it a success if it makes the reader think, not if it simply makes him agree with me. Bertrand Russell has said: 'It is the fate of rebels to found new orthodoxies'; it is not my ambition to do anything of the kind.

The main point of this book, however, will hardly be a controversial one, as it simply seeks to illustrate the obvious. For the past three hundred years we have succeeded whenever we have tried to apply scientific method to our problems, and we have failed when we have not done so. Most of these problems have been part of the physical and chemical sciences, but what is true there is also likely to be true of problems in the social sciences. Yet even where physics is concerned few people in administrative positions, or in the political field, have any realization of how all-pervading the influence of scientific method and the sovereignty of scientific law can be.

Consider Boyle's Law and the uniforms of B.O.A.C. air hostesses. These are tailored to fit like a glove on the ground, but, alas, the administrators had not remembered Boyle's Law according to which the volume and pressure of a gas vary inversely. Now in spite of the apparent lack of gallantry involved, an air hostess's tummy is simply a gas-filled container, and the lower cabin pressure, at 5,000 feet say, leads to a 20 per cent increase in volume of these containers, thus interfering drastically with the fit and convenience of the beautiful new uniforms. Thus does physics hold sway even in fields where one would least have expected it, and much expense and discomfort could have been saved had its laws been taken into account from the beginning.

Anyone suggesting the application of scientific laws and methods to the social field is immediately told that surely psychology does not possess any generalizations or laws sufficiently well founded to serve as a basis for action. Where, it is often asked rhetorically, is anything comparable to Boyle's Law in psychology? Strictly speaking one might, of course, proceed to fill the page with references to such things as the Bunsen-Roscoe Law, or Kapper's Law, or Korte's Law, or Marbe's Law, or any of the large number of well-known generalizations which, without detailed explanation, would unfortunately not mean very much to the questioner.

But at a less exalted level the best answer is probably to show in some detail how the generalizations of modern psychology can be and are being applied to problems of modern life. It is my hope that the reader of this book will consider at the end that while psychology is obviously still very much in its infancy, and centuries behind physics in its development, yet nevertheless it can already make a genuine, if small, contribution to the solution of social problems, while its potential, given suitable care and nourishment, is immense.

'But do not psychologists often quarrel and contradict each other?' is another favourite complaint. Well of course they do; so do mathematicians, physicists, chemists, and all other scientists. The quarrels of mathematicians are too unintelligible to the layman to make an impression on him whereas those of the psychologist obviously concern him rather more closely; that is the only reason why he knows of the latter and is ignorant of the former. The fact that light has sometimes been considered to be of the nature of a corpuscle, while at other times it has been considered more of the nature of a wave, has led to many disputes and 'crucial' experiments; it has never occurred to anybody to consider physics less of a science because of the different views to which this particular problem gives rise, including our present rather tolerant way of regarding light as partaking both of the nature of a particle and of that of a wave! There are many reasons why the phenomena of nature may appear contradictory at times, but usually continued research brings enlightenment.

Consider two hypotheses which are held equally strongly by popular imagination. One says that 'absence makes the heart grow fonder', i.e. it postulates a positive increase of F (heart's fondness) on L (length of absence). Exactly the opposite is postulated by those who believe 'out of sight out of mind'. Here you would seem to have the typical beginning of a quarrel between two psychological schools.

But perhaps both are right. Perhaps the relationship between F and L is curvilinear, as in Figure 1 overleaf. According to that figure absence at first leads to an increase in F but after a while the peak is past and out of sight becomes indeed out of mind. That would reconcile both theories and bring them together in a single law which could apply to the data.

Perhaps we may have to introduce further complications. Thus extraverted people might pass the peak of 'heart's fondness' after a relatively short absence whereas introverts might do so only after a much longer absence, as

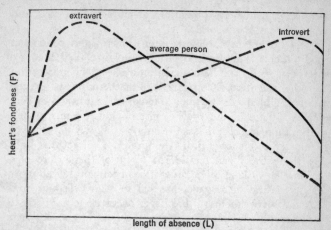

Figure 1. 'Absence makes the heart grow fonder' or 'Out of sight out of mind'? Diagram illustrating complications arising in formulating psychological laws.

indicated in the diagram; thus we might have to accommodate differences in personality in our law. These are only some of the most obvious complexities we shall have to face; many others will occur to the reader. But the fact remains that there is no obvious reason why a solution should not be found to all the questions associated with this problem, and even a partial and incomplete solution may be of considerable practical importance. The example I have chosen is, of course, an imaginary and rather light-hearted one, but the lesson it has to teach applies with even greater force to some of the more serious matters I have discussed in the body of the text. The reader must judge for himself whether the case I have made out is a good one or not.

I   Visit to a Psychological Laboratory

To most people, the notion of a psychological laboratory is almost a contradiction in terms. Psychology, so they believe, is essentially the study of the mind or psyche; how can such an immaterial thing be cribbed, cabined, and confined within the narrow limits of a room full of apparatus, or even – worse sacrilege – replete with rats and pigeons? Such questions deserve an answer, and in this chapter I shall take the reader into a few of the rooms in my own laboratory, point out the things that go on and, far more important, discuss the reasons *why* the people concerned are doing the things they are doing.

This, of course, is the crucial point which the ordinary visitor to any scientific laboratory will quite frequently miss. He will be shown impressive apparatus, giant pieces of electronic machinery, great rooms full of white-coated scientists looking through microscopes or watching the electrons go round in the cyclotron; but unless he knows the reason for the experiment, he may be impressed but he will not be very much the wiser. Psychologists, in taking visitors around their laboratories, have a tendency to dwell on the complexity of the apparatus and its physical perfection, rather than on the reasons for using it; there is an undoubted inferiority feeling in many members of the 'social sciences' group of studies, which leads them to believe that there is scientific respectability in apparatus which is not so easily found in theories and psychological experiments. I will here pass over the apparatus used in a few words of description, and will concentrate instead on the function the apparatus plays in uncovering some of the secrets of human behaviour.

This is an important point. The 'mind', or the 'soul', or the 'psyche' are a little too immaterial to be investigated as such by any scientific procedures; what the psychologist deals with, in fact, is *behaviour* which is palpable enough to be observed, recorded, and analysed. This hard-headed view is often criticized by people who say that this way of looking at things leaves out important qualities and aspects of humanity. Such an objection may or may not be true in the long run; this becomes almost a philosophical, rather than a scientific question, and there would be little point in arguing it here. Let us simply agree that you can go some way by paying attention to behaviour alone, and leave it to the future to show just what may be the limitations of such a view.

It will now be a little more obvious why the psychologist requires a laboratory. Behaviour may be analysed into three main components. On the one hand, we have the *stimuli* which impinge on the organism and which cause the organism to react. These stimuli may come from the outside (lights, sounds, smells, etc.), or they may come from the interior of the body itself, as, for instance, from the muscle spindles which are located in our arms and legs, and which mediate our awareness of the position of our limbs.

At the other end of the scale, we have the *responses* made by the organism. These may be muscular, i.e. movements of the body produced by the contraction or relaxation of the muscles; glandular, i.e. related to the secretions of the glands; or they may be produced by the autonomic nervous system, which governs a large number of involuntary re-actions, such as the dilatation of the pupil, or the sweating of the hands. So-called 'mental' activity may also be regarded as a response, although here, of course, we may get into difficulties when we try to record this response in any objective manner.

In between the stimulus and the response, we have the *organism*. Early in the history of psychology attempts were made to omit the organism from the account, and to describe behaviour entirely in terms of stimulus-response connexions. This became known as S-R psychology, but it soon became obvious that the same set of stimuli might produce an entirely different set of responses in different organisms, or even in the same organism at different times. This indeed is so obvious that it hardly needs saying, but obvious things are sometimes neglected, and the reinstatement of the organism has been a relatively recent occurrence.

It will now be clear why the psychologist needs a laboratory. In the first place, he has to produce stimuli, in order to be able to observe the effect which these stimuli have on the organism he is studying, whether it be a human being, a rat, an earthworm, or an amoeba. At first sight this may not seem a very difficult task, but when it is realized that human beings are so finely constructed that they can notice with their sensory equipment differences between stimuli which are not much greater than one single quantum of energy, then it will be seen that the utmost precision is required in producing exactly quantified sounds, colours, odours, etc., which can be specified in physical or chemical terms, and which can be duplicated by other investigators who may want to check on the results reported. What is more, the presentation of the stimuli often requires to be timed very accurately, within the limits of one thousandth of a second, or even better, and this is not an easy result to achieve. Extraneous stimuli have to be eliminated, to make sure that the organism under investigation is indeed reacting to the stimuli presented by the experimenter and not to others. This requires a sound-proof laboratory, fully air-conditioned, and preferably completely isolated from the building in which it is situated. There is even evidence that the predominance of negatively or positively charged ions in the air may affect people's responses to different kinds of stimuli, although few psychologists have gone to the length of controlling this particular variable!

When it comes to making a record of responses, we again find that considerable difficulties arise. It is easy enough to make a record of a person depressing a key as a reaction to a light which suddenly goes on, and even to measure his reaction time. It is a little more difficult to measure the actual pressure with which he depresses the key, and it gets quite complicated when you wish to take a recording of the neural innervation of the muscles before actual movement is observed. Or consider dreams – it is easy to ask a person when he is awake whether he had any dreams during the preceding night or not, but his answers would be of only limited value. It can be shown that dreaming is always associated with certain movements of the muscles connected to the eyeballs, and with certain electric patterns which can be recorded from the brain through the skull; thus to record such a simple thing as the occurrence of a dream may require quite complex instrumentation. Many responses which we would like to record we cannot at present measure at all, such as the secretion of hormones into the blood stream.

The study of stimuli and the study of responses is often difficult but not, in principle, impossible. Psychologists have suffered very much from an attitude common among university administrators when faced with requests for expensive apparatus, sound-proof rooms, and the like, to the effect that surely all a psychologist needs is pencil and paper, or perhaps a couch! Nevertheless, the situation is improving, and we are getting quite experienced in the precise application of stimuli and the precise recording of responses. When it comes to the organism itself, however, difficulties accumulate to such a terrifying extent that many psychologists have given up all hope of dealing with it in our lifetime, and prefer to regard it as what, in workshop parlance, is sometimes called a 'black box', i.e. a piece of apparatus into which you send an electric current and which responds with certain reactions, but the wiring and structure of which is unknown to you, and which you cannot open. To some extremists, this way of looking at things has led to the doctrine of the 'empty organism', i.e. a refusal even to speculate about the contents of the 'black box', and a return to the old notion of simply playing about with stimuli and responses, paying no attention to the organism itself. Now this doctrine of despair is not really justified by the facts of the situation. There are obvious similarities between the 'organism' we have been talking about and the notion of 'personality' which has formed the main part of

most of my own work, and consequently much of what I
have to say in this chapter will deal with ways and means of
getting round the difficulties presented by the 'black box',
and with attempts to make sure that the organism shall not
remain empty for ever.

After this little introductory sermon, let us go straight
away into the first room on the right. What you see there is
not very remarkable or very impressive; it is a rather simple
type of apparatus, called a pursuit rotor.

I hope to be able to show that this simple apparatus,
properly used, can lead to the elucidation of some very
important and difficult problems in psychology. Perhaps
the sceptical reader might like to listen to a quotation from
Faraday's famous *Chemical History of the Candle*, in which he
says: 'There is not a law under which any part of this
universe is governed which does not come into play and is
not touched upon in these phenomena. There is no better,
there is no more open door by which you can enter into the
study of natural philosophy than by considering the
physical phenomena of the candle.' Perhaps, in its own
modest way, the pursuit rotor may, in this presentation,
play the part that the candle did for Faraday.

The apparatus consists essentially of a gramophone turn-
table made of some plastic material, turning round at a
speed of sixty revolutions per minute. Set into it near the rim
is a small metal disc which thus goes round and round in
front of the subject, who holds in his hand a hinged stylus
with a metal tip (the hinge is there to prevent him from
pressing down too hard on the turn-table, thus slowing it
down). The task of the subject is simply to try to keep the
tip of the stylus in contact with the metal disc; in order to
do this, he has to move his hand and arm in a circular kind
of motion, in exact alignment with the movement of the
disc. This is more difficult than it may appear at first; most
people start off by being quite unable to catch the disc at all
with their stylus, only gradually learning the correct
movement. It will take something like between fifteen and
twenty minutes of practice before a reasonably good score
is achieved.

Performance on this task is measured by means of two electric clocks which are thrown into circuit alternately every ten seconds. While the subject is 'on target', i.e. while the stylus is in touch with the disc, a current flows through stylus, disc, and electric clock, causing the latter to move. When the contact is broken, through the failure of the subject to keep the stylus on top of the disc, the clock is stopped, only to start again when contact is made once more. After ten seconds, the first clock is disconnected and the second clock thrown into the circuit, so that we can read off, on the first clock, the exact period of time during which the subject has been 'on target'; this may, of course, be anything, from not at all to ten seconds if his performance has been perfect. The first clock is then automatically zeroed, ready to be thrown into the circuit again, while the second clock is read by the experimenter, to determine the amount of time 'on target' during the second ten-second period. In this way, the performance of the subject is plotted in terms of time on target during successive ten-second periods.

So much for the apparatus and the description of the method of using and scoring it. At first sight, both will appear utterly commonplace and of very little interest from the scientific point of view. It is precisely for this reason that I have selected the pursuit rotor as my first example, because before long I hope to be able to demonstrate that with its help we can measure, with some precision, human motivation and the drives which underlie certain types of activity; that we shall be able to measure a person's temperament; that we shall be able to analyse the effects of old age and brain damage; and that we shall be helped to unravel some of the causal factors in psychotic illness. Before doing all this, however, let us return to an analysis of performance on this instrument.

Supposing we allow our subject to work on this instrument for a period of five minutes and plot his performance; the result will be a rather jagged curve, starting at a very low level of between 0 and 0.5 seconds on target, and rising to anything from one second to four or five seconds on target at the end of five minutes. People differ very much in the speed with which they learn this task, and some remain very poor at it even after considerable practice (this applies particularly to women). If we average the results of a number of subjects, then we get a fairly smooth curve, rather like that shown in Figure 1, where all the chance irregularities, which form such an important part of the individual curves, have been averaged out.

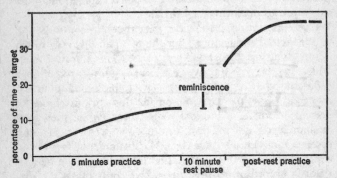

Figure 2. This diagram shows the average performance of a group of subjects on the pursuit rotor described in the text. Five minutes of practice are followed by a ten-minute rest pause, followed by some post-rest practice. The score is the percentage of time on target, and interest in the experiment lies in the so-called 'reminiscence' phenomenon, i.e. the improvement in performance after the rest pause and before any further practice has taken place.

Our subject is by now getting pretty tired of trying to follow the little disc on its circular adventures, and we let him take a ten-minute rest pause. This fatigue from which he is suffering is not, of course, the kind of muscular fatigue we would expect from someone running the mile in four minutes; the amount of muscular energy expended is so slight as to be not even equivalent to walking at a rather slow pace. We shall have to discuss in a minute just why it is that our subject feels bored and fatigued; for the time being, let us send him back to his task after his ten-minute rest pause, and make him go through it again for another period of five minutes. When we plot the second five-minute performance, we will find something rather unexpected and important. One might have imagined that our subject would start more or less where he left off; not having practised during the ten-minute rest pause, he would not be thought to have improved or learned anything during that period (we have made sure, of course, that he cannot practise the movement in any way during the rest period, by giving him something else to do, something quite irrelevant to pursuit rotor learning).

Our expectation, however, is very much in contradiction to the facts. Performance after the rest pause is very much better than just before the rest pause. This improvement, which has been found over and over again in many very different types of tasks, has received the rather puzzling name of *reminiscence*; the reason for this curious choice of nomenclature has historical roots which, while they may explain it, do not make it any more appropriate. In any case, we obviously have here a phenomenon requiring explanation, and this explanation takes us into the field of theory. According to this theory, we must make the distinction between performance (i.e. the act of carrying out a certain type of activity) and habit (i.e. the internal organization of the central nervous system which, due to previous learning, enables us to carry out the particular act in question). Performance only occurs when the habit is powered by a particular drive, so that we may write, almost in the form of an equation: performance = habit × drive. I may have acquired the ability to play tennis, speak French, or dance a mazurka, but these habits will only issue in performance if the appropriate drive is present as well.

Now, in addition to the positive drive to perform a given action, there also exist negative drives which would make us cease to perform that action. Boredom might be an example of such a negative drive; and when such negative drives equal or exceed in strength the positive ones, then the individual stops working; we encounter a 'block', or involuntary rest pause.

Now there is a good deal of evidence to suggest that the passage of nervous impulses through a particular pathway in the central nervous system causes a certain amount of inhibition; they make it more difficult, as it were, for an impulse of the same strength to pass through that particular set of neurons again. The position may be likened to that of a wire transmitting electricity. As the electricity passes through the wire its temperature is raised, and the increase in temperature in turn increases the resistance of the wire to the passage of the current. This phenomenon is known in psychology by the name of *reactive inhibition,* and is presumably the objective reality underlying our feelings of boredom and fatigue.

We now have a better understanding of what has been happening during the first five minutes of practice. Our subject, working under a certain drive, has acquired some proficiency in the habits needed to do well on the pursuit rotor. He has also, however, acquired a certain amount of inhibition, and this is felt subjectively in the form of boredom and fatigue. This inhibition, by detracting from his drive, has impaired his performance, thus reducing it below the level where it would have been had no inhibition been present. During the rest pause, the inhibition dissipates more or less completely, and performance, consequently, is much better than it was before the rest pause, when our subject was still bearing his load of inhibition.

From all this it follows that reminiscence is a good measure of the amount of inhibition which an individual has accumulated, provided that the rest pause is long enough to permit all, or nearly all, the accumulated inhibition to dissipate. It can easily be shown that rest pauses of eight or ten minutes are usually ample, so that our behaviour measurement of inhibition can be carried out adequately in a rather short period of time. We have thus succeeded in getting at least a peep into the 'black box'; the question arises whether we can use this limited amount of insight to obtain further information.

Let us go back for a moment to consider how inhibition builds up. We have already explained that inhibition is a negative drive, and there is some reason to assume that this negative drive keeps on growing, more or less as a straight function of time. Does it go on growing for ever? The answer to this must be 'No'. Clearly inhibition can only grow up to the point where its strength as a negative drive equals that of the positive drive under which the organism is working; when this point has been reached, our formula would read:

$$\text{performance} = \text{habit} \times 0$$

which means that performance should stop, and that we should get what we have, a paragraph or two back, called an involuntary rest pause, or block. During this involuntary rest period inhibition should dissipate until the positive drive was again sufficiently stronger than the negative drive to permit the resumption of activity. Inhibition would build up again until another rest pause was in force, and so performance would go on in a series of fits and starts as it were, with the work periods being periodically interrupted by short rest periods.

Do these involuntary rest periods actually occur? There are two lines of evidence which indicate that they do. In the first place, these involuntary rest periods can be observed in the record of performance of a given individual. This is often a difficult thing to do, particularly in tasks like the pursuit rotor, but it has been done successfully in a number of cases. In the second place, it has been found possible to discover physiological counterparts of the involuntary rest pause which can be recorded and measured. Thus the electroencephalograph, or E.E.G., a machine which records the electric activity of the brain, produces different patterns during sleep and in the waking state; it has been found that during prolonged practice on routine tasks the normal waking pattern is suddenly interrupted for brief periods by patterns which are typical of sleep. Furthermore, the occurrence of such sleep patterns coincides with a marked deterioration in performance. There seems to be little doubt that involuntary rest pauses do occur, and that their onset marks the moment when inhibition equals drive.

We have already seen that reminiscence is a good measure of inhibition. We have now shown that inhibition equals drive, once the critical point has been reached where the involuntary rest pauses begin to occur. It follows directly from this that reminiscence must be a good measure of drive once this critical point has been reached, and we would predict that if we were to compare two groups of people, one working under high, the other working under low motivation, the former would have higher reminiscence scores than the latter. This is a quite clear-cut and unambiguous prediction, and it is a kind of prediction which shows the value of theoretical analysis. It is unlikely that on the basis of common sense one would have hit upon reminiscence as a good measure of *drive*. Common sense would have more likely hit upon actual performance as being likely to measure degrees of *motivation*.

Actually it is possible to make a more detailed and quantitative prediction of what we would expect to find in comparing the reminiscence scores of high and low drive groups. Both groups should show an increase in reminiscence with time spent on working, until the low drive group reached the level at which inhibition equalled their (low) drive. At this point, which is reached roughly after two minutes, both groups should have roughly equal reminiscence scores, but from then on the inhibition, and, therefore, the reminiscence, of the high drive group should continue to rise, until this group also reached the point where inhibition equalled their (high) drive, while for the low drive group inhibition and reminiscence should remain pretty much at the same level they had reached after two minutes.

Figure 3 shows the results of such an experiment. Four high drive groups and four low drive groups were used, and rest pauses were scheduled for these groups respectively, after two, three, six, and eight minutes' work on the pursuit rotor. How was it possible to ensure that one group had a higher drive than the other? Both groups were made up of industrial apprentices, but, in the high drive group, the pursuit rotor test was given as one of the battery of admission tests to a training course, which for these youngsters was

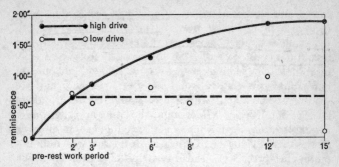

Figure 3. As explained in the text, the amount of reminiscence shown by a person should be a function of his drive, being greater for people working under a high level of motivation than for people working under a low level of motivation. This superiority of the high-drive group should become more apparent the longer the pre-rest work period, because the longer this period is, the more opportunity they have of accumulating inhibition. The diagram shows the results of large-scale experiments bearing out these predictions (from H. J. Eysenck, *Experiments in Motivation*).

probably even more important than is success at the eleven-plus examination for most children; if successful, they were sure of a well-paid, skilled job at the end of their training, as well as being paid for taking part in the training course itself. As far as the low drive group was concerned, its members had already been accepted and, under trade union rules, would now progress towards secure jobs, regardless of their performance on the training course or anything associated with it. Their motivation to perform the test was, therefore, minimal: just adequate to avoid a reprimand by taking part in the experiment, but without any particular interest in the result. Interestingly enough, the two groups of apprentices did not differ in their performance to any great extent, but they did differ very much with respect to their reminiscence scores, and, as shown in Figure 3, these scores behaved exactly as predicted on theoretical grounds. It would appear, therefore, that our theory is along the right lines, and that also it enables us to measure drive and motivation, which has always provided a rather elusive quality, at least as far as humans are concerned.

People differ with respect to the speed with which they build up inhibition, and the speed with which they dissipate inhibition. One would imagine that these differences would have important consequences for their general behaviour, not only in work situations but also in life as a whole. There is evidence to show that extraverted people, that is to say, people who are sociable, happy-go-lucky, impulsive, and generally interested in the outer world, generate inhibition more quickly and dissipate it more slowly than do introverted people, i.e. people who are socially shy, serious-minded, introspective, and generally interested in ideas more than in action. Can we account for the behaviour of introverts and extraverts, respectively, in terms of this difference of inhibition? I shall come back to this point a little later on, but I want to give just one example of the kind of argument which would link the experimental results with certain types of behaviour. The example I have chosen is called, on the experimental side, 'alternation behaviour', and it is investigated usually along these lines.

An experiment with rats (we will be visiting the animal laboratory in a little while, but for the sake of an illustration I must anticipate a little) may serve to demonstrate what is meant by alternation behaviour. Suppose you put a rat at the bottom of what is called a T-maze, i.e. essentially a runway leading the rat to a choice point where he can go either right or left. The rat is hungry, and he finds food either at the end of the right-hand lane or at the end of the left-hand lane, whichever he happens to choose. Once he has found and devoured the food, he is picked up and put at the starting point again (and the food he has eaten is, of course, replaced). Under these conditions, you might expect that a rat, having turned right, say, and been rewarded with food, would go on turning right each time it was put in the maze. Inhibition theory would predict, however, that this 'turning right' and ending up in the same food compartment each time would set up inhibition which would lower the drive to carry out this act, so that the rat would soon come to the point where it would turn left, i.e. in the previously not preferred and, therefore, not rewarded direction. This is precisely what happens, and the rat keeps changing his preference from right to left and from left to right as the experiment goes on. Actually the inhibition in this case seems to have two components. One of these may be called the muscular component, i.e. inhibition is set up against the turning in the same direction each time. The other component may be called a perceptual one; it arises from having to look at exactly the same food chamber time and time again. These two variables can, of course, be manipulated experimentally. Thus we can increase the complexity of the muscular movement by making the path rather twisted and tortuous, or by having the rat make several right or left turns before he reaches the choice point. Alternatively, we can emphasize the perceptual component by making the two food boxes as different as possible, i.e. by having them of different size, painting them in different colours, and so on. The main result to emerge from work of this kind appears to be that perceptual inhibition lasts much longer, and dissipates much more slowly than does muscular inhibition; this has been found to be true in human beings also.

It may be a long jump from the rat to the human, but there is no doubt that alternation behaviour is quite frequent among the latter also. Studies on food choice behaviour in real-life canteen situations has shown, for instance, as indeed one might have expected, that when confronted with the same menu day after day, people do alternate their choices; this alternation is much more marked for some people than for others. This is a relatively simple situation, but quite obviously the principle can be extended very much. Some people stay in the same place all their lives; others move from one place to another a large number of times. Some people stick to one firm, or even one job, throughout their lives; others chop and change continually. Some people stay happily married to the same person throughout life; others are constantly in and out of the divorce courts. Circumstances over which the individual has no control do, of course, play a part in all this, but so does personality. We would expect, other things being equal, that quicker arousal and slower dissipation of inhibition would make the extraverted person more changeable in all these different ways, and indeed there is much evidence to indicate that, by and large, this is true. The extravert needs new stimuli, new faces, different jobs, and frequent changes; the introvert is more likely to remain content with an established routine. It would be foolish to say that one was in any sense 'better' than the other; they are just different. Both types of behaviour can, of course, become pathological when taken to extremes; within the normal range there is nothing neurotic about either, although members of one of these two groups often have an uneasy suspicion about members of the other!

Let us now turn to a last application of the pursuit rotor experiment, this time to a problem on mental disorder. The most serious and most terrible mental disorders are those sometimes subsumed under the name 'psychotic'; schizophrenia and manic-depressive psychosis are the two best known groups of psychotic disorders. Among many other symptoms of mental derangement, along with ideas of persecution, inappropriate emotions, feelings of guilt not justified by the facts, disorders of thinking, and so forth, there is one which is highly characteristic of all psychotics, to wit, an extraordinary slowness which pervades thought and action alike. Now it is possible to speculate that this slowness may be due to an excess of inhibition in the psychotic person, and the possibility does not seem unlikely that this excessive inhibition, in turn, may be due to difficulties the organism has in dissipating and getting rid of the inhibition constantly accruing. If this hypothesis were true, then we would expect to find that psychotics in the typical pursuit rotor experiment would fail to show any reminiscence after a ten-minute rest pause (it will be remembered that reminiscence is the measure of the amount of inhibition dissipated during the rest pause; if no dissipation takes place, then there will be no reminiscence). Figure 4 shows that this prediction is indeed borne out in fact; psychotics show no reminiscence; a comparable normal group shows a great deal. Now even in psychotics, inhibition presumably must ultimately dissipate, although at a much slower rate, and we might expect that if we extended our rest pause to twenty-four hours, instead of restricting it to a mere ten minutes, then psychotics, too, would show reminiscence. This in fact has been found to be the case, showing that, quite possibly, we have here isolated one of the causal factors in psychosis. It is now possible to go on from there and search for drugs, or other methods of treatment, which will accelerate the rate of dissipation of reactive inhibition.

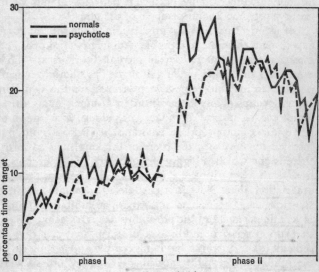

Figure 4. There are considerable differences between people in the amount of reminiscence they show. This diagram gives results obtained from normal and psychotic individuals. It will be seen that the psychotics have almost no reminiscence, whereas the normals have a considerable amount. This is probably due to the slow dissipation of inhibition in psychotic subjects (from an article by Gordon Claridge in H. J. Eysenck (Ed.), *Experiments in Personality*).

We have almost done with the pursuit rotor now, and it may be hoped that the reader will now look upon this very simple instrument with a little more interest and respect than may seem appropriate at first sight. It illustrates to perfection a point I am very much concerned to make in this book, namely, that it is not so much what you do as why you do it that makes a given experiment or piece of apparatus interesting and important. In this discussion, and in those that follow, I have, of course, stuck out my neck in a way one would not normally do in a scientific journal or monograph; I have done this in order to show the reader the kind of thinking which lies behind this type of experimental investigation. Much of this type of thinking may, of course, be quite wrong. It may be quite unjustifiable to argue from the alternation behaviour in the rat to the 'successive polygamy' which characterizes some of our more extraverted film stars. Other explanations come to mind and should, of course, be tested experimentally. But before an idea can be tested experimentally, there must be an idea, and this discussion may serve to illustrate the way in which such ideas may lead to experimentation. Scientists are usually rather chary of exposing the beautiful butterflies of their imagination to the powerful spotlight of public regard; this is a self-preservative habit which has much to say for itself. Nevertheless, without some degree of intellectual strip-tease, it is impossible to give any true idea of the sort of activity which is psychological research.

We have lingered much too long in the first room of our laboratory (this indeed is quite typical of conducted tours of this kind); we must now cast some hurried glances at the other rooms.

Here, in Room Two, we see in progress an experiment which is so simple that it hardly seems to deserve the name. The subject holds in his hand a simple metal stylus, and with it he is banging away on a metal sheet as fast as he can. The whole apparatus is very simple and extremely cheap; it cost exactly tenpence to produce. What can we hope to learn from such a very simple, straightforward type of activity? The reader may remember our discussion of involuntary rest pauses. These are rather difficult to demonstrate experimentally, and to measure accurately, and in this particular experiment it is our hope that by banging away for several minutes with the stylus, the subject will acquire a considerable degree of inhibition, and will thus be led into demonstrating a large number of involuntary rest pauses. In order to discover these, of course, we have to record his performance in considerable detail. Indeed, the apparatus for scoring his performance takes up a whole room by itself, and costs something like £1,500. What it does essentially is to measure, with an accuracy of a thousandth of a second, the exact length of time that the metal stylus is in touch with the metal plate; this we may call the length of a tap. It also measures the exact length of time that the stylus is in the air until it returns again to the plate; this we may call the length of a gap between the taps. Now there is not much learning to be done in a situation like this, and performance, on the whole, does not improve or deteriorate very much. Gaps and taps tend to be of pretty uniform length. Having recorded them in our apparatus, we can now plot them on paper and analyse them in detail.

When this is done, we find something rather interesting. On the whole, our expectation is fulfilled. The gaps, to concentrate on these (pretty much the same is true of the taps also), tend to be fairly uniform in duration for any given person, varying around the mean just a little. But occasionally we have a gap which is something like two or three times as long as the average; in other words, we have here made visible the involuntary rest pauses which we have been talking about. Later on, I shall show a picture of the involuntary rest pauses produced by extraverted and introverted people, respectively; the reader may remember that, in our hypothesis, extraverts, showing more inhibition, would be expected to produce far more involuntary rest pauses than introverts. For the moment, let us simply rest content with noting that there may be an important relationship between such a very simple task as tapping and certain dimensions of personality, and let us also note that a simple task of this nature may be used to make visible, almost as under a microscope, the working of our nervous system.

Let us now hurry to Room Three where we have what looks like a spiral painted on to a piece of cardboard which is being rotated in a clockwise direction at a speed of about 100 revolutions per minute. The room is blacked out and the spiral is picked out by a beam of light of a certain brightness. We are instructed to look fixedly at the centre of the spiral and to keep from blinking as far as possible. As the spiral goes round, it seems to have the effect of expanding and getting bigger. Suddenly the experimenter stops the spiral and asks us what we see. Surprisingly enough, the spiral, although stationary, seems to be contracting rapidly; indeed, if we cast a glance at the face of the experimenter – or indeed, any other object – it also seems to be contracting. Gradually this contraction fades and finally disappears. It is called the spiral after-effect, and is indeed quite a common observation after looking fixedly for a while at any moving object. It is also sometimes known as the waterfall illusion, because if you gaze for a minute or two at a waterfall, and then look away at a house or a car, this will appear to be moving in an upward direction, i.e. in an opposite direction to the downward-moving water. In the laboratory, this effect is sometimes obtained by rotating, in front of the subject, a drum painted with alternating black and white stripes around its horizontal axis. If you have not got a waterfall or one of these drums handy, you might like to look at one of the lists of credit titles which appear at the end of a play on television. These lists are usually moving from bottom to top of the screen, and you should get a beautiful after-effect in reverse, if you keep looking fixedly at the centre of the screen.

People differ very much with respect to the length of time during which these after-effects continue; this time is measured from the moment the spiral or the rotating drum is stopped until the subject fails to perceive any further apparent motion of the stationary stimulus. The length of the after-effect is obviously a function of the length of stimulation; the longer the original stimulation, the longer the after-effect. However, even with a standard stimulation period, there are still marked differences between one person and another. To explain these, we may have to cast a cautious look at psychological theory underlying this phenomenon.

We are handicapped by the fact that neither psychologists, physiologists, nor neurologists have any real explanation of why this after-effect occurs (there are indeed many theories, but none of them can be taken very seriously). It does seem likely, however, that the original rotation of the spiral, like all perceptual processes, produces some degree of inhibition, and that this would be greater in extraverts than in introverts. This inhibition, by decreasing the total stimulating effect, would act in the same way as would a decrement in the time during which stimulation was administered, thus leading to a shorter after-effect. Similarly, whatever physiological processes may underlie the after-effect itself, they also must be subject to inhibition, thus leading to the same prediction. The facts seem to bear out these notions, because it has often been found that extraverts do indeed report shorter after-effects than do introverts. It has also been found that these after-effects are shortened by the so-called *depressant* drugs, such as alcohol and sodium amytal, while they are lengthened by the so-called stimulant drugs, such as caffeine, dexedrine, and so forth. This is confirmatory evidence, because it has often been found that depressant drugs produce an inhibitory effect on the cortex and shift people's behaviour in an extraverted direction, while stimulant drugs have an excitatory effect on the cortex and shift people's behaviour in the introverted direction. Experiments with drugs of this type are, therefore, a useful complement to the study of individual differences.

The usefulness of this phenomenon, however, is by no means exhausted yet. It has been found, for instance, that people suffering from brain damage have greater difficulty in perceiving the after-effect and tend to perceive it for a shorter time. This is not unexpected; it has often been found that brain damage, whether occurring naturally or as a result of an operation, increases cortical inhibition and, therefore, produces extraverted behaviour. Similarly, old age is often accompanied by certain subtle forms of brain damage, and thus leads to greater cortical inhibition in the aged. We would expect, therefore, that young people would perceive the after-effect for longer periods than old people, and again this has been shown to be the case.

It might be thought that this test might be a good measure of brain damage and consequently of considerable clinical interest; this, unfortunately, is not necessarily true. The length of after-effect, as we have seen, is determined by many factors, of which brain damage is only one; the perfectly normal extravert might give results very similar to those of a brain-damaged introvert, to take one obvious example. One would have to know a person's score before and after the brain damage to make it possible to get over this difficulty.

It might be thought that perhaps old people, or patients with brain damage, or flighty extraverts, would not have the same motivation to keep on looking until the last flicker of apparent movement had died away, and would, therefore, report 'no movement' earlier than would normal young and introverted people. Experiments were, therefore, done with high drive and low drive groups similar to those mentioned in connexion with pursuit rotor experiments. The results show pretty conclusively that whatever effects low drive might have, the shortening of these after-effects is not one of them. Quite the opposite appeared to be the case; the high drive groups reported less after-effect than the low drive groups! As an exercise, the reader may himself try to tie this bit of information in with the theory linking inhibition and drive described a few pages ago!

Again we see that an apparently isolated and odd phenomenon in the psychological laboratory is related to many interesting and important features of the outer world. It mirrors personality patterns of extraversion and introversion, it reflects damage suffered by the brain through injury or old age, it may be used as a measure of

drive or motivation, and its more detailed study may be
related to many more interesting and important byways.
Its apparent simplicity should not beguile us into looking
upon it as unworthy of scientific analysis; in the end, it will
probably take the combined resources of many psychological, psychiatric, anatomical, neurological, physiological,
and pharmacological departments to lay bare the actual
mode of working of the spiral after-effect.

In addition to the spiral after-effect, there are several
other interesting experiments of a perceptual nature set up
in the same room. One of these deals with the so-called
C.F.F., or critical flicker fusion threshold. Essentially this
consists of a light which flickers on and off many times per
second; this light forms part of a circuit which enables the
experimenter to vary the rate at which it flickers, and also,
during each on-off period, the proportion of time that the
light is on and off respectively. At low rates of flicker, everyone sees a flickering light, but as the rate is increased, the
flicker gradually ceases and a steady light is perceived instead. The point of transition between flicker and steady
light is called the C.F.F. threshold, and it can be established
with considerable accuracy. (The ordinary light bulb, fed
by an alternating current of 50 cycles per second, is just
below this threshold and can be seen to flicker by some
people, particularly when they see it out of the corner of
their eye rather than straight on; similarly, the image on
the television screen may sometimes be seen to flicker.)

A high threshold may be regarded as a positive ability,
because it means, in effect, a high power of resolving stimuli
impinging on the eye in large numbers. This ability characterizes introverts as opposed to extraverts; it is increased by
stimulant drugs and decreased by depressant drugs; and it
is lowered by brain damage and old age. Here again, there
is no widely accepted theory to account for the facts of the
relationship with personality and drugs which has been
established time and time again (in addition to those mentioned above, it also appears that neurotics have lower
powers of resolution than do normal people).

Similar to this experiment is another, in which we study

the extremely interesting phenomenon of *apparent movement*. A well-known psychologist was once asked by a sceptical journalist to name a single psychological phenomenon on whose existence there was any agreement among psychologists, and the laws regarding which were sufficiently well known to make it of practical usefulness. He replied that not only was there such a phenomenon, but that it was so highly regarded by modern man that temples were put up to it in every town and village and that millions of people went to these temples every week, paying large sums of money in order to be admitted to view this phenomenon. The journalist was rather taken aback, until he realized that the psychologist was talking about the cinema. This whole flourishing industry (to which nowadays could be added television as well) is based on the phenomenon of apparent movement which, reduced to its simplest outline, consists of two lights in a dark room flashing on for a short period of time in such a way that the one comes on just before the other. Under these circumstances, the observer does not see two lights coming on at points A and B respectively; he sees one light moving from A to B. Translated into the terms of the cinema, he is shown two pictures, A and B, in rapid succession, separated by a gap of blackness; what he sees, of course, is a moving scene which appears to have no gaps at all.

There are several laws relating to this phenomenon, governing such things as the optimal interval between the two stimuli, the effect of their brightness, and of the distance they are apart; these form part of that large body of generally agreed experimental knowledge, the existence of which is so successfully concealed from laymen by the absurd stress on warring 'schools' and other inessentials, which tend to attract more attention than straightforward experimental work dealing with facts rather than fancies.

In dealing with apparent movement, we again have a threshold because, as we increase the speed with which light B follows light A, the point arrives where what the subject sees is not succession but simultaneity. (There is, of course, another threshold, too, namely that at which the interval between A and B has become so long that all we see is two unrelated lights, without any movement taking place. This threshold, however, is much more subjective and much more difficult to measure than the other, and it is usually ignored.) We might expect that the apparent movement threshold would, like the C.F.F. threshold, be affected by drugs and by personality variables, and while the evidence is much less conclusive, it does indeed seem to point in the same direction.

The instrumentation for the C.F.F. or the apparent movement type of phenomenon is relatively simple; that for the next experiment to be demonstrated is rather complex. Psychologists discovered very early that they needed instruments for the exhibition of stimuli where the time period in question could be controlled very accurately, perhaps to one thousandth of a second, and the variety of instruments constructed to do this all go by the name of *tachistoscope*. The one we are going to use now exhibits not only one stimulus but two, and, in addition to allowing us to control the length of exposure of each of the two stimuli, it also allows us to vary the length of time between the disappearance of the first and the appearance of the second. Suppose now that our first stimulus is a black circle and that we expose it for something like thirty milliseconds. There is no difficulty in perceiving this circle accurately, even for people with rather poor vision, so apparently the length of exposure is quite sufficient. But now let us follow the exposure of this circle, after a brief pause, with the exposure of a ring or annulus, the inner edge of which is shown in exactly the same position as had previously been occupied by the outer edge of the circle (cf. Fig. 5). Given a suitable timing of both circle and ring, and an interval between them, what is seen is not a circle followed by a ring, but simply a ring with an empty centre. This is called 'masking', or suppression of one stimulus by another which is adjacent to it, and it is one of many illustrations of the fact that what we see is not necessarily the same as that which we are shown.

circle   annulus

Figure 5. In this experiment, the subject is first shown the circle for something like 30 milliseconds and then the annulus after a very short period of time. The annulus is so positioned that its inner edge lies in precisely the same place as the outer edge of the circle. Under these conditions, and with a suitable time-interval, it is found that the circle is not seen but only the annulus; in other words, the annulus 'masks' the circle.

The explanation for this experiment is possibly the same as that of a slightly different one, in which the eye is successively stimulated by a red light (shown for about 20 milliseconds) followed by a white light. Given a suitable brightness of the two lights, the subject sees not a red light followed by white, but a green light! Apparently what happens is this. In the first place, we know that strong visual impressions produce after-images which tend to be of a different and complementary colour. Thus, if you look at a bright red light and then close your eyes, you will experience a bright green after-image of the same size and shape as the original red stimulus. This is supposed to be produced by a kind of reversible chemical process in the retina, according to which a mysterious substance is *depleted* by stimulation with red; this substance is restored when the red stimulus is withdrawn, and this restoration is experienced as green. (In a similar way, if the original stimulus had been green, this substance would have been augmented during the original period of stimulation, and it would have been restored to a lower level after cessation of the stimulation, thus producing the red image.)

The green we perceive in the experiment, therefore, can

be explained as being the after-image of the red which was, in fact, used to stimulate the eye. Why wasn't the red perceived at all? The reason seems to lie in the rather interesting phenomenon of *pre-excitatory inhibition*. It has been shown in physiological studies that when a stimulus impinges on the retina there arises a wave of excitation which corresponds with and mediates our perception of the stimulus. Before this wave of excitation, however, there arises a very rapid wave of inhibition which clears the deck, as it were, for the stimulus to come; it wipes out all existing traces of excitation so that there should be no competition with the later stimulus. This wave of inhibition arises more quickly than the wave of excitation and, with suitable time relations, the wave of inhibition from the white stimulus wipes out the wave of excitation from the preceding red stimulus before it has had time to rise above the threshold and become an active percept. All that is seen, therefore, is the after-image which arises after the wave of inhibition, set up by the white stimulus, has already passed.

If this wave of inhibition is in any way similar to the kind of inhibition we have been talking about hitherto, then its strength should be increased by a depressant drug and decreased by a stimulant drug. This is indeed so; a depressant drug increases the strength of a red light which can be neutralized by the pre-excitatory inhibition set up by the white, while a stimulant drug has the opposite effect. Similar drug effects have been found in relation to the 'masking' phenomenon mentioned above. Little has been done so far in using these phenomena in connexion with personality differences or the effect of brain damage and old age, but such work as has been done has shown personality differences very much in line with what we would have predicted.

To watch the next experiment, we have to go into a special sound-proofed room, because the experiment to be demonstrated can very easily be disturbed by slight sounds and other stimuli from the outside. It is, in a way, a duplication of Pavlov's famous conditioning experiment, in which he taught dogs to associate the sound of a bell with food given to them shortly afterwards. The details of this will be familiar to many people; to recapitulate briefly, the dog is standing on a table strapped to a stand, and is being observed from the outside by the experimenter whenever he enters the room during the course of the experiment. He can manipulate various stimuli, and he can also record the salivation which is being produced by the dog at any one moment of time. The experimenter first shows that the dog does not salivate to the sound of a bell. He then shows that the dog does salivate to the sight of some food. He then goes on to pair the bell and the food, always taking care that the bell precedes the presentation of the food. After a while, he presents the bell by itself, and is now able to show that, due to the pairing of the conditioned stimulus (that is to say, the bell) and the unconditioned stimulus (that is to say, the food) the bell has now acquired certain stimulant properties which previously belonged to the food alone; in other words, the dog now salivates to the sound of the bell. Figure 6 shows diagrammatically the set-up in Pavlov's laboratory.

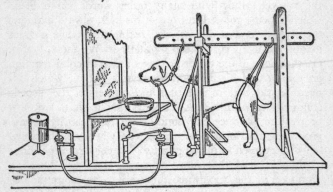

Figure 6. Diagrammatic drawing of Pavlovian conditioning experiment, with dog in stand and recording apparatus outside the room.

There are many ways of performing experiments of this type with human beings, and some of them actually use salivation. But this is a rather messy business, and we have chosen a quite different type of procedure. Our subject is sitting at a table, and we have strapped electrodes to the palms of his two hands. A very slight current goes through his body and the resistance the body makes to the current is accurately measured on a suitable device. It is well known that any kind of emotional or physiological stress or shock or upset will cause a slight degree of sweating in the palms of the hand, and sweat, being an electrolytic agent, will decrease the resistance of the body and can be measured, therefore, with great accuracy by our set-up. There are many ways of producing such a shock; we might, for instance, give the subject an electric shock, or we might produce a very loud noise right next to his ear. This is the unconditioned stimulus, so-called because it produces its effect without any previous process of learning or conditioning. Let us say that we have chosen a very loud tone delivered over earphones.

As our conditioned stimulus, that is to say the particular stimulus which we wish to associate with the unconditioned one, we have chosen the word 'cow'. This is presented to the subject, along with many other words, on a drum which is being rotated in front of his eyes, always exposing these words one at a time, and taking about five seconds before one word is replaced by another. We show, first of all, that none of the words produces any particular reaction on the part of his autonomic nervous system, which determines the rate of sweating and, therefore, the electric conductivity of his skin. Having shown that, we now proceed to produce our conditioned response by always producing the loud noise in his ear whenever the word 'cow' is exposed in our apparatus. After several repetitions of this, we find that now, whenever the word 'cow' is produced in the apparatus, there are quite unambiguous signs of stress in our record of the electric conductivity of the skin, even though we have temporarily suspended the sounding of the loud noise in his earphones. In other words, he has become conditioned to the word 'cow' and responds to it very much as he does to the loud noise.

He also shows certain other rather interesting phenomena which were first discovered by Pavlov. For instance, we can show that he produces the phenomenon of *generalization*. Pavlov showed that when a dog was conditioned to a particular sound, it also produced a conditioned response to other sounds which were similar to the original one but not identical with it. He showed that the greater the similarity between the sound to which the dog had become conditioned and the new sound, the larger was the salivation to the new sound. The more unlike the two sounds were, the less was the salivation to the new sound. In our present experiment, we can show that, although the subject had been conditioned to the word 'cow', he will also respond with an increase in conductivity to words like 'sheep' or 'goat', whereas he will not respond in any way to words like 'paper' or 'door'. In other words, he has generalized his responses along a gradient which is of an ideational kind. He responds with a conditioned reflex to words which are similar to the original one, because all of them denote farm animals, and does not respond to words denoting articles of furniture or parts of the house.

Apart from generalization, we can also demonstrate *extinction*. Pavlov showed that when a dog was given the bell a number of times without ever being reinforced by food, then, although he had been conditioned in the first place, he would now extinguish the response. In other words, salivation would get less and less after each stimulation, until finally the bell produced no salivation at all. Similarly here, if we exhibit the word 'cow' a number of times, without ever sounding our loud tone over the earphones, then gradually the response will die out, until finally it becomes completely extinguished.

The dog in Pavlov's experiment has no voluntary control over his salivation; he cannot determine whether he shall or shall not salivate, and is presumably relatively unconscious of the whole process. Similarly, our human subject has no control over his autonomic system, and over the slight degree of sweating which occurs and which mediates the drop in the resistance of his skin to the passage of the electric current. In fact, in the ordinary way, he is quite unconscious of this and does not even know what kind of response it is that we are recording. He is quite unfamiliar with the phenomenon, and he has no voluntary control over it. This, of course, is extremely useful to us, because it means that we do not have to worry about his 'faking' his scores in any way, or trying to impress us with either his quick conditioning or his inability to form conditioned responses. We are fairly safe in relying on the record as being one giving us an accurate impression of his physiological reactions.

The next room which we visit is quite empty, except for our subject who is sitting on a chair, and the presence of a tape recorder. The tape recorder is repeating a long list of digits, calling out one every second. Very occasionally, there is a sequence of three odd digits, such as 'one, nine, three', or a series of three even digits, such as 'eight, four, six'. Whenever that occurs, the subject presses a Morse key which he holds in his hand, and the response is recorded in the next room on an automatic ink writer. This is called a vigilance experiment, and it originated essentially during the war, when tasks of a rather boring and repetitive nature had to be performed with considerable accuracy. Radar operators, for instance, in the search for submarines or aeroplanes, often had to watch the radar screen for hours, searching for a pip that might never come, or which, if it did occur, might only come on for a very short period of time and then be lost for ever if it were not noticed. It was soon found that the abilities of people to detect signals of this kind deteriorated sharply even over such short periods of time as half an hour or so, and it was also found that people differed very much in their ability to maintain vigilance. To study this phenomenon, it was transferred to the laboratory, and various types of tasks rigged up to test a person's ability to maintain vigilance.

One typical experiment would ask him to fixate a clock with only one hand, moving one position every second. Very occasionally the clock hand would move two positions instead of one; this would constitute the stimulus to be signalled by pressing a key. The decreased efficiency on this task over time may reasonably be attributed to inhibition. Thus we can use this type of test to measure differences in personality, predicting that extraverts would show greater decrement in performance than would introverts, or we can study the conditions which aid vigilance, or, on the other hand, which make vigilance less effective. Last, but not least, we can also study the effect of drugs on the phenomenon, expecting, for instance, that caffeine and benzedrine would improve vigilance, whereas alcohol and barbiturate would decrease it. All these effects have, in fact, been found.

We just have time to look into one more room before making a quick visit to the animal laboratory. In this room we find another perceptual experiment going on. The subject fixates a sheet of paper upon which is marked a small cross at which he is looking, and to the left of this cross is a small, black square. After he has fixated the sheet of paper for about a minute, the experimenter says, 'Now', and immediately the subject transfers his gaze to another sheet of paper, also marked with a fixation point in the middle, but flanked on either side by a slightly larger white square. Both these white squares are exactly equal in size but, when asked by the experimenter, the subject reports that the left one looks larger than the right one. The experiment is illustrated in Figure 7, and the reader can try this experiment out for himself, although, of course, it is rather more difficult to reproduce at home than it is in the laboratory.

This effect is called the *figural after-effect*, and one hypothesis about its origin runs something like this. The transmission of the neural impulses set up by the small black square at which the subject was looking during the first minute of the experiment produces inhibition in the neural pathways; this inhibition is sometimes called *satiation*. When the subject now looks at the second set of figures, the two large white squares, the square on the left will lie outside the satiated area in the set of visual pathways leading from the eye to the brain, and these pathways,

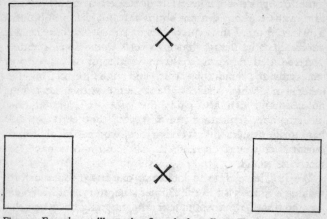

Figure 7. Experiment illustrating figural after-effects. To get this effect, fixate the cross at the top of the page for a minute or so, then transfer your regard suddenly to the other cross at the bottom of the page, and compare the size of the squares at either side of the fixation point. The one on the left should look larger, although in actual fact the two squares are identical in size. For explanation of this phenomenon, see text.

being as it were inhibited, will tend to 'push' the outline of the large white square away from this inhibited area, so that conduction will be undertaken by fresher, less inhibited parts of the visual pathways. It is for this reason that the left square looks larger than the right.

There are many more rooms to visit in the laboratory, but we must now rush away to spend at least a few minutes in the animal laboratory. We have already looked at one experiment, that dealing with alternation of behaviour. We now encounter a rather different type of experiment. In this we see a large circular area on the floor marked off in squares, and surrounded by a high wall. This area is brightly illuminated and above it are a number of loud-speakers which produce a constant level of white noise.* Into this area the experimenter puts a white rat, and then

---

*A heterogeneous mixture of sound waves extending over a wide frequency range.

notes down, on a sheet of paper, the exact movements of the rat as it goes from one square to another, and he also counts the number of faecal boluses the rat deposits in this arena, and the number of times that it urinates. This test, the so-called 'open field test', is essentially a measure of emotionality. When the rat is very much afraid, it tends to cower in a corner rather than ambulate about and go from square to square; he also tends to defaecate and urinate, very much as human beings would do in similar circumstances. Here, for instance, is a brief historical account of a battle in early Persian history, in which the flight behaviour of the enemy commanders is described as follows: 'To save their lives, they trampled over the bodies of their soldiers, and fled. Like young captured birds they lost courage. With their urine they defiled their chariots and let fall their excrement'. Similarly, in more recent studies of the Second World War, it was reported that in soldiers under battle conditions the need for elimination may become so strong that it broke through all cultural restraints. A whole continuum of physiological fear responses was found, in which loss of control over elimination was discovered to be the extreme fear symptom, nine per cent of the men reporting urinating in their pants and twenty-one per cent reporting loss of control over bowels when under fire. For comparison, it might be mentioned that fifty-seven per cent felt sick, and eighty-four per cent experienced a violent pounding of the heart.

We thus have here a test which objectively measures the amount of fear experienced by animals brought up under identical conditions and exposed to identical tests. It is noteworthy that animals differ very much from each other under these circumstances. Some will explore quite intrepidly and not urinate or defaecate at all, while others cower in a corner and may urinate several times and deposit as many as five or more faecal boluses during the course of a few minutes. This fact gives us a chance to investigate the inheritance of emotionality, and we shall see later that studies of this kind can be very informative indeed.

In the next room we have rather a different type of experiment. Here animals have been taught to expect a reward whenever a bell is rung. They rush to a trough in a corner of their cage where a tasty pellet of food has been deposited, and ravenously eat it. Having made them accustomed to going over to the corner and eating the pellets the moment the bell has rung, the experimenter now tries to teach them manners. The particular type of etiquette he wishes to establish is this: it is impolite for rats to start eating the moment the bell has rung; they should wait for at least three seconds before they are allowed to pitch in to their meal. In order to teach them this etiquette, the experimenter now arranges for an electric shock to be given to the rats through the metal bars which constitute the floor of the cage, whenever they start eating less than three seconds after the bell has given the signal and the food pellet has been deposited in the trough. This experiment has obvious relevance to the kind of training which goes on in human society to teach young children not to soil their pants, not to show evidence of overt aggression, and in many other ways, to conform to the mores of society. What do the rats do? They have three ways of responding to this training. The first we may call delinquent, or psychopathic: here the rat will go and eat the food immediately it is deposited, regardless of the punishment which it receives. The second type of reaction we might call the neurotic reaction: the rat is so terrified of the whole procedure that he cowers in a far corner and refuses to eat even when it is quite safe to do so. And the third reaction we might call the normal, or integrative, reaction: here the rat learns to wait for three seconds and then to eat his food in complete safety. Can we use experiments of this type to throw any light on criminal and neurotic behaviour in human beings? The answer is probably in the affirmative, but we will have to wait for a later chapter before we take up this question again. For the moment we must end our visit, by looking in very briefly on another experimenter in a neighbouring room. He is running animals along a straight way, beginning in a starting box and running to a food box right in the middle of the runway where they stop, eat one or two pellets of food, and then go on to the second food box which is at the other end of the runway, where they are fed again. This process is repeated a number of times, until the rat expects to be fed in the middle food box as well as in the terminal food box. The experimenter measures the speed with which the rat runs from the starting box to the centre food box and from the centre food box to the terminal food box. He then omits to put any food into the centre food box, expecting the rat to be severely frustrated by this. The object of the experiment is to study the effect of frustration on the rat, and the hypothesis is that frustration, being a strong emotional drive, will make him run faster on the second part of his way, from the second food box to the terminal one. This is indeed what we tend to find. Frustration has a very strong energizing effect and the rat does indeed run a good deal faster than he has done before. Again we may ask whether this is relevant to human conduct. Does the action of the frustrated rat resemble that of the frustrated driver who, after following another car for a long period of time during which he finds it impossible to overtake, then accelerates and rushes away, even though the conditions are still dangerous and such that, in normal conditions, he would not have overtaken? Again we must leave a discussion of this point to a later page.

On the way out, we may hear sounds of revelry, laughter, and the tinkling of glasses. It may come as a surprise to the reader that a party may act as a research instrument for the psychologist, but there are certain questions and problems in social psychology which can best be tackled by disguising the laboratory atmosphere in such a way that few people are aware of the fact that an experiment is being conducted. Let us join the party for a few minutes. What we see is essentially ten people enjoying themselves in the usual way, talking to each other, dancing, flirting, and generally having fun. There are also two rather more sober-looking individuals who circulate but do not seem to participate very much in the spirit of the occasion. These are the experimenters. What is the purpose of the experiment?

Essentially, what we are concerned with here is a study of the 'Can you tell margarine from butter?' type. Most people, whether Jews or anti-semites, assume that Jews constitute a kind of biological group and that they differ from the majority of Europeans and Americans in their physical configuration; that they have a certain type of nose, a certain type of hair, a certain way of speaking, and so on. Is this in fact true? I remember how this question was brought home to me many years ago when I was still at school. I was looking out into the street from the balcony of our house in Berlin, when a group of Storm Troopers were marching by. Walking in the opposite direction was a very Jewish-looking man, and the moment the Storm Troopers saw him they broke formation and started beating him up, with cries of, 'Hit the dirty Jew!' and so forth. I raced down the stairs, two at a time, trying to see what I could do for the man but, of course, without any definite plan in mind. However, when I got down to the ground floor the time for heroics had passed. The Storm Troopers had marched on and the man was lying on the ground, bleeding profusely. He was, as you might imagine, rather indignant about the whole thing, but his indignation revealed that I had really had no call to be concerned about him, because it appeared that he himself was by no means Jewish but was in fact a member of the Nazi party, with a very early accession number. His racial background, which had apparently been investigated very thoroughly, went back over several hundred years without any single Jew being present among his ancestors!

On another occasion, the Nazi Government sent specialists into the schools to look over the pupils and give them a kind of Aryan rating. From top to bottom, every one of us was carefully looked over, measured, and finally pronounced to be Aryan or otherwise. As it happened, the one who got the top rating was one of my best friends and a full-blooded Jew!

These are, of course, simply anecdotes which prove

nothing, except that occasionally we may be mistaken in our judgements. An experiment is necessary to decide just *how* mistaken the average person will be in a large number of cases, and consequently, for the purpose of the experiment, groups of ten people were invited to each of a series of parties, five of whom were Jewish, five of whom were definitely not. They were instructed to mingle, to talk to each other, to enter into the spirit of the party, but not to reveal their true names. They had no notion of the purpose of the experiment, but at the end, after several hours of really getting to know each other, they were asked by the experimenters to say which, if any, of their partners in this party had been Jewish and which had not. The answer, on the whole, was a complete fiasco. Nobody in fact did better than chance. These people found it completely impossible to tell a Jew from a non-Jew by personal appearance, by the way he dressed, the way he talked, the way he behaved, or in any other way. From previous work done in the United States, we had more or less expected that non-Jews who had no particular anti-semitic prejudice, would in fact be unable to tell a Jew from a non-Jew, but there had been some slight evidence that anti-semites and Jews might be better at the game.* Apparently, however, this is not so. In the whole group studied, Jews and anti-semites fared no better than non-Jews who had no interest in this question at all.

Some purists may feel that an experiment of this kind, while quite interesting, is different in nature from the typical laboratory experiment and that it has scientifically a different status. I do not believe that we can make any clear-cut distinction between laboratory experiments of the type described on the previous pages and this particular one and others like it. The essence of the experiment in science is that you should be able to exert control over the variables which influence the outcome of the experiment. Under certain conditions this may require a very elaborate laboratory set-up; in certain conditions it may require control over social variables of quite a different kind. There

*The American work had been done with photographs.

is no difference in principle between the two, and consequently I have included this particular experiment in our list.

This, I am afraid, will have to finish our conducted tour. We have only had time to look into something like ten rooms or so; there are still another forty to go which we will not have time to visit. But what we have seen will perhaps give the reader an idea of the kind of work which is going on and perhaps also show him some of the reasons why individual psychologists are doing the kind of things they are doing. It will be the task of the succeeding chapters, however, to try and spell this out in some detail, and to show the reader just how experiments of this type can be woven together into a theory which affects, or may affect, his life at very many points. It is, of course, a long jump from laboratory experiments of this type to the behaviour of the criminal, or the neurotic, or the person who is suffering an automobile accident. However long and complex the line of reasoning may appear between laboratory and real life, I am, nevertheless, convinced that there is a relationship, and I am also convinced, perhaps even more firmly, that we will never understand and control the events of everyday life unless we succeed in bringing them down to the level of the laboratory and studying them in the simplified conditions made possible by the control we can exert there over stimuli and responses. This outlook, of course, is quite foreign to those who prefer to study life in its full complexity. However desirable it might be to do this, unfortunately it does not seem to be a practicable proposition, and it seems safer to follow the path that physics has also had to take. The physicist, too, cannot study the behaviour of inanimate objects in all their complexity; he, too, is forced to take his problems to the laboratory, to simplify, and perhaps even to over-simplify conditions, until he gets the kind of answer which he is looking for and which he may then, in the form of scientific laws, apply to nature in general. Human behaviour is too impossibly complex to be tackled all at once; we must take it step by step, and if our first faltering steps appear to the critic to be ridiculously inadequate, then we can only say that there is no real alternative. Mankind has tried, for thousands of years, to control behaviour without having recourse to scientific manipulation and laboratory study, and has conspicuously failed to do so. Perhaps the scientific laboratory approach will fail also. It is impossible to make accurate predictions about what science can and cannot do; but at least we should let it have a try and, although its successes have been only small to date, I think they are sufficiently promising to suggest that this approach does indeed have something to offer.

2 Personality and Eysenck's Demon

The concept of personality is widely recognized as being quite central in psychology, yet its definition is a very nebulous affair indeed. There is some agreement that it refers to certain enduring dispositions in the constitution of the individual and that it is the basic reality underlying important individual differences in behaviour, but precisely what its nature is, how it originated, and how it can be defined and measured, are questions on which psychologists are in desperate disagreement. Many textbooks have been written to deal with these problems from many points of view; I shall not try to do anything of the kind here. What I shall try to do instead is to put forward a particular point of view which is probably a minority one, but which has the great advantage of tying psychology in closely with physiology, neurology, and the biological sciences generally. This, to my mind, is extremely important. T. H. Huxley, the comrade-in-arms of Charles Darwin in the great battles over evolution, once coined the phrase 'no psychosis without neurosis'. By this he meant that there are no mental events without some underlying physiological or neurological events which could be investigated and measured by physical science. The day is still far off when we shall be able to accomplish this reduction in an unambiguous fashion, as far as the concepts of personality are concerned, but I will endeavour to show, in this chapter, that the hope of being able to do so is not chimerical and that there is already some evidence to link certain structures in the nervous system with certain types of behaviour patterns.

Before entering upon a discussion of these relations, however, we must first attack a rather different problem. In studying personality, psychologists have found it necessary to make a distinction which, indeed, is customarily made in other sciences as well, and that is the distinction between descriptive and causal analysis. Astronomers, to take but one example from the oldest of the sciences, can and did for many centuries rest content with a simple, mathematical description of the orbit of the planets. Admittedly, they often advanced certain very rudimentary causal hypotheses, such as that the planets were carried along in crystal spheres, or other improbable theories of this kind, but these hypotheses were, one might almost feel inclined to say, of an aesthetic character; they had no direct relation to the problems of descriptive analysis. From this descriptive point of view, it makes relatively little difference whether we regard the sun or the earth as the centre of our planetary system; it is clearly possible to formulate equations which will describe the movements of the planets quite accurately, with reference to either one or the other. It may be easier and more convenient to refer the motions of the planets to the sun rather than to the earth, but there is no principle involved other than that of convenience. The situation changes, however, once we introduce, with Galileo and particularly with Newton, concepts of gravitational force and other causal hypotheses which, however imperfectly, are put forward to reveal to us the causal laws according to which planetary movements occur, and which explain, in a lawful fashion, why the planets move as they do. As long as Galileo was content to adopt the heliocentric point of view merely as a descriptive hypothesis, the Inquisition was happy enough to leave him alone. It was his realization, his insistence, that there were causal questions involved which led to his arraignment before the Inquisition, and to his enforced renunciation.

In psychology, too, we have these two problems. We can *describe* behaviour in terms of traits and types and attitudes and habits, and so forth, without necessarily having to answer questions as to *why* a person is behaving in a particular manner. Causal questions of this kind are important, but they are different from those of a descriptive type, and, one may add, they come historically later. We must first have some preliminary answers at least to the descriptive problem before we can properly tackle the causal problem. I have already, in *Sense and Nonsense in Psychology*, dealt, in some detail, with the descriptive problem, and will, therefore, here only discuss quite briefly the general outlines of the solution; I am more concerned in this chapter with the causal problem. Let us, therefore, look at Figure 8, which gives in brief outline the results

descriptive
before. causal

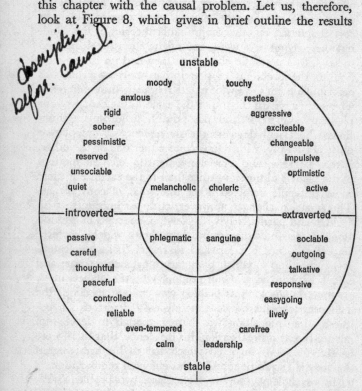

Figure 8. The inner circle of this diagram shows the famous doctrine of the four temperaments; the outer circle shows the results of numerous modern experiments involving ratings and self-ratings of behaviour patterns of large groups of people. It will be seen that there is considerable agreement and it will also be seen that a considerable part of personality can be described in terms of two major dimensions, here labelled introversion/extraversion and unstable/stable.

of a large amount of research. In the smaller circle at the centre of the Figure, the reader will see the four classical temperaments, as they were first put forward by Galen and later adopted by the famous German philosopher, Immanuel Kant, and later still, by the great German psychologist, W. Wundt. It will be seen that two of the temperaments, the choleric and the melancholic, are opposed to the phlegmatic and the sanguine, in the sense that the former have strong emotions, are relatively unstable and neurotic, whereas the latter have rather less violent emotions and are more stable in their behaviour.

Similarly, cholerics and sanguine people shared together a common set of traits which might perhaps, in modern terminology, be called extraverted, whereas melancholics and phlegmatics tend to be introverted. It will be obvious that this gives us two entirely different principles of classification, which we may call *categorical* and *dimensional*. According to the categorical system, we can put people into one of the four quadrants, calling them choleric, or melancholic, or phlegmatic, or sanguine. This is the principle originally adopted by Galen and later by Kant, and they clearly believed that a person could only belong to one or the other of these types, and that no intermingling was possible. 'There are no compound temperaments, e.g. a sanguine-choleric. In all there are only these four temperaments, each of which is simple, and it is impossible to conceive of a human being which mixes them all up.'

The alternative view is that one would assign each person a position on two continua or axes; in other words, a person can be anywhere on the introvert/extravert continuum and he can also have any particular position on the stable/unstable continuum. We would then describe him by referring to his position in this two-dimensional framework. All positions clearly are possible, in the sense that they can be occupied by a given person, and the majority will be likely to lie at the origin: that is to say, be neither melancholic, nor phlegmatic, nor choleric, nor sanguine. This was the view introduced by Wundt around the 1880s, and it is one which is now universally accepted. The doctrine of categorical personality types is not seriously held by any psychologist or psychiatrist nowadays.

How about the description of these four temperaments? Let us follow Kant, who first published his description in 1798. According to him, then, 'the sanguine person is carefree and full of hope; attributes great importance to whatever he may be dealing with at the moment, but may have forgotten all about it the next. He means to keep his promises but fails to do so because he never considered deeply enough beforehand whether he would be able to keep them. He is good-natured enough to help others but is a bad debtor and constantly asks for time to pay. He is very sociable, given to pranks, contented, does not take anything very seriously, and has many, many friends. He is not vicious but difficult to convert from his sins; he may repent but this contrition (which never becomes a feeling of guilt) is soon forgotten. He is easily fatigued and bored by work but is constantly engaged in mere games – these carry with them constant change, and persistence is not his forte.'

We next come to the melancholic temperament. 'People tending towards melancholia attribute great importance to everything that concerns them. They discover everywhere cause for anxiety and notice first of all the difficulties in a situation, in contradistinction to the sanguine person. He does not make promises easily because he insists on keeping his word, but has to consider whether he will be able to do so. All this is not so because of moral considerations but because interaction with others makes him worried, suspicious, and thoughtful. It is for this reason that happiness escapes him.'

Here now is what Kant has to say about the choleric temperament. 'The choleric person is said to be hotheaded, is quickly roused, but easily calmed down if his opponent gives in; he is annoyed without lasting hatred. Activity is quick but not persistent. He is busy but does not like to be in business precisely because he is not persistent; he prefers to give orders but does not want to be bothered with carrying them out. He loves open recognition and wants to be publicly praised. He loves appearances, pomp and formality; he is full of pride and self-love. He is miserly; polite but with ceremony; he suffers most through the refusal of others to fall in with his pretensions. In one word, the choleric temperament is the least happy because it is most likely to call forth opposition to itself.'

Last, the phlegmatic temperament. 'Phlegma means lack of emotion, not laziness; it implies a tendency to be moved neither quickly nor easily but persistently. Such a person warms up slowly but he retains the warmth longer. He acts on principle not by instinct; his happy temperament may supply the lack of sagacity and wisdom. He is reasonable in his dealing with other people and usually gets his way by persisting in his objectives while appearing to give way to others.' (The reader may perhaps guess that Kant considered himself a phlegmatic!)

What is the point in bringing up these old theories and hypotheses again? Have we not advanced beyond the level of the fifteenth century? The answer to this question is given by the ring of trait-names in the outer circle of Figure 8. These, briefly, represent the results of a considerable amount of empirical research, mostly carried out during the last twenty or thirty years, in which large numbers of subjects in America and England, and also on the Continent, have been rated, or have filled in questionnaires regarding a great variety of different traits and types of behaviour. The results of these studies were then treated by means of complex statistical analyses, correlation analyses, principal component analyses, factor analyses, and so on, in the hope that, by doing so, it would become possible to delineate the main dimensions of personality. The outcome of all this work is by now fairly widely recognized to be the emergence of two very strong, very powerful, and very influential factors, axes, or dimensions, which are, in essence, identical with those recognized by Wundt. One axis we have labelled introversion/extraversion, although by this we do not mean to suggest that this conception is identical with that advocated by C. G. Jung, the well-known Swiss psychiatrist. Contrary to common belief, he did not originate the terms extraversion and introversion, but took them over from common European usage, where indeed they had been widely employed for over two hundred years. Neither was he the first to describe these temperamental types, as is often believed; as pointed out before, they go back at least as far as Galen and probably even further, and all that can be said of Jung's own contribution to this typology is that what is new in it is not true, and what is true is not new.

The other dimension is called by many different names: neuroticism, or emotionality, or instability, as opposed to stability or normality. Descriptively, agreement between these modern studies and the old doctrine of the temperaments is quite surprisingly good. The trait-names printed in the outer ring give a rough indication of the results of modern research, in the sense that the closer the trait-names are together, the higher is the empirically observed relation between them. When the angle between them is about ninety degrees, there is no relationship at all, and as the angle grows from ninety to a hundred and eighty degrees, the relationship becomes negative. Thus there is no correlation at all between the trait of excitability and changeability, on the one hand, and that of 'easygoing' and 'responsive', on the other. There is a negative relationship between such traits as 'pessimistic' and 'sober', and 'talkative' and 'outgoing'. There is a very high correlation between traits such as 'moody' and 'touchy'. Thus the inner ring of Figure 8 depicts an ancient theory of personality description; the outer ring depicts the results of the most modern research in this field, and the reader must judge for himself whether the agreement between these two approaches is as close as the writer believes it to be.

The notion of emotional instability, or neuroticism, is perhaps too obvious to require much in the way of definition, and the trait-names given in Figure 8 will enable the reader to form a sufficiently close idea of what is meant, to dis: pense with a formal definition. I have given, in *Sense and Nonsense in Psychology* (pp. 195–6), a questionnaire for the measurement of this emotional instability which may be consulted by anyone who does not find this concept meaningful, or who does not quite understand its implications. For the moment, I shall rather turn to the concept of extraversion/introversion, and give a brief description of typical extraverts and introverts. It is not suggested, of course, that every person is either an introvert or an extravert, or that people are always as extreme as the one or the other description may suggest. Extraversion/introversion is a dimension ranging from one extreme to the other, and passing through a middle area where people are neither the one nor the other; and empirical data suggest that most people fall into this middle area. The position is very similar to that which obtains in the field of intelligence testing. We talk about intelligent and stupid people without implying that everyone is either the one or the other. We know perfectly well that there is a continuum ranging all the way from the lowest mental defective to the highest genius, with the majority of people falling in between, with I.Q.s of between 90 and 110. In order to understand the precise nature of the dimension, however, it is useful to have some idea in mind of what the extremes look like, and it is for this reason that the descriptions below are given.

The typical extravert is sociable, likes parties, has many friends, needs to have people to talk to, and does not like reading or studying by himself. He craves excitement, takes chances, often sticks his neck out, acts on the spur of the moment, and is generally an impulsive individual. He is fond of practical jokes, always has a ready answer, and generally likes change; he is carefree, optimistic, and likes to 'laugh and be merry'. He prefers to keep moving and doing things, tends to be aggressive, and loses his temper quickly. Altogether, his feelings are not kept under tight control, and he is not always a reliable person.

The typical introvert, on the other hand, is a quiet, retiring sort of person, introspective, fond of books rather than people; he is reserved and distant except with intimate friends. He tends to plan ahead, 'looks before he leaps', and distrusts the impulse of the moment. He does not like excitement, takes matters of everyday life with proper seriousness, and likes a well-ordered mode of life. He keeps his feelings under close control, seldom behaves in an aggressive manner, and does not lose his temper easily. He is reliable, somewhat pessimistic, and places great value on ethical standards.

Extraverts and introverts also differ with respect to their attitudes, particularly in the social and political fields. As I have pointed out in *Sense and Nonsense in Psychology*, extraverted people tend to have tough-minded attitudes, introverted people tend more towards tender-minded attitudes. If they are conservative, introverts tend towards religious attitudes and beliefs, whereas the extravert will tend to show such attitudes as believing in the death penalty and in the flogging of criminals, being against miscegenation – he will consider coloured people inferior, and so on. On the radical side, introverts tend towards pacifistic and Quaker-type ideals, whereas the extravert tends towards belief in companionate marriage, easier divorce laws, the belief that Sunday observance is old-fashioned, and so on. At the extreme, conservative extraverts tend to hold Fascist beliefs, and radical extraverts, Communist beliefs. We thus see that the differences between these personality types are quite real and extend into a great number of different fields.

In all that I have been saying, it is not suggested, of course, that these two dimensions are the only ones in terms of which personality can be described, or into which it can be analysed. There are presumably many others, but these are the only two which have been found again and again by many different investigators, using many different methods, and it may perhaps be agreed that these two dimensions are the most important ones in describing human behaviour and conduct. If we were reduced to describing a person in just three figures, then I have no doubt that we would get the closest approximation to his real nature by using these figures for an assessment of his intelligence, his extraversion, and his neuroticism. More than that is not claimed for the personality dimensions we are dealing with, and future research will undoubtedly un-cover many more, although it may be surmised that they will be of rather less generality and importance than the ones discussed here.

So much for the descriptive part of this chapter. How about the causal agents which we may make responsible for these behaviour patterns? In approaching this problem, let us consider, first of all, whether these behaviour patterns are determined more by heredity or more by environmental influences of one kind or another. The belief in the import-ance of environmental influences is very strong, particularly in the United States and in the Soviet Union. Many readers will know of J. B. Watson's famous remark that if a child were given to him at an early age, and if he could prescribe his exact environment, then he could make anything he wanted to of the child, including a famous musician, scientist, etc. Beliefs such as these are characteristic of manipulative societies, with a strong faith in the possibility of solving all problems in a technological manner. The experimental evidence, however, runs strongly counter to any such simple belief, and there is no doubt that we must take into account very decidedly the possibility of hereditary predisposition.

Experimental work in this field has largely made use of certain experiments that nature, as it were, undertakes her-self. As is well known, there are two types of twins, the so-called identical twins, who share identical heredity, and the so-called fraternal twins, in whom heredity is no more alike than it is in ordinary brothers and sisters, i.e. identity amounts to no more than fifty per cent. We may use these interesting natural phenomena in various ways, in our attempt to unravel the mystery of heredity and environ-ment. Let us consider, in the first place, a comparison between groups of identical and fraternal twins, with respect to any particular trait. If we assume that this trait is completely inherited, then the identical twins should show it to precisely the same degree. Fraternal twins, however, only sharing heredity to a much lesser extent, should deviate considerably from each other, although less so, of course, than people selected at random. Let us now look at another trait which owes nothing whatsoever to heredity. In respect to this trait, environment is all-important, and consequently identical twins should be no more alike than would fraternal twins. There are no difficulties in these two situations, and they are not of any particular interest. Our interest comes in when we encounter a situation intermediate between the two, i.e. where the trait is partly determined by heredity and partly by environment. Under these conditions, identical twins should be more alike than should fraternal twins, but the difference should be rather smaller than in the case of a trait completely inherited, and we could use the difference in resemblance between identical twins, on the one hand, and fraternal twins, on the other, to make an assessment of the precise importance which heredity has in the determination of this trait.

This experiment has been carried out several times with respect to various different assessments of neuroticism and of extraversion, and the result has always been to show that heredity does indeed play a large part in the determination of personality but that it does not do this to the complete exclusion of environmental factors. Experiments of this type have sometimes been criticized, on the grounds that identical twins, being so very much more alike, are probably also being treated more similarly by parents, schoolteachers, and others, than are fraternal twins who, after all, are no more alike than ordinary siblings. This is a reasonable criticism, although investigations into the way that twins are treated and the way they react to this have not, on the whole, borne it out. It is usually found that, if anything, identical twins rather dislike being merely mirror images of each other, and try to achieve individuality by developing along different lines as far as that is possible. Thus they react to their identity by trying to individualize each other and to become, as far as they can, different. Thus, if anything, the opposite to the criticism just mentioned might be true; the figures perhaps underrate rather than overrate the resemblance between identical twins.

We can use another method of investigation to study this

particular problem even more closely. What would happen if we took our identical twins and separated them at birth, or very soon afterwards, and had them brought up in entirely different conditions? When this is done, as it was done, for instance, in a recent study by J. Shields, who located a large number of such twins through an appeal over television, we find that identical twins are still very much more alike than are fraternal twins, although the latter have been brought up together. Indeed, Shields found, when he compared his identical twins brought up separately with his identical twins brought up together, that with respect to intelligence, extraversion, and neuroticism, the twins who had been brought up separately were more alike than were the twins who had been brought up together. This is a complete vindication of the twin method, and a powerful answer to the criticism of the studies using identical and fraternal twin comparisons, when both types of twin have been brought up together.

A third method of investigation is one in which personality traits are measured in various members of a family, the hypothesis being that if heredity plays an important part, then the degree of similarity between different members of the family should, to some extent, mirror the degree of relatedness. This experiment, too, has been done several times and has also given positive results; it does indeed seem that, with respect to extraversion and neuroticism, the degree of consanguinity is mirrored by a degree in resemblance. This has also been found to be true of intelligence, which, on the whole, appears to be inherited to pretty much the same extent as are emotionality or neuroticism, and extraversion/introversion.

There is one other avenue of experimentation which is open to us, and this, in many ways, is the most satisfactory. Human beings interbreed in a manner which does not admit of any form of scientific control; all our experimental and analytic work has to be *post hoc*. At best, we can make use of such experiments as nature performs for us, such as, for instance, the production of identical and fraternal twins, but we cannot plan investigations *de novo*. Things are different, of course, with animals, and here we can carry out experimental work to our heart's content, breeding for a variety of behaviour patterns which we have reason to believe may be determined, in part or completely, by hereditary factors. Let me give just one example of such a study, to illustrate the method.

The reader will already be familiar with the open field test for measuring emotionality in rats; it was described in passing in the first chapter, in our brief tour of the experimental rooms in the animal laboratory. It will be remembered that the chief score in this test is the number of faecal boluses deposited by the rat during his brief stay in the open field, with bright lights glaring down on him and loudspeakers pouring forth white noise above his innocent head. Now different rats vary greatly in their behaviour under these conditions, and it is possible to select rats of high emotionality – that is to say, those producing many boluses – and interbreed them, and at the same time, select rats of low emotionality – that is to say, depositing few boluses – and interbreed them. In this way, we can continue from generation to generation, always interbreeding the highly emotional with each other and, at the other end, those of low emotionality. In the course of this work, and assuming that heredity plays an important part in the genesis of emotionality, we should come to a point where the offspring of the emotional group were hardly overlapping in their behaviour with the offspring of the non-emotional group. Figure 9 gives the results of such an experiment, showing the mean number of boluses produced in the experimental situation by each successive generation. It will be seen that, as the breeding experiment progresses, the two strains draw apart more and more until, towards the end, they are very far apart indeed. There is, for all practical purposes, no overlap between the two strains, so that the most emotional offspring from the non-emotional strain are less emotional than the least emotional offspring from the emotional strain. There are, of course, technical ways of measuring the precise degree of inheritance present in these animals and even the degree of dominance, penetrance,* and so on, but we will not enter into these rather complex matters here. Suffice it to say that the fact that one can breed for a particular trait is sufficient to prove that heredity plays a strong part in the causation of this trait.

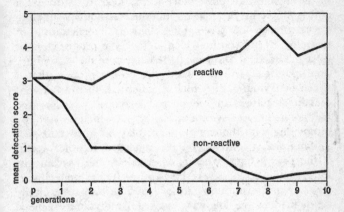

Figure 9. This diagram shows the results of an experiment in which rats were bred for high and low emotionality, respectively. Ten generations are shown, and it will be seen that the emotionally-reactive animals become progressively more reactive, whereas the emotionally-non-reactive animals become much less so. The tenth generation shows almost no overlap between the offspring of these two strains. (From an article by P. Broadhurst in H. J. Eysenck (Ed.), *Experiments in Personality*).

Isolation of this trait in animals does not mean, of course, that what is true of rats must necessarily be true of humans. But we have already seen, in the first chapter, that in humans, too, defaecation and urination are frequently the outcome of strong and powerful emotions of fear and that, therefore, there is a close similarity between the two; and we have seen that other methods, such as the twin method, when applied to humans, also show that emotionality or neuroticism is, in fact, inherited. We may say, therefore,

*Penetrance: the relative ability of a gene to produce its specific effect in any degree whatsoever in the organism of which it is a part.

that animal methods of this type may be used to support evidence derived from experiments with human beings.

These studies of inheritance are important, because they suggest very strongly that there must be some biological roots underlying personality and behaviour. It is clearly inconceivable that personality traits, such as extraversion and emotionality, should be inherited without postulating the existence of some physiological, biochemical, or neurological substratum which, in fact, was produced, or at least modified by the genes, the carriers of our hereditary predispositions. In other words, we do not propose that it is the behaviour itself which is inherited, but rather that certain structures in the central nervous system or the autonomic nervous system are inherited, which, in turn, by interacting with the environment, play an important part in determining conduct. What is inherited, in other words, is the *genotype*, and what is observed by the psychologist interested in behaviour, is the *phenotype*. These are technical terms in the scientific study of heredity, and may briefly be defined in the following way. An individual's genetic constitution is called his genotype, whereas his actual appearance, which is a product of genotype and environment as he has experienced it, is called his phenotype. The distinction, which is an important one theoretically, is, of course, not always easy to make, but should always be borne in mind in discussing these matters.

We have now come to the point where we have determined the existence, at a descriptive level, of two important dimensions of personality, extraversion/introversion and neuroticism/stability, and we have also decided that these dimensions are powerfully determined by heredity and are likely, therefore, to have some form of physiological, neurological, or biochemical basis in the nervous system of the individual. Can we go further than that and determine the precise nature of this causal agency? The answer is that this cannot be done with any great degree of accuracy or conviction, but that there are many leads nowadays which may take us to the edge at least of this promised land. Let us first of all deal with the concept of emotionality or neuroticism. Clearly, what we are dealing with here is an over-reaction on the part of the individual to a variety of stimuli; this over-reaction takes the form of very strong emotions being experienced under conditions where most people only feel weak emotion, if any at all. Now fortunately a good deal is known about the nature and causation of emotions, and as I have discussed this at some length in *Sense and Nonsense in Psychology*, I will only recapitulate it very briefly.

All mammals have a central nervous system which essentially consists of long, neural pathways going from all parts of the body to the brain, mediating information coming in through the sense organs, and which also contains other pathways going from the brain to the striped musculature of the body, initiating voluntary movements. In addition, however, to the central nervous system, we have the autonomic nervous system, which deals, as the name implies, with certain involuntary activities which are essential for the survival of the organism. It regulates the heart beat, for instance; it makes us continue breathing when we are asleep; it governs the flow of blood through the body and the very fine adjustments in this necessitated by changes in temperature; it governs the size of our pupil in response to incoming light, opening it wider when the light is poor and closing it down when the light is too bright; it determines the electric conductivity of the skin, increasing it under conditions of upset, or emotion, or danger, and reducing it under conditions of quietude. The autonomic system is itself subdivided into two parts, the so-called sympathetic and the para-sympathetic system; the former is the emergency system, preparing the body, as it were, for fight or flight; it stops the digestion, makes the heart beat faster, increases the rate of breathing, and in many other ways, prepares the body for reactions to dangerous situations. If the reader will try to remember an occasion when he was very much afraid or very angry, he will probably recall these reactions in terms of the action of the sympathetic nervous system – the rapid beating of the heart, the increase in the rate of breathing, and other similar reactions. The para-sympathetic system is antagonistic to the sympathetic and produces exactly opposite effects. It lowers the rate of breathing, it decreases the heart beat, and in all other ways, has precisely the opposite effect to the sympathetic. It is essentially a system of quiet, happy, peaceful existence, just enabling the organism to vegetate, as it were.

There seems very little doubt that differences between people in emotionality or neuroticism are mediated by inherited differences in the lability and excitability of the autonomic nervous system. Some people are constitutionally predisposed to react strongly with their sympathetic system towards incoming stimuli of various kind, whereas other people are predisposed to react much less strongly. These reactions, integrated as they are with ongoing activity, are experienced by the organism as emotions and are reacted to accordingly. There is very little mystery about the whole process in principle, although, as we shall see, there are certain specific difficulties when it comes to making precise predictions about the reactions of a particular person. One of these difficulties is that of response specificity. We have talked of the sympathetic nervous system as if it always acted as a whole, but this is, in fact, not true. Emergencies stimulate the whole sympathetic system, it is true, but there are still differences in rate of response between the different parts of the system. Thus, one person may be characterized by reacting particularly strongly with an increase in heart rate, whereas another one rather tends to react with a much more rapid rate of breathing. A third one, again, may react more in terms of an increase in muscular tension throughout the body, and a fourth may have yet another favourite pattern of reaction. It is unknown whether this patterning of reaction is itself inherited, or whether it is due to a process of early conditioning; probably both factors are involved in most cases. Investigation of a person's emotional reactivity, therefore, has to be relatively complex, and has to involve many more than one type of measurement. These, and other difficulties and complexities, have to be faced by the experimental psychologist studying these reactions, but they are not sufficient to detract, in any serious way, from the value of our identification of the autonomic system as the most likely biological basis for individual differences in emotional reactions.

It is when we turn to extraversion/introversion that difficulties have arisen in the past, and it is here that I wish to introduce the little demon that has given this chapter its title. The reader may, of course, like to question the propriety of introducing demons into a scientific book on personality, but there is good historical precedent for this. Readers with a background in physics may recollect Maxwell's demon, introduced by the famous originator of field theories in electricity, to illustrate certain types of behaviour of molecules in gaseous substances. What he postulated roughly was a little demon situated near a hole in a partition which separated the two halves of a large chamber filled with gas. The task of the demon was to let the molecules of gas pass from chamber A to chamber B, but not to allow them to come back from B into A. In this way, they would gradually build up an inequality of pressure between A and B, an inequality which would be unlikely to occur if the ordinary statistical laws of the movement of molecules were allowed their way. Maxwell's demon, of course, is non-existent, and was merely introduced as a teaching device to illustrate certain points. Eysenck's demon, however, is a much more robust fellow and I hope to be able to show that, in some form at least, he may have a real existence in the recesses of our hindbrain.

For the moment, let us simply regard this demon as a kind of homunculus, sitting near the point where the long pathways of the central nervous system enter into the lower parts of the brain. He has his hands on two levers, one marked 'excitation', the other marked 'inhibition'. Whenever sensory stimuli are coming in through these pathways, he presses sometimes one lever, sometimes the other, and sometimes both. Stimuli produced by the levers are then sent on into the brain, where they either facilitate

the passage and the interplay of the incoming neural
stimuli, or suppress and inhibit them. In part, therefore,
the demon acts as a kind of amplifying valve, and in part
as a suppressor; in both ways, the demon adds a good deal
of flexibility to the system of incoming and outgoing
messages.

Can we say more precisely what we mean by excitation
and inhibition? By excitation we mean, in neural and
behavioural terms, facilitation of perceptual, motor, learning, and thinking responses in the central nervous system.
By inhibition we mean the opposite of all these, i.e. the
depression of the central motor, learning, and thinking
responses. In this connexion, the reader may like to think
back on our first chapter, where we have already introduced some behavioural studies involving these concepts,
particularly that of inhibition. Let us, for the moment,
throw all the responsibility for producing inhibition on to
this little demon, and also make him responsible for its
opposite: facilitation, or excitation of neural impulses,
transmission, etc. Does this help us in any way in our search
for a biological basis for our behavioural concepts of
extraversion/introversion? Well, the answer is that it does
not by itself do so, but we have to make one further assumption which is indeed vital for the hypothesis I am
going to put forward in this chapter. Let us assume that
some demons are right-handed and that others are left-
handed, so that some demons have a tendency to pull the
inhibition lever more strongly than others, while other
demons have the opposite tendency: that is to say, to pull
the excitation lever more strongly. And let us make one
further assumption: that is to say that demons who are
left-handed and have a tendency, therefore, to pull the
inhibition lever more strongly, inhabit the central nervous
systems of extraverted people, while right-handed demons,
with a tendency to pull the excitation level more strongly,
inhabit the central nervous systems of introverted people.
Demons who are ambidextrous, and who have no pro-
pensity for pulling extra hard with either hand, would
then, of course, be found in the central nervous systems of

ambiverts, that is to say people who are neither extraverted nor introverted.

How can we supply some measure of experimental proof for a hypothesis of this type? Dismissing, for the moment, the daemonological aspects of our theory, what we are saying essentially is that inhibitory potentials are likely to be greater in extraverted people, excitatory potentials in introverted people. Now fortunately we have already had some acquaintance with experimental measures of these two forces, and these lead us immediately to a direct test of our hypothesis. For instance, in connexion with the pursuit rotor, we have shown in the first chapter how reminiscence, or the improvement in performance over a rest period due to the dissipation of inhibition, is a direct measure of the amount of inhibition accumulated prior to the rest period. We would expect, therefore – and it has indeed been found to be so – that extraverted people would accumulate more inhibition, dissipate more inhibition, and consequently show greater reminiscence. Findings of this type, precisely because they are so unexpected on commonsense grounds, must strongly support the general theory which enables them to be discovered in the laboratory.

We have also mentioned, in the first chapter, the fact that by simple tests of tapping, it is possible to measure the number of involuntary rest pauses induced by inhibitory potentials. This number would be expected to be greater in extraverted people than in introverts, and Figure 10 shows the actual performance of nine introverts and nine extraverts on the first minute's work of this test. These subjects were selected on the basis of a questionnaire, from about ninety male workers in a factory; they were not extreme in any kind of pathological sense, but were the sort of people one would easily meet in everyday life. Nevertheless, the discrimination between them, on the basis of this test, is very considerable. The mean number of involuntary rest pauses of the extraverted group is eighteen; of the introverted group it is only one. There is no overlap whatsoever between the two groups. The introvert with the largest number of rest pauses has many fewer than the extravert with the smallest number of rest pauses. No lengthy discussion is required: the diagram speaks for itself.

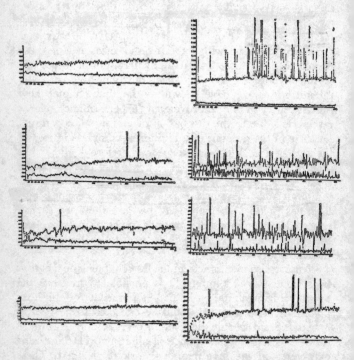

Figure 10. Results of an experiment in which nine introverted subjects (left of pages 72–3) and nine extraverted subjects (right of pages 72–3) were asked to tap as fast as they could for one minute. Length of tap (bottom line in each diagram) and length of gap (top line in each diagram) were recorded for each single tap and gap. It was anticipated that inhibition would be set up during this experiment and that this would lead to involuntary rest pauses; it was further anticipated that these would be much more numerous among the extraverted group. It will be seen that these expectations are borne out, particularly with respect to the gaps. For explanation see text (from an experiment by I. Spielman, in H. J. Eysenck, *Crime and Personality*). (Figure continued opposite.)

Also discussed in our first chapter was the spiral after-effect, and the prediction that here extraverts would have shorter after-effects than introverts, a finding which has been duplicated in many laboratories. Masking effects

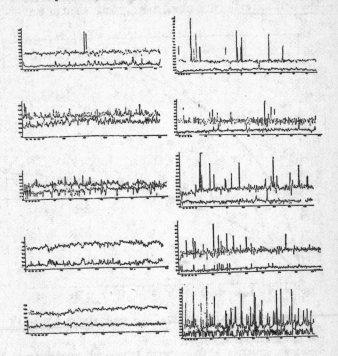

were also discussed, and we have seen that extraverts would tend to show inhibitory effects in this experiment, to a greater extent than do introverts: a finding which, once again, has found much support. A third visual measure, the figural after-effects test, can also be regarded as a measure of inhibition, and, as one would have expected, extraverts show greater after-effects than do introverts.

Of particular importance, however, for our argument, are differences between extraverts and introverts in conditioning. Pavlov was the first to show how strongly inhibitory effects can retard and upset conditioning schedules, and we would expect, therefore, that extraverted people, having strong inhibitory potentials, would condition less well and extinguish much more quickly than introverts.

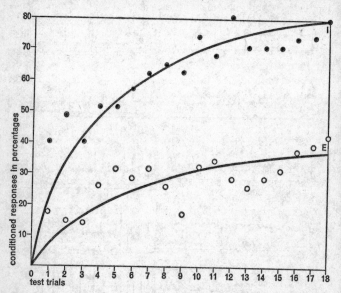

Figure 11. Performance on an eye-blink conditioning experiment by introverts (solid circles) and by extraverts (open circles). It will be seen that throughout the experiment introverts show about twice as many conditioned responses as do extraverts (from work reported by C. Franks).

Figure 11 shows the results of one such test carried out on groups of introverted and extraverted people, both normal and neurotic. (It was interesting to note that there are no differences between normals and neurotics as such, so that we can quite safely lump together extraverted normals and neurotics, on the one hand, and introverted normals and neurotics, on the other. Care was, of course, taken to see that the proportion of normals in each group was equal.)

Again the figure speaks for itself; it will be clear that introverts condition about twice as strongly as do extraverts.

It would be possible to go on a good deal longer showing that, on other tests, such as vigilance for instance, the predicted differences between extraverts and introverts do, in fact, occur. However, there would be little point in doing this; at the moment we are merely interested in illustrating the *kind* of differences which can be observed. It may be useful, however, at this point, to introduce one warning. Predictions in this field may sometimes be a little more complex than might appear at first sight. As an example, let us take the figural after-effects test. In this, as the reader will remember, the subject has to fixate a drawing for a period which may vary from one to four or five minutes, depending upon the experimental arrangements; he then transfers his gaze to another drawing, and the experimenter studies the after-effects of the first drawing on the perception of the second. Now, these after-effects, as we have said, are of the nature of an inhibitory potential and, in terms of our theory, we would expect extraverts to show them more strongly than introverts. However, there is one obvious complication here which may have occurred to the critical reader. The subject has to gaze upon the first drawing for a very long period of time; this activity itself requires a kind of concentrated effort, and we would expect, therefore, in terms of our theory, that inhibition would set in and make it more difficult for the subject actually to fixate the drawing. We would expect him occasionally to look away from it, quite involuntarily of course, and without any desire to disobey instructions; or his accommodation might vary, or he might, in other ways, give way to involuntary rest pauses of one kind or another, the effect of which would be to break up and interrupt the concentrated fixation of the picture on which the after-effect depends. Now the inhibitory potential set up by this long process of watching should be stronger in extraverts than in introverts and, consequently, we would expect them to fixate the original drawing less well than would introverts. This, however, should militate against the setting up of the satiation which we are measuring when we transfer the gaze from the first drawing to the second. In other words, we have here two contradictory effects; the first, regarding the fixation of the first drawing, would favour the introverts and would make us predict that they would have a longer effective period of fixation and that, therefore, their after-effects of fixating the second drawing should be longer. On the other hand, the accumulation of greater satiation during the fixation period on the part of the extraverts would lead us to predict that they would have longer visual after-effects. Apparently, then, almost anything can happen, and no direct prediction can be made from our hypothesis.

Fortunately, the position is not as dark as this might suggest. We know that inhibitions attaching to muscular movements, such as those which keep the eyes firmly fixed on the fixation point of the first drawing, are subject to an inhibition which takes much longer to develop than the kind of inhibition which is the basis of the perceptual satiation on which the figural after-effect depends. Consequently, we can alter our prediction, making it rather more complex, by saying that if the inspection period is relatively short, there will be little opportunity for muscular inhibition to set in, and satiation, by itself, will be the main determining factor in accounting for the length of the figural after-effect. Under those conditions, extraverts should show longer figural after-effects, and it is this type of experiment which I have been discussing so far. If, however, we prolong the inspection period unduly, then we would expect the opposite type of result, and intro-verted people should show greater figural after-effect. With intermediate length of inspection periods, we would expect a crossing over; that is to say, there should be one point of time when the two groups would, in fact, be equal. We thus have a much more complex type of prediction and one which, if it could be shown to be in fact correct, would give even greater support to the general theory for which we are arguing. Figure 12 shows the outcome of experiments specifically conducted in order to test this more general hypothesis.* On the baseline are plotted the six inspection periods used, ranging from 15 seconds to 210 seconds, and on the vertical axis are shown the amounts of after-effects. It will be seen that, with the short inspection periods, the extraverted groups in fact show greater after-effects, that there is a crossing over at the length of inspection period of about 135 seconds, and that with the long inspection period, as predicted, the introverts in fact show longer after-effects. Some additional complexities of the experiment have been omitted.

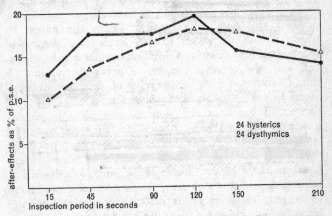

Figure 12. Satiation and inhibition effects according to theory are more pronounced in extraverts than in introverts. The time-course of satiation and inhibition, respectively, suggests that figural after-effects should be stronger in extraverts when short inspection periods are used, and longer in introverts when long inspection periods are used. This diagram demonstrates the predicted switch-over in an experiment using twenty-four neurotic extraverts (hysterics) and twenty-four neurotic introverts (dysthymics). For explanation, see text. (From an experiment by C. Blakemore.)

I have discussed this experimental complexity in some detail to give the reader an idea of the difficulties which attach to the direct proof of the predictions which can be made from a theory such as that we are considering.

*In this experiment, kinaesthetic rather than visual stimuli were used.

Similar difficulties and complexities attach, of course, to all the other experiments I have mentioned. I have, on purpose, refrained from going into too much detail, because that would be more appropriate in a textbook than in a popular discussion of this type.

How does our general picture of personality structure look now? I have tried, in Figure 13, to show roughly how we may regard the relations between the genotypic and the phenotypic levels of personality development. At the bottom – that is, the most fundamental level of all – we have a theoretical construct, the excitation/inhibition balance, or Eysenck's demon, if you like. This constitutes the constitutional part of personality: hence the letters P_C which I have appended to this level. This theoretical construct of the excitation/inhibition balance is to be identified with the genotypic aspect of personality, and it is this, of course, which we conceive of as being inherited along the ordinary lines of Mendelian inheritance. This theoretical construct can now be embodied in experimental phenomena of an observable nature by means of studying conditioning, vigilance, reminiscence, after-image duration, figural after-effects, and so forth. None of these phenomena, of course, is a pure measure of excitation or inhibition, and, consequently, one would not expect them to be pure measures either of the genotype that we are interested in. However, they are all determined, in part, by this theoretical construct, by our little demon with his right and left hands on the levers of excitation and inhibition, and, therefore, a reasonable collection of these different tests should give us a fairly good measure of the theoretical construct, or the nature of our demon, if you like.

Our organism, equipped with this particular genotypic constitution, now encounters a certain type of environment, and the interaction between environment and genotype then gives rise to phenotypic extraversion and introversion, and the various primary traits, sociability, impulsivity, ascendance, activity, and so on, which conjointly make up this concept. In the diagram I have put this in the form of an equation, to wit: $P_B = P_C \times E$; that is to say, behavioural personality equals constitutional personality times environment. In this formula, the multiplication sign, of course, does not have any particular mathematical implications; it merely suggests the interaction of these two forces.

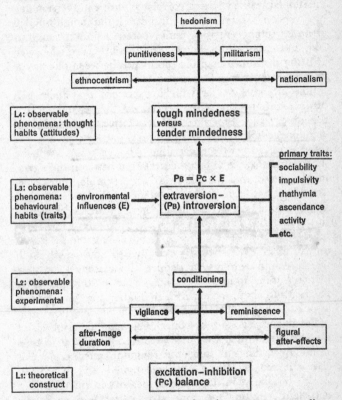

hedonism

punitiveness ←→ militarism

ethnocentrism ←————————————→ nationalism

L4: observable phenomena: thought habits (attitudes)

tough mindedness versus **tender mindedness**

primary traits:
sociability
impulsivity
rhathymia
ascendance
activity
etc.

$P_B = P_C \times E$

L3: observable phenomena: behavioural habits (traits)

environmental influences (E) → extraversion – (P_B) introversion

L2: observable phenomena: experimental

conditioning

vigilance ←→ reminiscence

after-image duration ←————————————→ figural after-effects

L1: theoretical construct

excitation–inhibition (P_C) balance

Figure 13. The influence of heredity and environment on personality. The balance between excitation and inhibition is presumed to be constitutionally determined; it can be measured with varying degrees of accuracy by experimental phenomena like conditioning, vigilance, reminiscence, and so on. These hereditary functions interact with environmental influences to produce behavioural traits like sociability, impulsiveness, ascendance, and so on, and also, at a higher level still, attitudes like hedonism, nationalism, ethnocentrism, and so forth.

The primary traits making up extraversion and introversion may be considered as habits, and we may go up
one more level to the one which, in the diagram, is labelled
L_4. This deals with thought habits or attitudes, such as
those of tough-mindedness and tender-mindedness, which I
mentioned before as being correlated with extraversion and
introversion. Here I have illustrated the tough-minded
attitudes: ethnocentrism, punitiveness, hedonism, militarism, and nationalism. These also, of course, are conceived
as being the outcome of the confluence between phenotype
and environmental influences.

The attentive reader will have noticed that there is a
distinct gap in our scheme between the second level –
the observable, experimental, laboratory phenomena of
vigilance, conditioning, reminiscence, and so on – and the
third level, that of the observable habits or traits. We have
shown that there is in fact a correlation between these two,
in the sense that people who are sociable, impulsive,
ascendant, active, and so on (in other words the extraverted
sort of people) show certain responses in the experimental
situations; they condition poorly, they show poor vigilance,
have short after-image duration, have long reminiscence,
and so forth. But we have not provided any causal chain
which would help us to deduce the existence of these
primary traits from what is known about the excitation
balance and about the experimental laboratory phenomena
associated with it. This is a task to which we must now turn.

Let us make a start by considering some descriptions of
the extravert which we have already quoted from Kant's
work. According to him, the sanguine temperament is
characterized by being 'easily fatigued and bored by
work'. Similarly, in the choleric 'activity is quick but not
persistent'. Putting the same ideas in terms of the traits
which modern research has found characteristic of the extravert, he is changeable and easygoing; he does not persist
in activities for any long period of time but switches over
to something else. Why should this be so? Now here the
relationship with our hypothetical demon pulling the inhibition lever particularly strongly is, of course, fairly clear.

Any activity the extravert indulges in sets up inhibition; this inhibition gradually builds up until it enforces a cessation of the activity – the involuntary rest pauses we have encountered so often before. If there is no prolonged rest, then ultimately the activity must come to a stop altogether, and if the person has any freedom of choice at all, he will then turn to something else. The introvert, on the other hand, having much less inhibition set up in the course of his work, is able to continue for a very much longer period.

This changeableness of the extravert affects a very large number of different types of activity. He is more likely to change his work, his profession, move from one company to another, or change departments within one company. He is more liable to change house, to move from one part of the town to another, or even from one city to somewhere else. He is more likely to change his food preferences from day to day, or even his clothes. He is more likely to change girl friends, or, at a later stage, to get divorced and change wives. He is less likely to stick to one and the same car for a long period of time, or to the same colour scheme in his house, or even to the same furniture. This all-pervading changeability, which is such a fundamental part of the nature of the extravert, is directly traceable to the powerful influence of inhibitory potentials.

It is striking how slight changes in schedule can make very large changes in the effectiveness of certain learning procedures as far as extraverts are concerned. Here, for instance, is an example from a clinic to which were referred two adolescents, one an extreme extravert, the other an introvert. Both had completely failed to learn to read, and the task of the psychologist was to find a way of getting over this difficulty. As far as the introvert was concerned, there was no real trouble; in his case, illness and lack of attendance at school had caused the difficulty, and could easily be overcome by coaching. As far as the extravert was concerned, however, there was no record of absence from school, and coaching had no effect on him at all. The hypothesis was formulated that, in the case of the extraverted boy, the difficulty lay in the quickly-mounting inhibition set up by any form of teaching, and it was decided to test this hypothesis by alternating for him lessons of the ordinary length and lessons cut in half. After each lesson an attempt was made to assess what he had learned. A similar schedule was followed for the introverted boy, and the outcome was very interesting. As far as he was concerned, length of lesson made no difference at all. Where the extravert was concerned, however, he learned nothing whatsoever when the lesson was of the ordinary length, but he learned perfectly adequately when the lesson was cut by half and when, therefore, inhibition did not grow to an unwieldy extent. This, of course, is merely an example, and does not prove that this method would always work in similar circumstances, but it does show the kind of difference which exists between the extravert and the introvert.

Related to this is another feature in the conduct of the extravert, whether in ordinary life or in the laboratory, which has often been noted, and that is the variability of his performance. When you plot a person's activities, either on a test or during a work period, you can discriminate between different people in terms of the average level at which they perform. Supposing you were concerned with measuring their reaction times to a particular stimulus, then A might have the following set of reaction times in milliseconds: 180, 184, 176, 181, 182, 178, 179; whereas B might have the following: 200, 160, 175, 185, 210, 180, 150. Now both A and B would have a mean reaction time of 180, but clearly A is very much more consistent in his reactions, never varying very much from the central figure; whereas B is very variable indeed, his reaction times varying from 150 at the one end, to 210 at the other. Now this variability can clearly be accounted for in terms of inhibition and involuntary rest pauses. The involuntary rest pause provides the occasion for a very poor, long-drawn-out performance, but the rest involved in this means that the organism is now refreshed and can perform particularly well immediately afterwards, so that we get exceptionally poor and exceptionally good performances mixed up in his record. A look at Figure 10 (p. 72) will remind the reader of how very marked this difference can be. Here we have the tapping records of extraverts and introverts, and even the most casual look will convince the reader that the introverts, in every case, perform at a steady level, with only very occasional departures from this level, whereas the extraverts are, as the saying goes, all over the place. Nevertheless, on the average, the two groups perform equally well; there is no difference in the number of taps between extraverts and introverts. It is the variability in performance which distinguishes between them and it is this variability which is so characteristic of the extravert and which we can blame directly on his high level of inhibition.

There is another range of behaviour patterns which we can deduce from our postulated differences in the conduct of Eysenck's demon. Let us look at incoming sensory stimulation of any kind. According to our hypothesis, the demon may either amplify and facilitate this incoming stimulation, or he may act in inhibitory fashion and depress the level of stimulation which gets through to the cortex. From this, very simple, hypothesis, we can make many deductions. Supposing that individuals are exposed to very strong, painful stimuli and that they are motivated to try and bear this painful stimulation as long as possible. We would predict that the pain tolerance of the extravert would be greater than that of the introvert, because, in his case, although the actual pain inflicted would be equal to that inflicted on the introvert, the actual pain experienced would be very much less because of the activity of Eysenck's demon in depressing and inhibiting it. Conversely, the pain experienced by the introvert should be greater because, if anything, excitatory and facilitative actions are taken by the demon. This is an easy prediction to test, and several studies have shown very great differences in the predicted direction between groups of extraverts and introverts.

We can make a precisely opposite prediction in relation to conditions of sensory deprivation. These have attracted a good deal of attention in recent years, possibly because of their relation to astronauts and their likely experiences in space. In a typical experiment, the subject is shut in, all by himself, in a little room; his eyes are blindfolded, his ears are stuffed with cotton-wool, and, in addition, the room in which he is is soundproofed so that he is quite incapable of receiving any form of auditory stimulation. Cardboard covers are tied round his hands so that he cannot feel anything, and he is left alone, for days on end, all by himself. In some experiments, an even stricter régime is introduced, and the subject is actually immersed completely in water of body temperature, breathing through a kind of snorkel tube, and completely isolated from all sensory experience whatsoever. Very few people can tolerate this kind of condition for any length of time, and the absence of stimulation can be as painful as quite considerable degrees of pain. We would expect that introverts would be much better able to tolerate conditions of sensory deprivation because whatever stimulation is going, as it were, they will get, whereas the extravert will receive much less of even the very slight stimulation which is still present, because of the inhibitory activities of his central nervous system. This again has been shown to be so in several different investigations.

We can extend this whole notion by postulating that the extravert would be affected by what is sometimes called 'stimulus hunger', i.e. a desire for strong sensory stimulation – a desire which would be very much less marked in the introvert. Again, we can make certain testable deductions. We would expect extraverts, for instance, to be fond of loud noise, jazz, and bright colours; we would expect them to be keen on alcohol and other drugs, to smoke more cigarettes, and to indulge more in fornication and in other types of sexual activity. There is a good deal of evidence that this is indeed so. Unmarried mothers have been tested, for instance, and have been found to be strongly extraverted. It has been shown that there is an almost straight line relationship between the degree of extraversion and the number of cigarettes smoked. It has also been found that drinkers tend to be more extraverted than non-drinkers. Studies involving aesthetic preferences have indeed shown that extraverts do have strong preferences for highly coloured pictures, as opposed to introverts, who prefer the more old-fashioned, less highly coloured type of picture. The very sociability which is so characteristic a part of the extravert picture is possibly related to this stimulus hunger; most of our stimulation, after all, derives from concourse with other people, and the well-known tendency of the introvert to settle down all by himself with a good book is certainly not conducive to providing the 'arousal jag' the extravert needs so badly!

One of the most important chains of argument relating the genotypic to the phenotypic level, however, goes by way of the conditioning process. As I shall discuss this in considerable detail later on, I shall only mention the argument very briefly here, leaving it to our later discussion to establish it more firmly. It will be suggested, then, that most neurotic disorders, particularly the anxieties, fears, phobias, or the obsessional and compulsive habits which characterize so many of our patients, are, in fact, nothing but conditioned emotional reactions which are acquired through a process of ordinary Pavlovian conditioning. Given that, on the whole, the traumatic and pain-producing events of everyday life which are responsible for the unconditioned stimuli, as it were, in this process are distributed roughly evenly over the whole population, then we would expect that those people who condition more easily – that is to say, the introverts – will tend to be the people who also are more likely to suffer these different types of neurotic disorder. There is so much evidence now to show that this is indeed the case – that introversion, conditioning, and anxiety, phobic, and obsessional disorders do indeed go together in the same people – that it is hardly necessary to document the point.

Similarly, it will be made plain that Pavlovian conditioning is also responsible for what is sometimes called the process of socialization; that is to say, the process by means of which society imposes on young children and adolescents the pattern of behaviour which it finds necessary for survival. This pattern includes, of course, a variety of types of behaviour ranging, at the very early stages, from learning to urinate and defaecate in the pot rather than in one's clothes or in the bed, down to the perhaps rather more important conceptions of ethical and moral behaviour, of compliance with legal requirements, of not expressing aggressive and sexual tendencies in too overt a manner, and so on and so forth. Now if conditioning is basically responsible for our acquisition of these social mores, then we would expect that those who have failed to acquire them – that is to say, juvenile delinquents, criminals, psychopaths (moral imbeciles), and similar types of people – should, on the whole, be extraverted and should also be found to be difficult to condition. Here again there is a great deal of evidence. Perhaps Figure 14 might be useful in this connexion. It shows the results of various questionnaire studies of different types of neurotic and criminal populations. It will be seen that, as predicted, the criminal and psychopathic groups tend to show high emotionality and high extraversion, whereas the neurotic groups tend to show high emotionality and high introversion. With this Figure I shall leave this point for the moment, but, as said before, it will be taken up again, in considerable detail, later on.

We have now painted a rough picture of Eysenck's demon and his various activities inside the central nervous system, and we have tried to trace a chain between these activities and the ordinary, everyday-life behaviour of the people in whom he dwells. Can we now endeavour to give the demon a local habitation and a name? I shall try to do so, but the reader should be warned that we are now on rather dangerous and speculative ground, and that much work is going on at the moment in the physiological study of the structures I shall be discussing, so that what I am saying today may already be old-fashioned and out-of-date by the time the book comes from the printers. However, with this danger ever-present in mind, let us try and see whether we cannot bring the demon down to earth a little more than we have done hitherto.

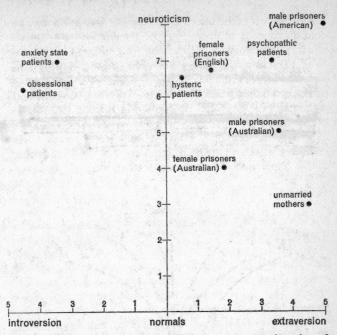

Figure 14. In this diagram are plotted the scores on questionnaires of neuroticism and extraversion/introversion of various neurotic groups and also of various criminal groups. It will be seen that anxiety state and obsessional patients tend to be high on neuroticism and high on introversion, whereas criminals and psychopaths tend to be high on neuroticism and high on extraversion. (From H. J. Eysenck, *Crime and Personality.*)

Let us have a brief look at the structure of the central nervous system. In the first place, we have the long neural pathways from the receptors to the brain, bringing in information about the state of the outer world. We also have a set of long motor pathways coming from the brain to the striped muscles, leading to activities geared to the information received via the sensory pathways. To this very simple pattern, however, it has been found necessary, in recent years, to add another structure, the so-called ascending reticular formation which is located in the brain stem and the lower part of the brain. This reticular formation may be considered as a pathway for the conduction of impulses which is accessory to the classical long afferent pathways. Whilst the impulses transmitted along these classical pathways appear, in the main, to be concerned with the carriage of detailed sensory information, those travelling through and elaborated in the reticular formation appear to be concerned with the facilitatory and suppressor effects capable of modifying the transmission of impulses through other centres. Figure 15 shows a rough picture of the sort of thing that is happening. The reticular formation (R.F.) is shown

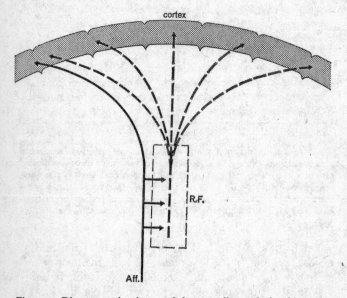

Figure 15. Diagrammatic picture of the ascending reticular formation (R.F.). It will be seen that the large afferent fibres reaching the cortex from the periphery of the body send impulses into the reticular formation which, in turn, sends impulses to the cortex which may either facilitate or inhibit cortical activity. These impulses are sent not only to the projection area to which the original afferent impulses have gone, but also to other areas of the cortex (from an article by R. Gooch, in H. J. Eysenck (Ed.), *Experiments with Drugs*).

as an alternative pathway for impulses proceeding from the receptor organs to the cortex of the brain. Impulses travelling to the cortex along the classical afferent pathways (Aff.) also enter the reticular formation through collateral nerve fibres from the afferent pathway, giving rise to impulses which are not only directed to the particular area in the cortex to which the afferent nerve is going, but may also be projected diffusely over a wide area of the cerebral cortex.

These impulses from the reticular formation are of the greatest importance. It has been found that the arrival of specific sensory impulses in the brain is not sufficient for the conscious perception of the impulses in the absence of activity from the reticular formation. It is particularly important, in this connexion, to note that wakefulness cannot be maintained without the integrity of the brain stem reticular formation, because, in its absence, activation will not last longer than the actual stimulus. Thus the reticular formation has a kind of arousal function which may be identified fairly closely with the notion of 'excitation', which we have employed hitherto.

However, certain portions of the reticular formation also provide an active kind of inhibitory influence. This is particularly true of the portion of the reticular formation known as the 'recruiting system'. The activity of this system corresponds very closely to what we have so far called 'inhibition', and it can thus be seen that the reticular formation exerts both suppressor and facilitatory influences of a kind very similar to our hypothetical demon. Figure 16 gives a very rough and ready diagram, showing different parts of the reticular formation. Putting it all very briefly and crudely, therefore, we would say that there is a distinct possibility that there are certain structures in the central nervous system, the various parts of the so-called ascending reticular formation, which seem to fulfil the functions which we have hitherto ascribed to the right and left hands, respectively, of our demon. We may, therefore, now take leave of this very useful little homunculus, dismissing him with thanks and handing over his functions to the rather less ethereal, more robust, physical structures which we can detect in our nervous system. We seem to have here a point of interaction between behaviour, in the gross psychological sense, and physiological and neurological activity, and it is reasonable to assume that those parts of personality which are related to extraverted and introverted behaviour may find their *fons et origo* in the structure of this particular system.

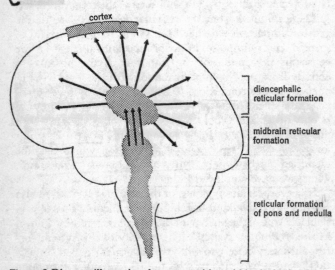

Figure 16. Diagram illustrating the exact position within the brain of the various parts of the reticular formation (from an article by R. Gooch in H. J. Eysenck (Ed.), *Experiments with Drugs*).

Is there any more direct evidence that there is indeed some sort of tie-up of this nature between the reticular formation and personality? One attempt to find such a proof has been made, by reference to the action of drugs on the central nervous system. It is well known that the so-called central nervous system stimulant and depressant drugs – drugs such as alcohol, and the barbiturates, for instance, on the depressant side, and amphetamine or caffeine on the stimulant side – have a direct action on the various parts of the reticular formation, and it has also been postulated that depressant drugs have an extraverting effect, increasing inhibitory potential and decreasing excitatory potential, whereas the stimulant drugs have an introverting effect: that is to say, decreasing inhibition and increasing excitation. Is this drug postulate in fact true?

There is a great deal of evidence that we can, in fact, shift a person's position on the extraversion/introversion continuum by means of these drugs. The proof essentially lies along the following lines. Let us take any of the tests we have described so far which show a difference in performance between extraverts and introverts, and let us administer this test to a group of people who have been given a placebo tablet which has no pharmacological effect at all on their performance. We use this group as a kind of control, because it has often been found that the simple administration of a dummy drug tablet has some effect on the performance and feeling of some subjects, the so-called 'placebo reactors' – probably through some process of suggestion or conditioning. In addition to this placebo control group, we have two other groups, one of whom is given a stimulant drug, the other a depressant drug. We would now give these three groups the particular test with which we are concerned, in the expectation that the group which had been given the stimulant drug would perform more like a group of introverts, whereas the group which had been given the depressant drug would perform more like a group of extraverts, with the placebo control group, of course, being relatively unaffected and lying between the others.

There is a great deal of evidence that this is, indeed, what happens. Stimulant drugs have, in general, provided us with evidence of excitatory effect, and depressant drugs with evidence of inhibitory effects. To take the simplest example: on tests of conditioning, it has uniformly been found that conditioning is improved and facilitated by stimulant drugs, and depressed and inhibited by depressant drugs. Practically all the tests described in the first chapter of this book have been given under drug conditions, and the uniform finding has been that our expectation has been borne out by the experimental results. This considerably strengthens our belief that the reticular formation is indeed the physiological and neurological basis of the phenotypic behaviour patterns we have identified as extraversion and introversion, and it gives us a welcome means of controlling behaviour.

Consider just one of two applications of the principles discussed above to a practical problem. Assume that we are concerned with people showing extremely psychopathic or delinquent behaviour patterns which have become so bad that some kind of action, on the part of the State, is required. In line with our discussion above, we may assume that we are here dealing with extraverted people, and that a partial solution, at least, to the problem could be found if only we could shift them on our continuum some way towards the introverted side. To do this, all we would need to do presumably would be to administer a certain quantity of stimulant drugs to them. Would this, in fact, help?

Consider a study carried out at a training school for Negro delinquent boys. Some of these were given a stimulant drug; others, no treatment. It was found that the untreated, control subjects displayed a steady increase in symptoms during the study period, whereas those who had received the stimulant drug showed a very significant decline in symptoms. This study had also included a group receiving placebo treatment, and the boys who had received these placebos also showed a decline in symptoms which clearly could not be due to any drug action. Consequently, it was decided to repeat the study under rather better controlled conditions. The results of the study are shown in Figure 17. There are three groups of boys – a control group who received no drugs at all, a placebo group (that is to say, boys who received dummy tablets), and the drug group receiving the stimulant drug called dextro-amphetamine. This was administered in increasing doses from the fortieth day of the experiment to the hundredth, as shown in the black figure at the bottom of the diagram. The behaviour of the boys was rated by raters who did not know which boys had received which drug. The study began with a period of observation; then followed the administration of the drug; and finally the

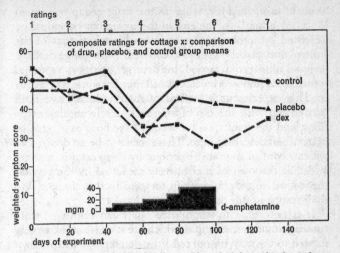

Figure 17. Diagram illustrating the results of giving stimulant drug (amphetamine) to criminals. The amount of amphetamine given at various stages is blocked out at the bottom of the diagram. In addition to the experimental group receiving the drug, there was also a control group receiving no drug and a placebo group receiving dummy tablets. The subjects of the experiment were rated on their behaviour, a high score indicating bad behaviour, a low score indicating good behaviour. It will be seen that at the beginning of the experiment all three groups had roughly equal scores; at the beginning of the drug administration all groups improved; this is probably due to the fact that they were feeling that they were being closely observed. However, very soon the control and the placebo groups returned to their previous poor conduct, whereas the amphetamine group continued to improve. When drug administration ceased on the hundredth day, the amphetamine group began to deteriorate again in its conduct but would still seem to be superior to its original behaviour (from an article from L. Eisenberg, *et al., American Journal of Orthopsychiatry,* 1963).

drug was withdrawn and observation continued. It will be seen that, at the beginning of the drug-administration period, there is a general improvement in performance in all three groups, probably due to the fact that an experiment was being carried out on the boys, and that they responded in some way to the social atmosphere. However, very soon the control and placebo groups returned to their previous

levels of misbehaviour, whereas the drug group continued
to improve, until by the end of the treatment period, their
weighted symptom score was only about half that of the
control and placebo groups combined. After the end of the
drug-administration period, the drug group shows a gradual
return to its previous level, but still remains some way below
it. This experiment is typical of many which have been
carried out with the use of amphetamine in similar situations, and the results, on the whole, have been as good as or
better than described here. There seems to be no doubt that
we can control human behaviour by drug administration,
and that this control is effectively mediated by the general
theoretical considerations put forward in this chapter. We
shall return to this point in a later chapter.

It is now time to summarize our main findings before
turning to some other topics which are somewhat less closely
related to the activities of our little demon. We have shown
that a good deal of behaviour which gives rise to the concept
of personality can be described in terms of two main dimensions or factors, or axes, or continua, one being that of
extraversion-introversion, the other being that of emotionality or neuroticism as opposed to stability or normality,
both of which are independent of intelligence. We have
shown that these two personality factors are, to a considerable degree, determined by hereditary factors, and we
have also postulated that this determination must have some
kind of basis in the nervous system of the individuals concerned. Lastly, we have tried to show that such a basis can
indeed be found, and is most likely to be associated with the
so-called ascending reticular formation, and that we can
use stimulant and depressant drugs to change the behaviour
of this formation, and thereby change a person's position on
the extravert/introvert continuum, in any desired direction.
In the next chapters we shall try and apply some of the
knowledge gained so far to a consideration of the causes and
cures of neurotic disorders, of criminality, of accident-
proneness, and various other concepts.

There are two well-known and important 'cases' in modern psychology which can be seen almost as paradigms for two contrasting ways of attempting to understand human behaviour. They are the case of 'Little Hans' and the case of 'Little Albert'. The former illustrates the approach of Freud and psychoanalysts in general, the latter the point of view of Pavlov and behaviourism. This contrast pervades much of modern psychology and also extends to other fields such as anthropology, sociology, literature, and the interpretation of history. Here we shall be concerned with the form this conflict has taken in the field of neurotic behaviour, and particularly with the causes of such behaviour postulated by these two schools respectively.

This chapter then deals with the topic of 'neurosis', a word which is on everybody's lips nowadays, and about which there is more misinformation current than about almost any other concept. We are told by reputable psychiatrists that we are all neurotic, or that half of all the patients visiting general practitioners are not physically ill, but are suffering from neurosis, or that the incidence of neurosis has risen sharply over the last hundred years – perhaps because of the accelerated speed of living. We are told that neuroses are due to long-forgotten events of early childhood; that they can be cured only by 'uncovering' these early complexes; and that psychoanalysis can accomplish in this way the most miraculous changes of personality. Any or all of these statements may be true, but when we ask for convincing evidence of a scientific nature, we find that none in fact exists. In other words, in this field we are dealing with theories, hypotheses, hunches, surmises, opinions, beliefs – often held with great tenacity and proclaimed with considerable vigour, but none the less not based on incontrovertible evidence. Films, novels, plays, and other popular media have given the public an entirely erroneous picture of the situation, by assuming that certain theories about the *causes* of neurosis had, in fact, already been demonstrated to be true by scientific tests, and that certain methods of treatment had been shown to work. This is not true, and where experts disagree, the layman – even where he would like to plead artistic licence – may, with advantage, study the evidence before committing himself.

This disagreement among experts extends even to the very definition of the term, neurosis. Most people agree that it has something to do with emotional reactions of a maladaptive character, but beyond this even the most elementary points are in dispute. Thus many psychiatrists believe that neurosis and psychosis are two entirely disparate and separate types of mental disorder; the former, characterized by emotional reactions, is not supposed to deprive the patient of insight into his condition, or to render him 'insane' in the legal sense, while the latter, characterized by delusions, hallucinations, and other mental derangements, leads to certification and hospitalization. But other psychiatrists dispute this easy and obvious division, and maintain that neurosis may change into psychosis as stresses accumulate, and that both types of disorder are, in any case, due to the selfsame set of causes.

Equally in dispute are the subdivisions of 'neurosis' into such disorders as anxiety state, hysteria, phobia, obsessional illness, compulsions, or psychopathy; in question are not only the actual diagnoses used, and their definition, but also the ability of psychiatrists to apply the labels in any consistent fashion. Several experimental studies have shown that when different psychiatrists in one and the same hospital are asked to give independent diagnoses of a set of neurotic patients, agreement among them is not much in excess of what would occur on a chance basis; this must inevitably make one wonder about the usefulness of the diagnostic labels employed. Even the distinction between neurosis and psychosis is not accomplished with any great reliability; disagreements are frequent, and consistency rare. It will be seen that this is not a field where dogmatic statements, even when made by experts, can be accepted with safety; we must, in each case, ask to see the evidence, and decide whether what has been demonstrated is indeed sufficient to make the conclusion reasonable. In spite of, or perhaps because of this state of affairs, we find that most people have adopted the opposite course: they follow without criticism and without doubt one of the contesting parties, looking neither to the right nor to the left, repeating to themselves the famous wartime slogan: 'Don't confuse me with facts, my mind is made up.' It is this attitude that has led, in the words of a famous social scientist, to the premature crystallization of spurious orthodoxies so characteristic of this field.

What, then, about the definition of 'neurosis'? Perhaps we have started off on the wrong foot; science does not usually succeed in giving widely accepted definitions of natural phenomena until it has reached a fairly advanced understanding of their causes. It is easier to describe and recognize an elephant than to define one, and perhaps it would be better to start with a description of certain types of behaviour which most people would readily agree to be truly neurotic. The so-called phobias will make a good beginning, as they embody some fairly obvious abnormalities. A neurotic suffering from a strong, unreasoning fear of certain things, places, persons, or animals, is usually called 'phobic'; open spaces, heights, small enclosed spaces, spiders, snakes – these are some of the most frequent objects of these violent and quite unreasonable fears. But literally anything can be the object feared by the phobic patient; what is required for the diagnosis is merely the presence of this strong, unreasoning fear. The patient, of course, recognizes the fact that his fear is without a reasonable cause; he has full insight into the fact that his behaviour is odd and unreasonable. Nevertheless, he is quite unable to overcome his fears, however much these may interfere with his leading a normal life. And so, comic as the description of a phobia sometimes sounds, the reality is sad and indeed often tragic, as far as the sufferer is concerned. By making impossible the patient's going out into the open, or into enclosed spaces, or up above ground level, his phobias effectively make it impossible for him to carry on with his job, or with his private life; everything has to be geared to the prevention of his phobic fears.

Much the same is true of obsessional and compulsive symptoms, which also may be of a bewildering variety. The patient may feel the need to wash his hands fifty times a day, or he may require to do certain other things, such as touching every door he passes, or only stepping on the cracks in the pavement. Alternatively, he may repeat every job three or four times, just to make certain that he has not made any mistake – driven to do this although he knows perfectly well that in fact no mistake has been made. The patient usually knows that his behaviour is unreasonable and indefensible, but he cannot help himself – something seems to drive him on which is stronger than his will-power, or, sometimes, even his instinct of self-preservation. Disaster may follow disaster; he may be sacked from his job and left by his wife, because of his odd behaviour, yet he cannot bring himself to stop it.

Anxiety is the central feature of the most common of all neurotic troubles, often accompanied by depression. This anxiety may be related to real problems, such as war, 'the bomb', job difficulties, money troubles, sexual insufficiencies, or family upsets, but the characteristic of neurotic anxiety is that it is out of proportion to the real features of the situation. It is not unrealistic to worry about 'the bomb', but it is unrealistic to get into such a state that the actual setting off of the bomb comes almost as a release from unbearable tension and anxiety. Often the anxiety sets off a vidious circle, some minor upset leading to exaggerated anxiety, which in turn makes the individual incapable of coping properly with the situation, which then deteriorates, leading to even greater anxiety, and so on. We shall later on be concerned with the actual mechanisms which cause this reciprocal action; at the moment, we need only note the fact that anxiety is a very disruptive emotion, and that in excess it can be extremely painful and indeed literally unbearable – many people attempt suicide rather than continue living in this way. Unfeeling and insensitive people often denounce neurotics of this type as 'malingerers' who are trying to get out of doing their fair share of the work; nobody at all acquainted with the acute misery suffered by neurotic patients could possibly hold any such view.

Reactive depression, so-called to distinguish it from endogenous depression which is an apparently uncaused and psychotic illness, is another quite frequent neurotic symptom, usually, though not always, accompanying anxiety. It is called 'reactive' because it represents a reasonable reaction to some external event, such as the loss of a relative; it is neurotic because it is much stronger and longer-lasting than would be appropriate. Depression, like anxiety, represents an emotional over-reaction; unlike anxiety, which is forward-looking and concerned with fears for the future, depression is backward-looking and concerned with sadness about the past. The differences are probably less important than the similarities, and the two states are usually found together in the same person, either simultaneously or alternating. Indeed, all the symptoms so far discussed tend to occur together in the same person; they are seldom found as tidily separated in nature as they are in psychiatric textbooks. Often they are accompanied by excessive tiredness and fatigue; this is sometimes said to be due to the 'expenditure of nervous and emotional energy' caused by the anxieties, fears, and depressions of the patient – an analogy with physical principles of 'energy conservation' which has little scientific value. Other frequent accompaniments of all these symptoms are over-concern with ethical and religious matters, constant introspection and self-questioning, guilt feelings, and feelings of unworthiness. We may call this constellation of neurotic symptoms 'neuroses of the first kind'; another term which has recently come into frequent use is 'dysthymia', emphasizing that we are dealing here with a profound dysfunction of the person's mood, a malfunctioning of his emotional apparatus. As we shall see in a moment, there are also 'neuroses of the second kind', which are characterized rather by disorders of behaviour: to these we must now turn.

Some neurotics appear to be rather free from the heavy burden of anxiety, fear, and depression which characterizes the dysthymic, although their troubles seem to be as real and oppressive. Into this group come, above all others, the hysterics and the psychopaths. Both these terms are used in many different ways, but there appears to be a general core of symptoms and personality traits in each case which is common to most patients so diagnosed. Hysterics tend to suffer from apparently organic troubles – loss of sensation in a limb, or loss of function of sight or hearing, or paralysis, or loss of memory; when a proper medical investigation is undertaken, no real physiological or other cause is found. Sometimes such patients are said to have 'converted' an emotional conflict into a physical symptom; thus the soldier who is afraid of combat may 'convert' this fear into some physical disorder which will effectively remove him from the battle zone. No wonder, then, that he is able to survey his resulting incapacity with the 'belle indifference' which is said to be a frequent feature of hysteria. However, here too it would not be true to say that these people are simply malingerers; hysterics have been shot as malingerers without giving up their symptoms, so that any notion that they were simply 'shamming' cannot reasonably be maintained. Hysterics are said to have characteristic personality features, such as impulsiveness, histrionic behaviour patterns, changeableness and inconstancy, lack of moral fibre and responsibility, which may, in mild cases, be the only presenting symptoms.

Psychopaths are people who show no 'symptoms' in the ordinary sense, but whose whole behaviour is such that it cannot be accounted for at all easily in the same terms as that of ordinary people. They are 'moral imbeciles'; although of standard or even of good intelligence, they seem unable to assess the consequences of their actions, and behave in an a-social or antisocial manner, regardless of punishment. They seem to prefer lying to speaking the truth, even though they derive no apparent benefit from it and are certain to be found out and punished. The impulse of the moment seems to be paramount, without counting the cost;

there is no feeling for other people, no taking into account the rights of others, and no guilt feeling once society has caught up with them. To emphasize the essentially social nature of their troubles, these people are sometimes called 'sociopaths', and they are an equal headache to society as they are to psychiatrists trying to cure them. They are often criminal, but not necessarily so; detailed case histories show that such a man can go on year after year seducing women, living on their money, tying them to the bed and beating them with whips, without any of these women coming forward to complain to the police. On the other hand, criminals are by no means always, or even usually, psychopaths; we shall return to this point later on, when we have gained some insight into the reasons for psychopathic behaviour.

These 'neuroses of the second kind' are obviously different in many ways from those of the first kind, particularly in the absence of the long-drawn-out emotional reactions, the anxieties, and the depressions; why do we call both types of syndromes 'neuroses'? There are, of course, historical reasons; psychiatrists have been in the habit of subsuming all these reactions under one concept. But there are also good experimental reasons. When we administer various types of personality test to patients showing these various different types of reactions, they are all differentiated from normal people in the same manner; neurotics of the first and neurotics of the second kind both show a uniformity of reaction which suggests that underneath all that external diversity there is some similarity of underlying causation. And we may gain a clue as to the nature of this underlying causation by noting that hysterics and psychopaths do resemble other neurotics in showing a similar emotional over-reaction to various painful or frightening stimuli; it is the lack of persistence of these over-reactions that distinguishes our hysterics and psychopaths from our anxiety states, depressives, and phobics. Other similarities and differences will become apparent later.

Neuroses 'of the first kind' are sometimes referred to as *personality problems*, and neuroses 'of the second kind' as *conduct problems*; both can be observed in children as well as

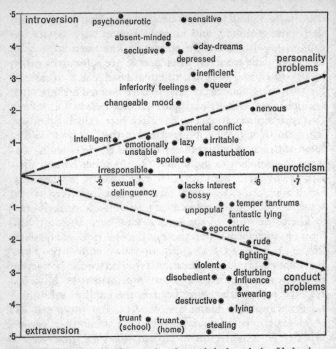

Figure 18. Diagram showing results of a statistical analysis of behaviour patterns of disturbed children (from an analysis by H. Himmelweit, in H. J. Eysenck, *The Structure of Human Personality*).

in adults, and indeed the child is very much the father of the man in this respect, as adult behaviour patterns can be predicted with some accuracy from childish ways. Consider Figure 18, which shows the occurrence in a large group of children of a variety of personality and behaviour problems. The diagram is based on a detailed statistical analysis, and has been so constructed that items which are usually found together in the same child are found close together in the diagram, while items seldom found together in the same child are found far apart in the drawing. Thus the child who is 'absent-minded' will nearly always be 'sensitive', 'inefficient', and full of 'inferiority feelings'. The child who is 'disobedient' will nearly always be 'destructive', 'rude', and 'egocentric'. The child who steals or plays truant will seldom day-dream or be seclusive. Children of the first kind, i.e. those with personality problems, seem to have a personality which is essentially introverted, while those with conduct problems seem to have a personality which is essentially extraverted; children showing either set of symptoms and personality traits may be called 'neurotic' at this purely descriptive level. These personality correlates of neurotic behaviour are here merely mentioned; we shall have to discuss them in much greater detail later on.

The symptoms so far mentioned do not, of course, exhaust the variety of complaints seen in the clinic by the practising psychiatrist. This book is not meant to be a psychiatric textbook, and this chapter is merely intended to set the stage for our discussion of the causes and cures of these disorders. Let me simply state that there are many 'disorders' which are often called 'neurotic' where it is very difficult to know whether the term is being applied in any meaningful way. Is a homosexual a neurotic? His emotional reactions are directed towards a sexual object which is unusual and disapproved of by society, but suppose he had lived in a society where homosexuality was accepted and indeed considered an ideal state by many? Are people whom we call sexual perverts 'neurotic'? We consider it natural for men to obtain sexual excitement by kissing women and fondling their breasts; in many South Sea Islands such behaviour is considered perverse, and the female breast has a purely functional significance. Socialists are often considered 'neurotic' in the United States, because their beliefs are unusual and contrary to those held by the majority; would they become 'normal' by being transported to Sweden? Is the excessive consumption of alcoholic beverages a 'neurosis', and what is 'excessive'? Is the jay-walker or the traffic violator a neurotic or a psychopath? Is the convict? How strong do maladaptive emotional reactions have to be to qualify a person for diagnosis and treatment? If I have a phobic fear of cats which makes me stay locked up in my room because of fear that if I went out I might meet a feline; which makes

me shun television in case a cat should be shown on it;
which makes me keep the curtains drawn, in case such an
animal should accidentally jump on to the window-sill –
then there would be considerable agreement that I was a
neurotic. But if I had a mild fear of spiders, equally unreasoning, would I still qualify? The descriptive tack has got
us on a little way, but we must now change course and try a
more systematic approach.

Historically, the study of the neuroses originated within
the medical field, and our nomenclature and our whole
orientation still bears many traces of this. Medicine deals
with diseases; diseases have their causes, which are different
from their symptoms; diseases have their treatments, which
are directed at the causes, rather than the symptoms.
Psychiatry unquestioningly took over these notions into the
field of neurosis, but it may be questioned whether they are
really appropriate. Consider here just the first question: are
neuroses diseases? An answer is difficult because physicians
have never given a definition of the term 'disease'; we are,
therefore, trying to do the impossible by asking whether one
unidentified and unidentifiable term can be subsumed under
another equally unidentified and unidentifiable term! But
let us use common sense. By 'disease' we traditionally mean
a state of an individual which, in some categorical way,
differs from his normal state. He is suffering from malaria, a
broken arm, syphilis, scarlet fever, thrombosis, or a stroke;
in each case there is a clear discontinuity between the normal and the (medically) abnormal. Furthermore, there is a
specific cause for each disorder; we have been invaded by a
germ, or we have been damaged physically in some way.
None of this is true of neurosis. There is no categorical state
of 'neurosis' which can be equivocally distinguished from
'normality'; psychiatrists have given up the search for any
such way of identifying the disease-entity 'neurosis'. There
is only a quantitative change in certain aspects of behaviour;
there is complete continuity from one extreme of 'normal'
behaviour to the other of 'neurotic' behaviour. It is time
we gave up the erroneous notion of neurosis as a disease, and
realized that neurotic behaviour is continuous in every way

with normal behaviour. This *dimensional* approach, as contrasted with the categorical approach, is much closer to the facts, even though it requires us to break with the age-old habits of medical semantics.

Let us begin by considering an essential feature of neurotic conduct which has been labelled by O. H. Mowrer the 'neurotic paradox'. Talking about the central problem in neurosis and therapy, he says, 'Most simply formulated, it is a paradox – the paradox of behaviour which is at one and the same time self-perpetuating and self-defeating! Ranging from common "bad habits" through vices and addictions to classical psycho-neurotic and psychotic symptoms, there is a large array of strategies and dynamisms which readily fit such a description but defy any simple, commonsense explanation. Common sense holds that the normal, sensible man, or even a beast to the limits of his intelligence, will weigh and balance the consequences of his act: if the net effect is favourable, the action producing it will be perpetuated; and if the net effect is unfavourable, the action producing it will be inhibited, abandoned. In neurosis, however, one sees actions which have predominantly unfavourable consequences; yet they persist over a period of months, years, or a lifetime. Small wonder, then, that common sense has abjured responsibility in such matters and has assigned them to the realm of the miraculous, the mystical, the uncommon, the preternatural.'

Indeed, the easiest and the earliest way out of the difficulty has been that of inventing special Satans, devils, or demons which were made responsible for actions constituting the neurotic paradox. Clearly such explanations are unacceptable to our modern scientific way of thinking, and it fell to Sigmund Freud to give the first completely naturalistic explanation of such behaviour. One of his early attempts to deal with this problem involved the concept of erotic fixation. He held that because of early libidinal attachments, either to another person, often of an incestuous nature, or to the self, some individuals were arrested in their development and consequently persevered in abortive, self-defeating actions which a normal person, not so fixated, would soon abandon. Thus, instead of devils and demons, we now have Oedipus and Electra complexes to account for the paradoxical behaviour of the neurotic. There is a gain, in that the postulate of the total determination of conduct by ascertainable factors in the outer world is maintained, but the gain is not as great as it might have been because, as has often been pointed out, the complexities of psychoanalytic reasoning effectively preclude any scientific testing of these theories. Furthermore, when we look at the evidence upon which Freud's theories are based, we find that it is not the kind which would recommend it to the scientist. Instead of experimentally tested deductions from clearly stated hypotheses, all that we find is anecdotal evidence collected in a relatively haphazard manner from individual case histories. This lack of true evidence is often disguised from the reader by the superb quality of Freud's writing, which deservedly won him the Goethe Prize in Germany, which is awarded for literary endeavour; however, in science persuasion should not take the place of proof, and we must examine Freud's attempts at proof a little more closely before we can come to any conclusions about the truth of his hypotheses. For the purpose of examination, I have chosen a paper published in 1909 by Freud with the title, 'An Analysis of a Phobia in a Five-year-old Boy'. This case is commonly referred to as 'the case of little Hans'. As Ernest Jones, in his biography of Freud points out, it was 'the first published account of a child analysis'. He adds: 'The brilliant success of child analysis was indeed inaugurated by the study of this very case.' The fame achieved by little Hans is one of the reasons for selecting the case. Thus, the best-known English psychoanalyst, E. Glover, has given it as his opinion that, 'In his time, the analysis of little Hans was a remarkable achievement and the story of the analysis constitutes one of the most valued records in psychoanalytical archives. Our concepts of phobia formation, of the positive Oedipus complex, of ambivalence, of castration anxiety and repression, to mention but a few, were greatly reinforced and amplified as a result of this analysis.'

Another reason for looking at little Hans in some detail
is the fact that an alternative theory to that of Freud was
elaborated by J. B. Watson, and he, too, put it in the form
of a story relating to a little boy, this time little Albert. It is
difficult to bring out the differences between psychoanalysis and modern psychology better than by contrasting
the cases of little Hans and little Albert, and to see what the
one has to teach us about the other.

Lastly, we have the great advantage that the case of little
Hans has been examined with very great care by two
modern psychologists, Joseph Wolpe and Stanley Rachman, in a paper which has become a classic.* In what
follows, I shall simply follow their discussion, quoting and
paraphrasing as I go on. The reader who wishes to follow
this discussion properly may be advised to have a look at
Freud's original paper as well, to see whether in fact the
criticisms made are, or are not, justified.

Wolpe and Rachman start out by saying that in their
paper they will 're-examine this case history and assess the
evidence presented. We shall show that although there are
manifestations of sexual behaviour on the part of Hans,
there is no scientifically acceptable evidence showing any
connexion between this behaviour and the child's phobia
for horses; that the assertion of such a connexion is pure
assumption; that the elaborate discussions that follow from
it are pure speculations; and that the case affords no factual
support for any of the concepts listed by Glover above.
Our examination of this case exposes in considerable detail
patterns of thinking and attitude to evidence that are well-
nigh universal among psychoanalysts. It suggests the need
for more careful scrutiny of the bases of psychoanalytic
"discoveries" than has been customary; and we hope it
will prompt psychologists to make similar critical examina-
tions of basic psychoanalytic writings.'

The first interesting feature of the case is that the case
material on which Freud's analysis was based was collected
by little Hans's father, who kept in touch with Freud by

*I have to thank the authors and the publishers, as well as the editor of the *Journal of
Nervous and Mental Disease*, for their permission to quote in such detail the paper in
question(op. cit., 1960 pp. 130, 135–48).

means of regular written reports. The father had several discussions with Freud concerning little Hans's phobia, but during the analysis Freud himself saw the little boy only once!

The following are the most relevant facts noted of Hans's earlier life. At the age of three, he showed 'a quite peculiarly lively interest in that portion of his body which he used to describe as his widdler.' When he was three and a half, his mother found him with his hand to his penis. She threatened him in these words, 'If you do that, I shall send for Dr A. to cut off your widdler. And then what will you widdle with?' Hans replied, 'With my bottom.' Numerous further remarks concerning widdlers in animals and humans were made by Hans between the age of three and four, including questions directed at his mother and father asking them if they also had widdlers. Freud attaches importance to the following exchange between Hans and his mother. Hans was 'looking on intently while his mother undressed'.

MOTHER: What are you staring like that for?
HANS: I was only looking to see if you'd got a widdler, too.
MOTHER: Of course. Didn't you know that?
HANS: No, I thought you were so big you'd have a widdler like a horse.

When Hans was three and a half his sister was born. The baby was delivered at home and Hans heard his mother 'coughing', observed the appearance of the doctor, and was called into the bedroom after the birth. Hans was initially 'very jealous of the new arrival' but within six months his jealousy faded and was replaced by 'brotherly affection'.

At the age of four and a half, Hans went with his parents to Gmunden for the summer holidays. On holiday Hans had numerous playmates including Mariedl, a fourteen-year-old girl. One evening Hans said, 'I want Mariedl to sleep with me.' Freud says that Hans's wish was an expression of his desire to have Mariedl as part of his family. Hans's parents occasionally took him into their bed and Freud claims that, 'there can be no doubt that lying beside them had aroused erotic feelings in him*; so that his wish to sleep with Mariedl had an erotic sense as well.'

Another incident during the summer holidays is given considerable importance by Freud, who refers to it as Hans's attempt to seduce his mother. It must be quoted in full.

Hans, four and a quarter. This morning Hans was given his usual daily bath by his mother and afterwards dried and powdered. As his mother was powdering round his penis and taking care not to touch it, Hans said, 'Why don't you put your finger there?'

MOTHER: Because that'd be piggish.

HANS: What's that? Piggish? Why?

MOTHER: Because it's not proper.

HANS (laughing): But it's great fun.

Another occurrence prior to the onset of his phobia was that when Hans, aged four and a half, laughed while watching his sister being bathed and was asked why he was laughing, he replied, 'I'm laughing at Hanna's widdler.' 'Why?' 'Because her widdler's so lovely.' The father's comment is, 'Of course his answer was a disingenuous one. In reality her widdler seemed to him funny. Moreover, this is the first time he has recognized in this way the distinction between male and female genitals instead of denying it.'

In early January, 1908, the father wrote to Freud that Hans, then five years old, had developed 'a nervous disorder'. The symptoms he reported were: fear of going into the streets; depression in the evening, and a fear that a horse would bite him in the street. Hans's father suggested that 'the ground was prepared by sexual over-excitation due to his mother's tenderness' and that the fear of the horse 'seems somehow to be connected with his having been frightened by a large penis'. The first signs appeared on 7 January, when Hans was being taken to the park by his nursemaid as usual. He started crying and said he wanted to 'coax' (caress) with his mother. At home 'he was asked why he had refused to go any further and had cried, but he would not say.' The following day, after hesitation and

*This is nothing but surmise – yet Freud asserts 'there can be no doubt' about it.

crying, he went out with his mother. Returning home Hans said ('after much internal struggling') '*I was afraid a horse would bite me*' (original italics). As on the previous day, Hans showed fear in the evening and asked to be 'coaxed'. He is also reported as saying, 'I know I shall have to go for a walk again tomorrow,' and, 'The horse'll come into the room.' On the same day he was asked by his mother if he put his hand to his widdler. He replied in the affirmative. The following day his mother warned him to refrain from doing this.

At this point in the narrative, Freud provided an interpretation of Hans's behaviour and consequently arranged with the boy's father 'that he should tell the boy that all this nonsense about horses was a piece of nonsense and nothing more. The truth was, his father was to say, that he was very fond of his mother and wanted to be taken into her bed. The reason he was afraid of horses now was that he had taken so much interest in their widdlers.' Freud also suggested giving Hans some sexual enlightenment and telling him that females 'had no widdler at all'.*

'After Hans had been enlightened there followed a fairly quiet period.' After an attack of influenza which kept him in bed for two weeks, the phobia got worse. He then had his tonsils out and was indoors for a further week. The phobia became 'very much worse'.

During March 1908, after his physical illnesses had been cured, Hans apparently had many talks with his father about the phobia. On 1 March, his father again told Hans that horses do not bite. Hans replied that white horses bite and related that while at Gmunden he had heard and seen Lizzi (a playmate) being warned by her father to avoid a white horse lest it bite. The father said to Lizzi, '*Don't put your finger to the white horse*' (original italics). Hans's father's reply to this account given by his son was, 'I say, it strikes me it isn't a horse you mean, but a widdler, that one mustn't put one's hand to.' Hans answered, 'But a widdler doesn't bite.' The father: 'Perhaps it does, though.' Hans then 'went on eagerly to try to prove to me that it was a

---

*Incidentally contradicting what Hans's mother had told him earlier.

white horse'. The following day, in answer to a remark of his father's, Hans said that his phobia was 'so bad because I still put my hand to my widdler every night.' Freud remarks here that, 'Doctor and patient, father and son, were therefore at one in ascribing the chief share in the pathogenesis of Hans's present condition to his habit of onanism.' He implies that this unanimity is significant, quite disregarding the father's indoctrination of Hans the previous day.*

Some time later the father again told Hans that girls and women have no widdlers. 'Mummy has none, Hanna has none, and so on.' Hans asked how they managed to widdle and was told, 'They don't have widdlers like yours. Haven't you noticed already when Hanna was being given her bath?' On 17 March Hans reported a phantasy in which he saw his mother naked. On the basis of this phantasy and the conversation related above, Freud concluded that Hans had not accepted the enlightenment given by his father. Freud says, 'He regretted that it should be so, and stuck to his former view in phantasy. He may also perhaps have had his reasons for refusing to believe his father at first.' Discussing this matter subsequently, Freud says that the 'enlightenment' given a short time before to the effect that women really do not possess a widdler was bound to have a shattering effect upon his self-confidence and to have aroused his castration complex. For this reason he resisted the information, and for this reason it had no therapeutic effect.†

For reasons of space we shall recount the subsequent events in very brief form. On a visit to the zoo Hans expressed fear of the giraffe, elephant, and all large animals. Hans's father said to him, 'Do you know why you're

---

*The mere fact that Hans repeats an interpretation he has heard from his father is regarded by Freud as demonstrating the accuracy of the interpretation; even though the child's spontaneous responses noted earlier in the paragraph point clearly in the opposite direction.

†It is pertinent at this point to suggest that Hans 'resisted' this enlightenment because his mother had told him quite the opposite and his observations of his sister's widdler had not been contradicted. When he was four, Hans had observed that his sister's widdler was 'still quite small'. When he was four and a half, again while watching his sister being bathed, he observed that she had 'a lovely widdler'. On neither occasion was he contradicted.

afraid of big animals? Big animals have big widdlers and you're really afraid of big widdlers.' This was denied by the boy.

The next event of prominence was a dream (or phantasy) reported by Hans. 'In the night there was a big giraffe in the room and a crumpled one; and the big one called out because I took the crumpled one away from it. Then it stopped calling out; and then I sat down on the top of the crumpled one.'

After talking to the boy the father reported to Freud that this dream was 'a matrimonial scene transposed into giraffe life. He was seized in the night with a longing for his mother, for her caresses, for her genital organ, and came into the room for that reason. The whole thing is a continuation of his fear of horses.' The father infers that the dream is related to Hans's habit of occasionally getting into his parents' bed in the face of his father's disapproval. Freud's addition to 'the father's penetrating observation' is that sitting down on the crumpled giraffe means taking possession of his mother. Confirmation of this dream interpretation is claimed by reference to an incident which occurred the next day. The father wrote that on leaving the house with Hans he said to his wife, 'Goodbye, big giraffe.' 'Why giraffe?' asked Hans. 'Mummy's the big giraffe,' replied the father. 'Oh, yes,' said Hans, 'and Hanna's* the crumpled giraffe, isn't she?' The father's account continues, 'In the train I explained the giraffe phantasy to him, upon which he said, "Yes, that's right," and when I said to him that I was the big giraffe and that its long neck reminded him of a widdler, he said, "Mummy has a neck like a giraffe too. I saw when she was washing her white neck."'

On 30 March, the boy had a short consultation with Freud who reports that despite all the enlightenment given to Hans, the fear of horses continued undiminished. Hans explained that he was especially bothered 'by what horses

*Hans's baby sister, *not* his mother. Again, the more spontaneous response directly contradicts Freud's interpretation. Thus Freud's subsequent comment that Hans only confirmed the interpretation of the two giraffes as his father and mother and not the sexual symbolism transgresses the facts.

wear in front of their eyes and the black round their mouths'. This latter detail Freud interpreted as meaning a moustache. 'I asked him whether he meant a moustache', and then, 'disclosed to him that he was afraid of his father precisely because he was so fond of his mother.' Freud pointed out that this was a groundless fear. On 2 April, the father was able to report 'the first real improvement'. The next day, Hans, in answer to his father's inquiry, explained that he came into his father's bed when he was frightened. In the next few days further details of Hans's fear were elaborated. He told his father that he was most scared of horses with 'a thing on their mouths', that he was scared lest the horses fall, and that he was most scared of horse-drawn buses.

HANS: I'm most afraid too when a bus comes along.
FATHER: Why? Because it's so big?
HANS: No. Because once a horse in a bus fell.
FATHER: When?

Hans then recounted such an incident. This was later confirmed by his mother.

FATHER: What did you think when the horse fell down?
HANS: Now it will always be like this. All horses in buses fall down.
FATHER: In all buses?
HANS: Yes. And in furniture vans too. Not often in furniture vans.
FATHER: You had your nonsense already at that time?
HANS: *No* [italics added]. I only got it then. When the horse in the bus fell down, it gave me such a fright really: that was when I got the nonsense.

The father adds that, 'all of this was confirmed by my wife, as well as the fact that *the anxiety broke out immediately afterwards*' (italics added).

Hans's father continued probing for a meaning of the black thing around the horses' mouths. Hans said it looked like a muzzle but his father had never seen such a horse 'although Hans asseverates that such horses do exist'.* He continues, 'I suspect that some part of the

*Six days later the father reports, 'I was at last able to establish the fact that it was a horse with a leather muzzle.'

horse's bridle really reminded him of a moustache and that after I alluded to this the fear disappeared.' A day later Hans, observing his father stripped to the waist, said, 'Daddy, you are lovely! You're so white.'

FATHER: Yes, like a white horse.

HANS: The only black thing's your moustache. Or perhaps it's a black muzzle.*

Further details about the horse that fell were also elicited from Hans. He said there were actually two horses pulling the bus and that they were both black and 'very big and fat'. Hans's father again asked about the boy's thoughts when the horse fell.

FATHER: When the horse fell down, did you think of your daddy?†

HANS: Perhaps. Yes. It's possible.

For several days after these talks about horses Hans's interests, as indicated by the father's reports 'centred upon lumf (faeces) and widdle, but we cannot tell why.' Freud comments that at this point 'the analysis began to be obscure and uncertain'.

On 11 April Hans related this phantasy. 'I was in the bath and then the plumber came and unscrewed it. Then he took a big borer and stuck it into my stomach.' Hans's father translated this phantasy as follows: 'I was in bed with Mamma. Then Pappa came and drove me away. With his big penis he pushed me out of my place by Mamma.'

The remainder of the case history materials, until Hans's recovery from the phobia early in May, is concerned with the lumf theme and Hans's feelings towards his parents and sister. It can be stated immediately that as corroboration for Freud's theories all of this remaining material is unsatisfactory. For the most part it consists of the father expounding theories to a boy who occasionally agrees and occasionally disagrees. The following two examples illustrate the nature of most of this latter information.

----

*A good example of the success of indoctrination.

†One of many leading questions, the positive answer to which of course proves nothing. It is worth noticing how the same question, differently phrased, elicits contrasting answers from Hans. When asked earlier what he thought of when the horse fell down, Hans replied that he thought it would always happen in future.

Hans and his father were discussing the boy's slight fear of falling when in the big bath.

FATHER: But Mamma bathes you in it. Are you afraid of Mamma dropping you in the water?

HANS: I am afraid of her letting go and my head going in.

FATHER: But you know Mummy's fond of you and won't let you go.

HANS: I only just thought it.

FATHER: Why?

HANS: I don't know at all.

FATHER: Perhaps it was because you'd been naughty and thought she didn't love you any more?*

HANS: Yes.

FATHER: When you were watching Mummy giving Hanna her bath perhaps you wished she would let go of her so that Hanna should fall in?*

HANS: Yes.

On the following day the father asks, 'Are you fond of Hanna?'

HANS: Oh, yes, very fond.

FATHER: Would you rather that Hanna weren't alive or that she were?

HANS: I'd rather she weren't alive.

In response to close, direct questioning, Hans voiced several complaints about his sister. Then his father proceeded again:

FATHER: If you'd rather she weren't alive, you can't be fond of her at all.

HANS (assenting†): Hm, well.

FATHER: That's why you thought when Mummy was giving her her bath if only she'd let go, Hanna would fall in the water . . .

HANS (taking me up): . . . and die.

FATHER: And then you'd be alone with Mummy. A good boy doesn't wish that sort of thing, though.

On 24 April, the following conversation was recorded.

FATHER: It seems to me that, all the same, you do wish Mummy would have a baby.

HANS: But I don't want it to happen.

*Leading questions.
†A very questionable affirmation.

FATHER: But you wish for it?

HANS: Oh, yes, *wish*.*

FATHER: Do you know why you wish for it? It's because you'd like to be Daddy.

HANS: Yes. How does it work?

FATHER: You'd like to be Daddy and married to Mummy; you'd like to be as big as me and have a moustache; and you'd like Mummy to have a baby.

HANS: And Daddy, when I'm married I'll have only one if I want to, when I'm married to Mummy, and if I don't want a baby, God won't want it either when I'm married.

FATHER: Would you like to be married to Mummy?

HANS: Oh, yes.

Having recounted the facts of the case, Wolpe and Rachman look at the value of the evidence. First they say there is the matter of selection of the material; the greatest attention is paid to material related to psychoanalytic theory, and there is a tendency to ignore other facts. Freud himself says, speaking of the father and mother, that 'they were both among my closest adherents'. Hans himself is constantly encouraged, directly and indirectly, to relate material of relevance to the psychoanalytic doctrine.

Secondly, there is the question of the value to be placed on the testimony of the father and little Hans. The father's account of Hans's behaviour is in several instances suspect. For instance, he tries to present his own interpretations of Hans's remarks as observed facts. This, for instance, is the father's report of a conversation with Hans about the death of his sister, Hanna. Father: 'What did Hanna look like?' Hans (hypocritically): 'All white and lovely. So pretty.' The comment in parentheses in this extract is presented as an observed fact. Another example of this has been quoted already, when Hans observed that Hanna's widdler is 'so lovely', the father states that this is a 'disingenuous' reply and that 'in reality her widdler seemed to him funny'. Distortions of this kind are common in the father's reports.

*Original italics suggest a significance that is unwarranted, for the child has been manoeuvred into giving an answer contradicting his original one. Note the induced 'evidence' as the conversation continues.

Hans's testimony itself is, for many reasons, quite un-
reliable. There are numerous lies which he told in the last
few weeks of his phobia, and in addition he gave many
inconsistent, and occasionally conflicting, reports. Most
important of all, however, much of what purports to be
Hans's views and feelings is simply the father speaking.
Freud himself admits this, but attempts to gloss over it. He
says: 'It is true that during the analysis Hans had to be
told many things which he could not say himself, that he
had to be presented with thoughts which he had so far
shown no sign of possessing and that his attention had to be
turned in the direction from which his father was expecting
something to come. This detracts from the evidential
value of the analysis, but the procedure is the same in every
case, for the psychoanalysis is not an impartial scientific
investigation but a therapeutic measure.' To sum this
matter up, Wolpe and Rachman say: 'Hans's testimony is
subject not only to "mere suggestion" but contains much
material that is not his testimony at all!'

Freud's interpretation of Hans's phobia is that the boy's
oedipal conflicts formed the basis of the illness which
'burst out' when he underwent a time of 'privation and the
intensified sexual excitement'. Freud says, 'These were
tendencies in Hans which had already been suppressed
and for which, so far as we can tell, he had never been able
to find uninhibited expression: hostile and jealous feelings
against his father, and sadistic impulses (premonitions, as
it were, of copulation) towards his mother. These early
suppressions may perhaps have gone to form the predisposition for his subsequent illness. These aggressive
propensities of Hans's found no outlet, and as soon as there
came a time of privation and of intensified sexual excitement, they tried to break their way out with reinforced
strength. It was then that the battle that we called his
"phobia" burst out.'

This, of course, is the familiar Oedipus theory, according
to which Hans wished to replace his father, whom he could
not help hating as a rival, and then complete the sexual act
by taking possession of his mother. Freud refers for con-

firmation to the following. 'Another symptomatic act
happening as if by accident involved the confession that he
had wished his father dead; for just at the moment that his
father was talking of his death wish, Hans let a horse that he
was playing with fall down – knocked it over in fact.'
Freud thus claims: 'Hans was really a little Oedipus who
wanted to have his father "out of the way", to get rid of
him, so that he might be alone with his handsome mother
and sleep with her.' The predisposition to illness provided
by the oedipal conflicts is supposed to have formed the basis
for 'the transformation of his libidinal longing into anxiety'.

What is the link between all this and the horses? Hans,
we are told, 'transposed from his father on to the horses'.
At his sole interview with Hans, Freud told him, 'that he
was afraid of his father because he himself nourished
jealousy and hostile wishes against him. In telling him this
I have partly interpreted his fear of horses for him; the
horse must be his father – whom he had good, internal
reasons for fearing.' Freud claims that Hans's fear of the
black things on the horses' mouths and the things in front of
their eyes was based on moustaches and eyeglasses and had
been 'directly transposed from his father on to the horses'.
The horses 'had been shown to represent his father'.
Freud interprets the agoraphobia element of Hans's phobia
thus. 'The content of his phobia was such as to impose a
very great measure of restriction upon his freedom of
movement, and that was its purpose ... After all Hans's
phobia of horses was an obstacle to his going into the street,
and could serve as a means of allowing him to stay at home
with his beloved mother. In this way therefore his affection
for his mother triumphantly achieved its aim.'

Freud interprets the disappearance of the phobia as
being due to the resolution by Hans of his oedipal conflict,
by 'promoting him (the father) to marriage with Hans's
grandmother ... instead of killing him.' This final interpretation is based on the following conversation between
Hans and his father. On 30 April, Hans was playing with
his imaginary children.

FATHER: Hullo, are your children still alive? You know quite well a boy can't have any children.

HANS: I know. I was their Mummy before, *now I'm their Daddy* [original italics].

FATHER: And who's the children's Mummy?

HANS: Why, Mummy, and you're *their Grandaddy* [original italics].

FATHER: So then you'd like to be as big as me, and be married to Mummy, and then you'd like her to have children.

HANS: Yes, that's what I'd like, and then my Lainz Grandmamma [paternal side] will be their Grannie.

'It is our contention,' say Wolpe and Rachman, 'that Freud's view of this case is not supported by the data, either in its particulars or as a whole. The major points that he regards as demonstrated are these:
(1) Hans had a sexual desire for his mother; (2) he hated and feared his father and wished to kill him; (3) his sexual excitement and desire for his mother were transformed into anxiety; (4) his fear of horses was symbolic of his fear of his father; (5) the purpose of the illness was to keep near his mother; and, finally, (6) his phobia disappeared because he resolved his Oedipus complex.

Let us examine each of these points.

(1) That Hans derived satisfaction from his mother and enjoyed her presence we will not even attempt to dispute. But nowhere is there any evidence of his wish to copulate with her. The 'instinctive premonitions' are referred to as though a matter of fact, though no evidence of their existence is given.

The only seduction incident described (see above) indicates that on *that particular occasion* Hans desired contact of a sexual nature with his mother, albeit a sexual contact of a simple, primitive type. This is not adequate evidence on which to base the claim that Hans had an Oedipus complex which implies a sexual desire for the mother, a wish to possess her and to replace the father. The most that can be claimed for this 'attempted seduction' is that it provides a small degree of support for the assumption that Hans had a desire for sexual stimulation by some other person (it will be recalled that he often masturbated). Even if it is assumed that stimulation provided by his mother was especially desired, the two other features of an Oedipus complex (a wish to possess the mother and replace the father) are not demonstrated by the facts of the case.

(2) Never having expressed either fear or hatred of his father, Hans was told by Freud that he possessed these emotions. On subsequent occasions Hans denied the existence of these feelings when questioned by his father. Eventually, he said, 'Yes' to a statement of this kind by his father. This simple affirmative obtained after considerable pressure on the part of the father and Freud is accepted as the true state of affairs and all Hans's denials are ignored. The 'symptomatic act' of knocking over the toy horse is taken as further evidence of Hans's aggression towards his father. There are three assumptions underlying this 'interpreted fact' – first, that the horse represents Hans's father; second, that the knocking over of the horse is not accidental; and third, that this act indicates a wish for the removal of whatever the horse symbolized.

Hans consistently denied the relationship between the horse and his father. He was, he said, afraid of horses. The mysterious black around the horses' mouths and the things on their eyes were later discovered by the father to be the horses' muzzles and blinkers. This discovery undermines the suggestion (made by Freud) that they were transposed moustaches and eye-glasses. There is no other evidence that the horses represented Hans's father. The assumption that the knocking over of the toy horse was meaningful in that it was prompted by an unconscious motive is, like most similar examples, a moot point.

As there is nothing to sustain the first two assumptions made by Freud in interpreting this 'symptomatic act', the third assumption (that this act indicated a wish for his father's death) is untenable; and it must be reiterated that there is no independent evidence that the boy feared or hated his father.

(3) Freud's third claim is that Hans's sexual excitement

and desire for his mother were transformed into anxiety. This claim is based on the assertion that 'theoretical considerations require that what is today the object of a phobia must at one time in the past have been the source of a high degree of pleasure'. Certainly such a transformation is not displayed by the facts presented. As stated above, there is no evidence that Hans sexually desired his mother. There is also no evidence of any change in his attitude to her before the onset of the phobia. Even though there is some evidence that horses were to some extent previously a source of pleasure, in general the view that phobic objects must have been the source of former pleasures is amply contradicted by experimental evidence.

(4) The assertion that Hans's horse-phobia symbolized a fear of his father has already been criticized. The assumed relationship between the father and the horse is unsupported and appears to have arisen as a result of the father's strange failure to believe that by the 'black around their mouths' Hans meant the horses' muzzles.

(5) The fifth claim is that the purpose of Hans's phobia was to keep him near his mother. Aside from the questionable view that neurotic disturbances occur for a purpose, this interpretation fails to account for the fact that Hans experienced anxiety even when he was out walking *with his mother*.

(6) Finally, we are told that the phobia disappeared as a result of Hans's resolution of his oedipal conflicts. As we have attempted to show, there is no adequate evidence that Hans had an Oedipus complex. In addition, the claim that this assumed complex was resolved is based on a single conversation between Hans and his father (see above). This conversation is a blatant example of what Freud himself refers to as Hans having to 'be told many things which he could not say himself, that he had to be presented with thoughts which he had so far *shown* no signs of possessing, and that his attention had to be turned in the direction from which his father was expecting something to come'.

There is also no satisfactory evidence that the 'insights' that were incessantly brought to the boy's attention had any therapeutic value. Reference to the facts of the case shows only occasional coincidences between interpretations and changes in the child's phobic reactions. For example, 'a quiet period' early followed the father's statement that the fear of horses was a 'piece of nonsense' and that Hans really wanted to be taken into his mother's bed. But soon afterwards, when Hans became ill, the phobia was worse than ever. Later, having had many talks without effect, the father notes that on 13 March Hans, after agreeing that he still *wanted* to play with his widdler, was 'much less afraid of horses'. On 15 March, however, he was frightened of horses, after the information that females have no widdlers (though he had previously been told the opposite by his mother). Freud asserts that Hans resisted this piece of enlightenment because it aroused castration fears, and therefore no therapeutic success was to be observed. The 'first real improvement' of 2 April is attributed to the 'moustache enlightenment' of 30 March (later proved erroneous), the boy having been told that he was 'afraid of his father precisely because he was so fond of his mother'. On 7 April, though Hans was constantly improving, Freud commented that the situation was 'decidedly obscure' and that 'the analysis was making little progress'.*

Such sparse and tenuous data do not begin to justify the attribution of Hans's recovery to the bringing to consciousness of various unacceptable unconscious repressed wishes. In fact, Freud bases his conclusions entirely on deductions from his theory. Hans's latter improvement appears to have been smooth and gradual and unaffected by the interpretations. In general, Freud infers relationships in a scientifically inadmissible manner: if the enlightenments or interpretations given to Hans are followed by behavioural improvements, then they are automatically accepted as valid. If they are not followed by improvement we are told the patient has not accepted them, and not that they are

*By Freud's admission Hans was improving despite the absence of progress in the analysis.

invalid. Discussing the failure of these early enlightenments, Freud says that in any event therapeutic success is not the primary aim of the analysis,* thus side-tracking the issue; and he is not deflected from claiming an improvement to be due to an interpretation even when the latter is erroneous, e.g. the moustache interpretation.

Readers not familiar with the psychoanalytic literature will by now have acquired some insight into the reasons why psychologists with a scientific background tend to look rather askance at the type of proof which is offered in case histories of this kind, and why psychoanalysis has never been taken very seriously by people with some regard for the principles of scientific method. Why then, has psychoanalysis established such a strong position, in spite of the many criticisms which have been levelled against it? One reason has been given by Conant, the well-known philosopher of science, when he pointed out that no amount of factual refutation is sufficient to kill a theory in science or medicine; that what is required is, rather, a better theory. As long as no alternative interpretation of the facts was available, so long psychoanalytic reasoning continued to flourish. Fortunately, the position has changed now, and alternative theories are available to account for facts such as those presented in the case history of little Hans. Before we attempt to re-interpret this particular phobia, let us have a look at another little boy, this time an American, one who was studied by J. B. Watson, the famous founder of the school of Behaviourism. Watson argued that it should be possible to produce phobias experimentally by means of Pavlov's paradigm of simple conditioning, and he tried to prove that this was so by making use of little Albert, an orphan, eleven months of age. Little Albert was quite fond of white rats, used to play with them a lot, and showed no sign of fear whatsoever for these animals. Watson set out to establish a phobic fear for white rats in little Albert, and he did so by imitating Pavlov's procedure, by means of which he had trained dogs to salivate to the sound of a bell by

*But elsewhere he says that a psychoanalysis is a therapeutic measure and not a scientific investigation!

simply pairing the bell with the presentation of food for a number of times.

Watson's method was simple and direct and very ingenious. He stood behind little Albert with a metal bar in one hand and a hammer in the other. Whenever little Albert reached out for the rats, in an attempt to play with them, Watson would bang the metal bar with the hammer, thus making a loud noise. Now, in this situation, the rats, as it were, are the conditioned stimuli, the loud noise produced by the metal bar is the unconditioned stimulus which produces a fear response. By always seeing to it that the sight and touch of the conditioned stimuli – that is to say, the rats – just preceded the onset of the unconditioned stimulus – the noise – Watson hoped to produce a conditioned fear reaction, so that the infant would react to the rats in the same way as he did to the noise produced by the metal bar; that is to say, with signs of fear and withdrawal. This is precisely what happened. After a number of repetitions, little Albert became afraid of rats, would whimper, try to crawl away from them, and, in a word, behaved exactly as if he were suffering from a severe rat phobia. Watson, therefore, had succeeded brilliantly in doing what he had set out to do; that is to say, to produce a phobic reaction by experimental means. This phobia did not pass away after a day or two but continued unabated. Furthermore, it showed another characteristic of conditioned responses; that is to say, it showed a generalization gradient. Little Albert became afraid, not only of rats, but also of other furry animals, just as one might have predicted from what is known of the genesis and generalization of conditioned responses in animals and man.

We cannot, of course, leave little Albert with his phobia, and we shall have to see, in the next chapter, what we can do to cure him of it. Before doing that, however, we must return now to little Hans, to see whether we can interpret his particular disorder along the lines of Watson's experiment. If we may generalize from Watson's data, we may regard it as conditioned anxiety or fear reactions. Any neutral stimulus, simple or complex, that happens to make an impact upon a person at about the time that a fear reaction is evoked, acquires the ability to evoke fear subsequently. If the fear of the original conditioning situation is of high intensity, or if the conditioning is many times repeated, then the conditioned fear will show the persistence that is characteristic of *neurotic* fear; and there will be generalization of fear reactions to stimuli resembling the conditioned stimulus.

Now Hans, we are told, was a sensitive child who 'was never unmoved if someone wept in his presence'. And long before the phobia developed, he became 'uneasy on seeing the horses on the merry-go-round being beaten'. Wolpe and Rachman contend that the incident to which Freud refers as merely the exciting cause of Hans's phobia was, in fact, the cause of the entire disorder. Hans actually says, 'No. I only got it [the phobia] then. When the horse and the bus fell down, it gave me such a fright, really! That was when I got the nonsense.' The father says, 'All of this was confirmed by my wife, as well as the fact that the anxiety broke out immediately afterwards.' In addition, the father was able to report two other unpleasant incidents which Hans experienced with horses, prior to the onset of the phobia. It was likely that these experiences had sensitized Hans to horses or, in other words, he had already been partially conditioned to fear horses. The first was the warning given by the father of Hans's friend, to avoid the horses lest they bite, and the second when another of Hans's friends injured himself (and bled) when they were playing horses.

Wolpe and Rachman go on to say:

Just as the little boy, Albert, in Watson's classic demonstration, reacted with anxiety, not only to the original conditioned stimulus, the white rat, but to other similar stimuli, such as furry objects, cotton wool, and so on; Hans reacted anxiously to horses, horse-drawn buses, vans, and features of horses such as their blinkers and muzzles. In fact he showed fear of a wide range of generalized stimuli. The accident which provoked the phobia involved two horses drawing a bus and Hans stated that he was more afraid of large carts, vans, or buses than small carts. As one would expect, the less close the phobic stimulus was to that of the original incident, the less disturbing Hans found it. Furthermore, the last aspect of the phobia to disappear was Hans's fear of large vans and buses. There is ample experimental evidence that when responses to generalized stimuli undergo extinction, responses to other stimuli in the continuum are the less diminished the more closely they resemble the original conditioned stimulus.

Hans's recovery from the phobia may be explained on conditioning principle in a number of possible ways, but the actual mechanism that operated cannot be identified, since the child's father was not concerned with the kind of information that would be of interest to us. It is well known that, especially in children, many phobias decline and disappear over a few weeks or months. The reason for this appears to be that in the ordinary course of life generalized phobic stimuli may evoke responses weak enough to be inhibited by other emotional responses simultaneously aroused in the individual. Perhaps this process was the true source of little Hans's recovery. The interpretations may have been irrelevant or may even have retarded recovery by adding new threats and new fears to those already present. But since Hans does not seem to have been greatly upset by the interpretations it appears more likely that the therapy was actually helpful, for phobic stimuli were again and again presented to the child in a variety of emotional contexts that may have inhibited the anxiety and in consequence diminished its habit strength. The *gradualness* of Hans's recovery is consonant with an explanation of this kind.

It may be rather rash to try, at this distance of time, to re-interpret a child's phobia that was treated fifty years ago. However, the facts fit in remarkably neatly, and at least we are provided with an alternative theory here which, to many people at least, will seem more plausible than the original one produced by Freud. However, what is clearly required is a method of proof which will decide between these alternative interpretations, not so much with regard to little Hans, but with regard to cases which may come up nowadays and which may be treated by methods deriving either from Freud's or from Wolpe's type of theory. We will discuss these developments in the next chapter. Here, let us simply quote the conclusions to which Wolpe and Rachman come, on the basis of their examination of the case of little Hans.

The chief conclusion to be derived from our survey of the case of little Hans is that it does not provide anything resembling direct proof of psychoanalytic theorems. We have combed Freud's account for evidence that would be acceptable in the court of science, and have found none ... Freud believed that he had obtained in little Hans a direct confirmation of his theories, for he speaks towards the end of 'the infantile complexes that were revealed behind Hans's phobia'. It seems clear that although he wanted to be scientific ... Freud was surprisingly naïve regarding the requirements of scientific evidence. Infantile complexes were not *revealed* (demonstrated) behind Hans's phobia: they were merely hypothesized.

It is remarkable that countless psychoanalysts have paid homage to the case of little Hans, without being offended by its glaring inadequacies. We shall not here attempt to explain this, except to point to one probable major influence – a tacit belief among analysts that Freud possessed a kind of unerring insight that absolved him from the obligation to obey rules applicable to ordinary men. For example, Glover, speaking of other analysts who arrogate to themselves the right Freud claimed to subject his material to 'a touch of revision', says, 'No doubt when someone of Freud's calibre appears in our midst he will be freely accorded ... this privilege.' To accord such a privilege to anyone is to violate the spirit of science.

With this conclusion, the present writer is in complete agreement.

Psychoanalysts, curiously enough, are not. They tend to argue that subjective experiences such as the therapist has in treating a particular case, are undervalued by those who base their conclusions on statistical analysis of many trials, and they further suggest that the meaning of 'science' normally accepted should be extended to bring into it their particular type of work. Argument along these lines is not particularly useful. It reminds one of the famous story told by Sydney Smith. He was visiting Aberdeen and was walking through the harbour with a friend, when they found two fishwives, one on each side of the street, leaning out of their windows and shouting abuse at each other. 'These two will never agree,' said Sydney Smith to his companion, 'they are arguing from different premises.'

Even though there is little point in trying to preach to the converted, the reader who is not too familiar with scientific method and who, on the other hand, has no axe to grind for psychoanalysis either, may wonder why a certain amount of subjectivity may not be permissible. There is ample evidence in the history of science of the blunders and errors that result from placing too much faith in the trustworthiness of human beings as recording instruments. An interesting example of this are the 'N-rays' claimed to have been discovered in 1902 by Professor M. Blondlot, an eminent physicist at the University of Nancy and a member of the French Academy of Sciences. Coming six years after the discovery of X-rays by Roentgen, Blondlot's discovery was quickly confirmed in other laboratories by quite eminent physicists. The presence of these rays was defined by the decrease of the resistance of a spark gap, the increased glow of a platinum wire, and the increased luminosity of a phosphorescent surface. All these determinations had to be made by eye, since the N-ray could not be recorded by photographic apparatus. E. Z. Vogt and R. Hyman, who record this history in their book *Water Witching U.S.A.* tell of many applications of the N-rays.[*] Thus Corson applied them to chemistry, Lambert and Meyer studied their effects on biological phenomena and also on plants, and Charpentier found that compression of a nerve was accompanied by emission of N-rays. Broca, the famous brain specialist, examined the relationship between N-rays and the brain.

Other physicists, however, tried to duplicate the N-ray effect but obtained negative results. The discussion nearly created an international incident when it was found that N-rays could only be found by French scientists. Finally, the famous physicist, R. W. Wood, of Johns Hopkins University, visited Blondlot's laboratory in person, to see why other physicists had failed to obtain his results. This is an account in his own words of his visit.

So I visited Nancy before rejoining my family in Paris, meeting Blondlot by appointment in his laboratory in the early evening. He spoke no English and I elected German as our means of com-

[*] I have followed their excellent account closely.

munication, as I wanted him to feel free to speak confidentially to his assistant who was apparently a sort of high-class laboratory janitor. [Wood, of course, understood and spoke French perfectly well.]

He first showed me a card on which some circles had been painted in luminous paint. He turned down the gas light and drew my attention to the increased luminosity when the N-ray was turned on. I said I saw no change. He said that was because my eyes were not sensitive enough, so that proved nothing. I asked him if I could move an opaque lead screen in and out of the path of the rays while he called out the fluctuations on the screen. He was almost one hundred per cent wrong and called out fluctuations when I made no movement at all and that proved a lot but I held my tongue.

Wood made a number of other tests, clearly demonstrating that Blondlot's rays existed only in his imagination. Thus Blondlot claimed to be able to see the face of a dimly-lighted clock through a metal phial with the aid of N-rays. He agreed to Wood's holding the metal phial in front of his eyes, but unknown to Blondlot, Wood secretly substituted a wooden ruler for the metal phial; in the darkened laboratory Blondlot did not notice this switch. Instead he continued to 'see' the clock through the ruler, even though the wood was one of the few substances that allegedly was impervious to N-rays.

The whole conception of N-rays was immediately dismissed from physics after Wood had published his findings that they were merely the result of faulty human observation coupled with suggestion. The consequences for Blondlot were, of course, tragic. Just preceding the exposure the French Academy had awarded him the Lalande Prize of 20,000 francs and its gold medal for 'the discovery of N-rays'. After Wood's account had appeared in print, the Academy went through with the award, but changed the announced reason to other contributions made by Blondlot previously; but this was not enough, and Blondlot eventually went mad and then died as a result of his disgrace. If such things can happen in physics, the queen of the sciences, and if human beings cannot be relied upon as observers, even under the very simple conditions of Blondlot's experiments, then how much less can we place reliance on psychoanalysts observing very much more complex and difficult phenomena and armed *a priori* with a system which prescribes to them, in complete detail, what they should find and what they must look for!

There are, of course, many examples in history which show how such preconceived notions can deceive even experienced and well-known scientists. The development of phrenology, the science of reading the bumps on a person's head, is one such example. For many years, the most famous brain surgeons and medical people in Europe firmly believed in the accuracy of the prognostications made on the basis of this system, originated by Gall and Spurzheim, although we now know that none of their claims has any basis whatsoever in reality. Astrology, of course, is another example, and we may note that even some quite famous astronomers such as Kepler, for instance, were firm believers in the reality of the influences which the planets can bring to bear on our lives. Nevertheless, we now recognize that this is nothing but superstition. Water witching is another example, for even nowadays many honest people, and even some scientists, believe that through the movements of a twig held in both hands, the dowser can indeed discover water under conditions where all other sensory impressions are eliminated. Alack, this belief, too, has not stood up to experimental investigation, and as Vogt and Hyman, in the book mentioned above, have shown quite conclusively, when experimental conditions are arranged in such a way that subjective errors and chance effects are ruled out, then the dowser is completely unable to fulfil his claims.

The truth seems to be, very simply, that during its early stages every science has to go through an ordeal by quackery. Astrology was probably as necessary to the development of astronomy as phrenology was to the modern development of the study of the properties of different parts of the brain. This development has always been accompanied by a shift from subjective to objective impressions, and there can be no doubt that only by practising the maximum amount of objective checking and re-checking of all the data available can we begin to develop theories which have some hope of standing up to future investigation. Scientists have to do two things; they have to formulate new theories which will advance the field in which they are working, but they must also strive to provide proof for these theories. Freud's contribution was entirely of the former kind. He was a rich source of theories, throwing them off almost like a Catherine wheel throws off sparks, but he was totally lacking in the ability to suggest and perform experiments which would put these hypotheses to a crucial test. Indeed, he was openly contemptuous of experimental work and his reply to an American psychologist, who had written to him to suggest the possibility of verifying some of his hypotheses in the experimental laboratory, is well known. He said, 'My theories are proved on the couch. They do not require experimental evidence.' This is not the attitude of a scientist, and it is unfortunate that Freud's example has been copied by his followers who lack not only a scientific attitude, but also that tremendous ability to formulate far-reaching hypotheses which was so uniquely the gift of Freud's.

Perhaps I may end this chapter by quoting Karl M. Dallenbach, who, in 1955, delivered a striking lecture, comparing phrenology and psychoanalysis. He ended it by saying, 'What does the future hold for psychoanalysis? In the light of our knowledge of the past I could make a prediction but prefer to let Freud speak for his own therapy. He said, according to Ernest Jones, his biographer, "That in time to come it should be possible to cure hysteria and nervous diseases by administering a chemical drug without any psychological treatment." If that should come to pass, as many believe it will, (and as we have some evidence today), what will that do to psychoanalysis? What then will be Freud's niche in history? Will it, like Gall's, become a roost for charlatans? Is it not already occupied by some? I leave these questions with you.'

In the last chapter, we left little Albert suspended somewhat uneasily between heaven and earth, with his conditioned phobia. Does our theory suggest any ways of curing him of this unfortunate habit? On the face of it, it seems reasonable that if our knowledge of the acquisition of conditioned responses has made it possible for us to induce a phobic reaction in little Albert, then our experimental knowledge of the extinction of conditioned responses in the laboratory should enable us to make some suggestions, at least, regarding the elimination of this phobia. Before doing so, let us look first of all precisely at just what it is that we have done.

We have explained, in a previous chapter, that the autonomic nervous system, which mediates emotional responses, is divided into two antagonistic portions, the sympathetic or 'fight and flight' reactive system, and the parasympathetic, or vegetating system. Now clearly, the conditioned response which we have inculcated in little Albert has been one involving the sympathetic nervous system; in other words, we have conditioned a sympathetic response to the sight, feel, and sound of the white rats. One obvious way of getting rid of this conditioned response and extinguishing it completely would be to condition a parasympathetic response to the sight, smell, and sound of the white rats. Parasympathetic responses, being antagonistic to sympathetic ones, should cancel them out, and the infant should then be left without any conditioned responses to white rats at all, and should, therefore, go back to his original state of liking white rats and playing with them happily. How can we induce a parasympathetic reaction? There are many ways of doing this, but the one suggested by Watson was a very simple one, of offering him some chocolate to eat when he was fairly hungry. As mentioned

before, there is a strong relationship between parasympathetic reaction and digestive functions, and Watson
suggested capitalizing on this relationship.

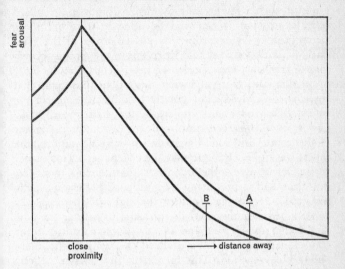

Figure 19. This diagram illustrates the decrease in the amount of fear
experienced (shown on the vertical axis) as the feared object is taken
further and further away from the person concerned (horizontal axis).
Each time a successful attempt is made to de-condition the fear, the total
curve is lowered, as indicated by the lower line, and on the next attempt
the feared object can be brought a little nearer. For explanation, see text.

One difficulty arose immediately when an attempt was
made to put this plan into action. Mary Cover Jones, who
carried out the experiment, found that the conditioned
sympathetic fear response was so strong in the boy that
when he was offered the chocolate he paid no attention to
it at all, but simply tried to get away from the rats. Under
these circumstances, she made use of a very simple device
which will appeal to the common sense of the reader. When
we are afraid of a particular person, or animal, or thing,
then our fear is roughly proportional to the nearness of the
object in question; the nearer it is, the more we are afraid.

Figure 19 shows this in rough, diagrammatic form, the amount of fear experienced being represented on the vertical axis, and the distance away of the object of our fear from ourselves on the horizontal axis. It is possible to establish such a relationship by means of introspection and observation, but it can also be done in a rather more scientific way by recording the actual upset of the sympathetic, autonomic system by means of polygraph recordings of the heart-beat, breathing rate, electric conductivity of the skin, and so on; and when this is done, it is found that these all do indeed show greater emotion, the nearer the object is moved to the subject of the experiment. Mary Cover Jones, therefore, simply put the rats in the far corner of the room, and found that under those conditions, the infant was quite willing to take the chocolate, although still casting a wary eye at the rodents. At this moment, therefore, she succeeded in producing a conditioned parasympathetic response, i.e. linking together the sight of the rats, the conditioned stimulus, and the pleasure in eating, the flow of the digestive juices, and so on, which constituted the conditioned response of generalized parasympathetic, more pleasurable reaction. This increment in parasympathetic conditioning would now subtract from the sum total of the sympathetic conditioning which had taken place, and the whole curve depicted in Figure 19 would be lowered, so that the next time the rats could be brought a little nearer, and the same parasympathetic conditioning process could be gone through again. Each time this was done, there would accrue a certain amount of parasympathetic conditioning, lowering the fear-distance curve a little, and enabling the experimenter to bring the rats a little nearer; until, finally, they could be brought right up close to the infant, who would then play happily with them, the sympathetic conditioning completely extinguished by the parasympathetic conditioning which had taken place. Once extinguished the phobia has gone, never to return – no further administrations of chocolate are required!

This process has been called therapy by *reciprocal inhibition* by J. Wolpe, who was the first to take up these laboratory experiments and apply them successfully to serious cases of neurotic disorder in human adults.

Watson's and Mary Cover Jones's experiments were done upon a very small number of cases and they were done in the laboratory. Would it be possible to generalize their findings a little and apply them to phobic fears which were not the product of laboratory conditioning but present before the beginning of the experiment?

THE CASE OF THE CAT WOMAN

This case, which was reported by Drs H. L. Freeman and D. C. Kendrick, concerns a married woman of thirty-seven years of age, who is suffering from a phobia for cats associated with tension, anxiety, and, occasionally, depression. Her father had been very strict with his children, dominated his wife, and made the family conform to his ideas. She was afraid of him as a child and felt that she never had any love for him. Her mother was a simple, rather garrulous, old woman, subject to 'nerve rashes'. She was given to threatening her children in their early years with action by their father. The woman married, at the age of twenty-two, having known her husband for four years. He is a schoolteacher, and is a placid, easygoing, good-natured sort of person. He has always been very concerned about the patient's symptoms, and has done his best to protect her from cats. They have two children, a daughter aged fourteen and a son aged twelve. The woman is sociable and outgoing, has many friends, and likes to be active at home, in evening classes, and so on. She is rather houseproud, perhaps excessively so. She is also sensitive, irritable, and readily shows her feelings. She is fond of all animals except cats, and her children have guinea pigs, tortoises, and birds, none of which upsets her.

The patient's fear of cats has existed as long as she can remember. The fear may date from the age of four, when she remembers her father drowning a kitten in a bucket in front of her. She remembers sitting at the table as a child with her legs stretched out straight in front of her if a cat was prowling about the floor, and screaming outside the front door of the house if there was a cat to be seen. When she was fourteen, her parents put a fur inside her bed on one occasion, and she became quite hysterical on finding it. At the age of eighteen, the patient had another fright when a cat got into her bedroom. The fear became worse after her marriage, and remained pretty much the same for a period of almost ten years, but had recently become steadily worse. The patient was terrified by the thought that cats would spring on her and attack her, although she knew that this was very unlikely in fact. At the sight of a cat panic would overcome her, and she would sometimes be completely overwhelmed with terror. She always walked on the roadside edge of the pavement, to avoid cats on the walls, and would never go out alone at night. She would never go into any room where there was a cat if it was possible to avoid doing so. She was afraid to go into her garden alone, and wash-days were a torment to her. 'She could not bear to touch any cat-like fur, or wear fur gloves, and felt uneasy sitting next to anyone wearing a fur coat on public transport. Pictures of cats in books, or on television or the cinema, made her feel uneasy. In recent months her life was filled with fear of cats, and she could think of nothing else. She interpreted any unexpected movement, shadow, or noise as due to a cat. She would be upset by her daughter's koala bear if she saw it or touched it unexpectedly. On waking in the morning, her first thought was how many cats she would meet during the day. From time to time she had terrifying nightmares, concerned with cats.'

Psychological investigations showed her to be reasonably intelligent, with an I.Q. of 112 and with a mildly extraverted personality. Her fear of cats was so strong that it was quite impossible to start the treatment by putting a cat, however small, into the same room with her, at however large a distance; it simply produced a paroxysm of terror in her. Consequently, it was decided to extend the distance gradient in another way; that is to say, not by putting a greater physical distance between subject and object, but rather by taking objects which were only slightly like the fear-producing cats, and which were, therefore, removed along a gradient of ideational distance. A series of pieces of material were, therefore, prepared, graded in texture and appearance from most unlike cat fur to very like cat fur (rabbit). The patient was then asked to handle these materials, in order of similarity to cat fur, and before she proceeded with the next piece in the series she was required to feel no uneasiness whatsoever in handling it. After overcoming the fear reactions to handling cat-like fur, she was then presented with a toy kitten, pictures of cats, and so on, until finally all these stimuli caused no anxiety at all. Once this state had been achieved, she was shown a live kitten, which gradually she was asked to approach and touch, and which she was asked to take home and keep when she was ready to do so. It was hypothesized that as this desensitization to cats became more marked, generalization to large cats would occur, and finally she would be free of her phobia for cats altogether.

The method of treatment was discussed with the patient, who was agreeable to try it, but who felt very sceptical about the outcome; she could not conceive of herself as ever being able to touch even a kitten. At the end of three weeks, fur, toys, and pictures had all been fully assimilated and a significant lessening in anxiety had already occurred. The patient was much less preoccupied with cats in general, and her family noticed that she was much more cheerful. She could walk within about ten yards of a cat without flinching, and when opening the curtains in the morning, her first reaction was no longer to look around the garden for cats.

The rapidity of response seemed so far remarkable, and the patient now felt ready to deal with a live kitten. One of a suitably placid disposition was obtained and the patient was brought into the room, where she saw it resting on the lap of one of the nurses. She sat down next to the nurse, stroked the kitten herself, and then took it on to her own lap. During this process she became very emotional, was laughing and crying, but this passed off in a few minutes, and she explained afterwards that it was not from distress, but from relief at having done something of which she imagined herself incapable. She later described this as 'one of the greatest days of my life'. In the next two days she looked after the kitten in the hospital and then took it home, where it has remained since. This occurred one month after her first attendance and during the next two months she continued to attend twice weekly, but mainly for the art classes, in which she was very interested. During this period she was assessed weekly by the psychiatrist, and her improvement was seen to be continuing. She said that she felt as though a cloud had been lifted from her, and she had stopped biting her nails for the first time in her life. She no longer walked along the edge of the pavement, could wear fur gloves, and sit next to people in fur coats without feeling uneasy. She was no longer upset by pictures or films of cats and could consider some of them as beautiful creatures. She could pass near to a full-grown cat without panicking and she felt that she would be able to go out alone at night. She had stopped having cat nightmares and dreamed without distress of kittens and later of full-grown cats. Ten weeks after beginning treatment she touched a full-grown cat for the first time. She states that her life has been completely transformed, and that she no longer goes round in a state of fear. Nor does she feel the need any longer to occupy herself in constant activity inside the house to relieve her anxiety. At the end of the fifth month from beginning treatment she had been out by herself at night, even in dimly-lit streets. It should be noted that throughout the treatment both direct suggestion and reassurance had been avoided. Interviews by the psychologist and by the psychiatrist were confined to explaining the procedure, administering the stimuli, and assessing the position reached. It is also interesting that once the treatment broke through the vicious circle of the phobic reactions there was not only a remission of the behavioural symptoms but also a reduction in the general level of anxiety.

This case is typical of many others in which phobias have been treated, except that it is perhaps a little simpler and more straightforward than most. Before turning to more detailed discussions of some of the problems involved, let me recount another case, rather different in nature, to wit, that of the wallpaper man.

This is a middle-aged patient who came to therapy because of sexual impotence. He was impotent with his wife, but only in their own house; whenever they went to an hotel or on holiday, he had no difficulty at all in consummating the sexual act. He was treated for several years by psychoanalysis, which succeeded in unearthing many childhood memories, and which resulted in the diagnosis of an unresolved Oedipus complex, an explanation which satisfied the analyst, but which did not result in any improvement in the symptom. Finally, the patient turned to a psychologist who was interested in the methods of deconditioning neurotic disorders. The psychologist elicited the following bit of information from the patient. When he had been an adolescent he had had sexual relations with the wife of another man, who once happened to interrupt the pair in the middle of intercourse. Being much the stronger of the two, he had beaten the patient to within an inch of his life. This beating may be regarded as constituting an unconditioned stimulus, leading to very strong sympathetic fear, pain, and anxiety reactions. According to learning theory, anything that the patient happened to see or hear in this situation might be the conditioned stimulus. As it eventuated, it had been the wallpaper which the patient had been looking at during his rather uncomfortable few minutes, and accordingly we have a very simple conditioning paradigm, in which the wallpaper plays the part of the conditioned stimulus which, through pairing with the beating-up, should now become the source of strong sympathetic anxiety reactions. As it happened, the patient's bedroom had a wallpaper which was very similar to that of the room in which he had been originally beaten up, and accordingly the psychologist reconstructed the reasons for his impotence in this room as being due to a conditioned sympathetic reaction making impossible the occurrence of a proper erection, which, as is well known, is mediated by the parasympathetic nervous system. (It should be noted, in this connexion, that the patient was in the habit of making love while the lights were on; he was, of course, French!) This explanation also provided the reason for the lack of impotence on the patient's part whenever he made love to his wife outside this particular room, and the recommendation of the psychologist was not a prolonged psychoanalysis, but rather that the patient should engage the services of a paper-hanger. When a new wallpaper was put up in the room, the impotence vanished completely and the patient had no further trouble. In his case also the removal of the symptom was followed by an all-round improvement in his behaviour, a lessening in anxiety, and much better marital adjustment. This case, too, of course, is not typical – perhaps we may say parenthetically that no cases ever are typical – but it does demonstrate very clearly the power of the conditioning paradigm in relation to the occurrence and the removal of neurotic symptoms.

Consider next the case of the water girl.

THE CASE OF THE WATER GIRL

This is of interest, not because it presents a very serious neurotic disorder, but rather because, in its small way, it exemplifies the way in which neurotic fears are learned and unlearned, and it also shows very clearly indeed the close relationship between the methods described by modern learning theory and the kind of commonsense approach which no doubt many mothers – and perhaps fathers, too – have, in the past, used in dealing with such fears arising in their children. This case, reported by P. M. Bentler, is of an eleven and a half months-old girl called Margaret, who loved wading in her small swimming pool, bathed with evident delight, and never objected to being washed. On one occasion, Margaret tried to stand up in the bath tub and slipped, and then began screaming. She refused further bathing with violent screams, and had to be removed from the tub. During the next few days she reacted with vehement emotion, not only to the bath tub, the faucet, and the water in the tub, but also to being washed in the hand-basin, to faucets, or water in any part of the house, and to the wading pool. Clearly, the fear produced by the slipping, and possibly other, unknown, concomitant events, had caused a conditioned fear response in Margaret, and during the next week it became apparent that she would continue this behaviour unless systematic steps were taken to overcome her fear.

Distraction, affective responses towards toys, body contact and other mother-related stimuli, were used to produce responses incompatible with anxiety. Treatment, which lasted approximately for a month, consisted of four parts. In the first part, toys were placed in the empty bath tub and Margaret was given free access to the bathroom and to the toys. She would enter the bathroom and remove a toy from the tub but did not stay near the tub, and refused to play with the toys whilst leaning over the tub. She continued to scream if any washing was attempted, but her behaviour towards the tub became less emotional. In the second part of the treatment, Margaret was twice placed on the kitchen table surrounding the sink, while the sink was filled with water and toys floated in it. At first she screamed when near the water, but then all the toys were placed on the other side of the basin, and on to a ledge above it, so that Margaret would have to walk through the basin in order to reach the toys. Finally, she entered the water reluctantly; she cried a little when she became wet, but the kitchen sink helped desensitize Margaret to water.

The third part of the treatment consisted of washing Margaret, at diaper-changing time, in the bathroom sink. She was given a favourite toy to play with, but the mirror hanging over the sink proved more interesting, and initial crying soon turned to happy squeals. She also started playing with the water, and during this time, began to play with the sprinkler in the yard. The fourth and final step was washing Margaret at diaper-changing time in the tub, with the water running. At first she objected to this with screams, but parental hugging and firmness caused her to stop crying after two days. One month's treatment, therefore, saw Margaret recovered, and playing normally in the tub while taking baths. Her fear of faucets, tubs, or water anywhere around the house had gone, and she was not only willing to take baths and be washed, but gleefully initiated playful behaviour with water, running madly towards the wading pool in the backyard, entering it, and splashing about joyously while playing. Follow-up studies showed that these changes were quite permanent and that there was no residue of her original fear.

This case may seem too slight to be mentioned at all, but I have seen children going from bad to worse after a very slight beginning such as this, and I have also seen a good number of children treated psychoanalytically for fears of this kind, with most unfortunate consequences. On the other hand, I have also seen a good number of children showing fears of this type who were treated with equal success by their parents, who showed a very good intuitive understanding of this method of reciprocal inhibition. In simple cases, no doubt, this parental understanding works extremely well in extinguishing the conditioned fear response; it is only in more complicated cases that the services of an expert and the use of learning theory will become necessary.

Before turning to a description of some more complex cases, we must first look a little more closely at the theoretical rationale underlying such treatment, as elaborated particularly by J. Wolpe, the South African originator of this particular type of therapy. We have already seen that the simple device used with children, of transferring the fear-object to the other end of the room, and thus reducing anxiety by putting a good deal of distance between the child and the feared object, is difficult, if not impossible, to execute with the more complex disorders of adults. The fears are usually too strong to make this device feasible, at least to begin with, and, furthermore, many fears are not of a kind that make it possible to employ this particular technique. A person may be afraid of heights, or of open spaces, or of blood; he may have anxieties relating to the state of the world, or the hydrogen bomb, or Communist spies. It is difficult to manipulate these stimuli in the same way in which we can manipulate little Albert's white rats, and we have to have recourse, therefore, to their ideational representation, i.e. through the use of words, through the use of mental imagery, and through the use of pictures. Furthermore, it is unusual for a phobic reaction to be as completely monosymptomatic as that of little Albert, or of the cat woman. Usually, anxieties and fears are aroused not just by one object, but by a good many; and these objects may not always be similar to each other. What is necessary, Wolpe points out, is to order all the fear-producing stimuli in a number of habit-family hierarchies. By this he means that first of all the fears are grouped according to the particular stimuli which give rise to them: say, all stimuli associated with dogs, all stimuli associated with people, all stimuli associated with heights, and so on. Within each of these groups, a hierarchy is then formed, starting with the most severe fear-producing stimulus, and going down to the least fear-producing stimulus. As an example of such a hierarchy, consider the case of the frightened tram driver.

THE CASE OF THE FRIGHTENED TRAM DRIVER

This case was treated by J. Wolpe, who reports that the twenty-three-year-old man entered the consulting room in a state of acute anxiety. Some hours before, a woman had walked straight into his slowly-moving tram, and had been knocked out, with her head bleeding. Although a doctor had told him that the woman's injury was not serious, he had become increasingly shaky, and had developed severe stomach pains. He had recovered from previous accidents in an hour or two, but in these no human injury had been involved. This statement was significant, because when the patient was thirteen, his father had died after an accident, and since then he had had a fear of human blood. Even the tiny bead of blood which might appear on his face during shaving gave him an uncomfortable feeling. He was quite indifferent to animal blood, and it was clear that his grossly excessive reaction to the particular accident in which he had been involved was due to his phobia for human blood.

The central aim of therapy was, therefore, to overcome this phobia. Various situations involving human blood were staged, in ascending order of their disturbing effect. At each interview, while the patient was in a state of hypnotic relaxation, he was made to visualize 'blood situations'. The feeblest was a slightly blood-tinged bandage lying in a basket. When this failed to disturb his relaxation, he was presented with a tiny drop of blood on his own face while shaving. In this way, with the presentation of two or three images at each session, it was possible gradually to work up to the stage in which the patient could visualize a casualty ward full of carnage and not be disturbed by it. The success of this method, in real-life situations, was revealed, in his case, in a most dramatic manner. Two days before his last interview, the patient saw a man knocked over by a motor-cycle. The victim was seriously injured and was bleeding profusely. The patient was quite unaffected by the blood, and when the ambulance arrived, helped to load the victim on to it.

In this case, only one hierarchy was necessary, but, as pointed out before, in more complex cases, two, three, or even as many as ten such hierarchies may be required. Each has to be worked through from the bottom to the top. This may sound more difficult and a much lengthier procedure than it actually is, because in actual fact, it has been found that higher levels of the hierarchy are reduced in their anxiety-producing properties by the elimination of the lower ones, and anxieties in one hierarchy are again reduced by the elimination of anxieties in other hierarchies.

I have purposely omitted a detailed discussion of one very crucial point which arises in reciprocal inhibition therapy, and that is the production of those responses which are antagonistic to anxiety, and which reciprocally inhibit it. The most important, from a practical point of view, is probably the category of relaxation responses. It had been experimentally shown by Jacobson that intense muscle relaxation is accompanied by autonomic effects antagonistic to the characteristic effects of anxiety. Jacobson worked out a method of 'progressive relaxation' which essentially is a training in relaxing the whole body by concentrating on relaxing parts of it, one at a time, until finally complete relaxation is achieved. Anxiety-producing stimuli also produce a great deal of muscle tenseness, and, therefore, persistent relaxation implies some measure of reciprocal inhibition of the effects of any anxiety-producing stimuli that happen to appear. Usually it takes several interviews of training in progressive relaxation, possibly aided by hypnotic techniques, before complete relaxation can be achieved. After the preliminaries have been completed, the patient is asked to imagine a scene embodying the feeblest member of the anxiety hierarchy, and he is instructed to signal if, at any time, he feels more than the slightest disturbance. The relaxation counteracts the slight anxieties which are produced by these imaginings, and, therefore, reciprocally inhibits them. Usually, two or three items from the hierarchy are presented at each session, the speed of progression depending, of course, on how much disturbance is shown or reported by the patient afterwards. An item is presented several times, until the reaction aroused by it disappears completely. It usually takes between ten and thirty desensitization sessions before the highest items in the hierarchy are accepted by the patient without disturbance.

Russian workers have used a rather different technique, recently also introduced into the United States. It is an attempt to induce deep relaxation through the utilization of a variable, low-frequency, low-intensity current transmitted to the human cortex through appropriately designed electrodes. This method derives from Pavlov's theory of inhibition, and may take the place of relaxation in cases where this is difficult to achieve, or where there is no time to indulge in the lengthy practice periods which may occasionally be required.

Feeding responses may, of course, also be used with adults and adolescents, as with children, but, in the past, they have usually been rather neglected. As Wolpe points out, 'What is required is that in the presence of the anxiety-evoking stimulus food must be given under so intense a hunger drive that in the act of eating there will be an inhibition of anxiety. Probably, it is precisely this which is the explanation of the beneficial effects on neuroses of sub-coma doses of insulin.'

Quite a different method again involves the inhalation of high concentrations of carbon dioxide. Processes antagonistic to anxiety can be found both in the excitation which goes with intense respiratory stimulation through this gas, and also in association with the complete muscle relaxation that high concentrations of carbon dioxide produce. Wolpe has reported that this method usually produces dramatic and, under certain circumstances, lasting relief from pervasive (free-floating) anxiety. This is a particularly interesting method of treatment which has not been used to anything like its full effect.

Quite different again to the preceding methods is one which Wolpe calls that of assertive responses. They are used for overcoming unadaptive anxiety aroused in the patient by other people during his direct dealings with them.

To take a common example, a patient feels hurt when members of his family criticize him, and responds by trying to defend himself, by sulking, or by an outburst of petulant rage. Such responses are expressive of anxiety and helplessness. But some measure of resentment is, understandably, almost invariably present at the same time. The patient is unable to express this resentment because, for example, through previous training, the idea of talking back to his elders produces anxiety. Now just because this anxiety inhibits the expression of the resentment, it might be expected that if the patient could be motivated to express the resentment, the latter would, in turn, be reciprocally inhibitory to the anxiety and thus suppress it, to some extent at least. The therapist provides this motivation by pointing out the emptiness of the patient's fears, while emphasizing how his fearful patterns of behaviour have incapacitated him and placed him at the mercy of others, and informing him that, though expression of resentment may be difficult at first, it becomes progressively easier with practice. It usually does not take long for patients to begin to perform the required behaviour, although some need much initial exhortation and repeated promptings. Gradually the patient becomes able to behave assertively in progressively more exacting circumstances and reports a growing feeling of ease in all relevant situations. A conditioned inhibition of the anxiety responses is clearly developing, presumably on the basis of the repeated reciprocal inhibition.

Somewhat similar to this method is that called by Wolpe the method of sexual responses. These responses, of course, are mainly of use when anxiety responses have been conditioned to various aspects of sexual situations. Usually the inhibition of sexual responsiveness is partial and not complete; it varies according to variations in definable properties of the relevant situations.

The patient is told that he must, on no account, perform sexually unless he has an unmistakable positive drive to do so, for otherwise he may very well consolidate, or even extend, his sexual inhibitions. He is instructed to wait for, or to seek out, situations in which pleasurable sexual feelings are aroused and in these he must 'let himself go' as freely as possible. If he is able to act according to plan, he experiences a gradual increase in sexual responsiveness to the kind of situation of which he has made use, with varying degrees of generalization to sexual situations of other kinds. Such favourable consequences occur, it seems, because each time a positive sexual feeling occurs and is intensified by the sexual approach there is reciprocal inhibition of whatever anxieties are being invoked by the situation, and the strength of the anxiety-evocation tendency is each time slightly weakened.

These two types of therapy may be illustrated by the following cases.

THE CASE OF THE SUBMISSIVE WOMAN

Wolpe recounts it thus:

An attractive woman of twenty-eight came for treatment because she was in acute distress as a result of her lover's casual treatment of her.

Every one of her numerous love affairs had followed a similar course. First she would attract the man, then she would offer herself on a platter. He would soon treat her with contempt and after a time leave her. She lacked assurance, was very dependent, and was practically never free from feelings of tension and anxiety. At her fifth interview, the unadaptiveness of her anxieties and the rationale of the reciprocal inhibition principle were explained to her, and she left feeling optimistic. At the next interview she was told how to behave with firmness and take independent courses of action with her lover. She performed well according to prescription and was able to terminate her relationship with him with dignity and with relatively little disturbance, and, indeed, with a certain feeling of triumph. Meanwhile, she was shown how to counterattack her nagging mother, and to deal with her boss, and other people who easily upset her. Through action, she gradually developed a feeling of mastery, both at home and at work, until she found that she was beginning to hold the reins in a variety of sexual situations. After her thirtieth interview she went on holiday and returned six weeks later, to say that she had made continued efforts to control inter-personal situations, and was feeling much more stable emotionally. She was much better poised and had been a social success for the first time in her life. About this time she met a man who attracted her and now her feelings had an adult independent character. After handling many difficulties admirably, she married him three months later. She had forty interviews in all and a year later was reported to be well and happy.

There was a general disappearance of all the neurotic traits and tendencies which had characterized her previously.

Next we have the case of the impotent accountant.

THE CASE OF THE IMPOTENT ACCOUNTANT

This forty-year-old man was sent for treatment by a psychoanalyst who had been told by him that he could not wait the two years estimated to be necessary for psychoanalytic treatment. At twenty-two, this man had had a regular girl friend with whom he indulged in frequent petting, which usually culminated in non-copulatory orgasm for both of them. He noticed, with some perturbation, that he was ejaculating increasingly quickly, and an uncle further upset him by telling him that this was 'partial impotence'. During the succeeding years, his sex life was characterized by very premature ejaculations, until the patient married at the age of twenty-nine. In the marriage relation, too, premature ejaculation was almost invariable and, after nine years, the marriage was dissolved. For some time the patient had a physically satisfactory sexual affair with a married woman, but finally, after an attack of influenza, he became completely impotent. Over the years, his effort at coitus with many women was consistently bedevilled by erectile failure or premature ejaculation.

Finally, the patient fell in love with a girl of twenty-four, but in his sexual relations with her again the same pattern of impotence and premature ejaculation was repeated. Once he was successful and managed to deflorate her but, as his failures began to increase, the girl began to show signs of coolness towards him, and he became more and more anxious to find a quick solution of his sexual difficulties. The reciprocal inhibition principle was explained to the patient and he was given lessons in progressive relaxation, and instructed to adopt a relaxed attitude in the sexual situation. He was not to attempt coitus unless he had a strong erection beforehand, and after intromission was not to aim at any set level of performance but was to let himself go. 'These instructions are based on the rationale that since penile erection is a parasympathetic function and ejaculation a sympathetic function, the predominantly sympathetic discharges of anxiety will tend both to inhibit erection and to precipitate ejaculation prematurely. If the anxiety can be brought down to a low level, the sexual responses will reciprocally inhibit it.'

At the fourteenth interview, the patient stated that he had twice had successful intercourse – slightly premature on the first occasion, but very prolonged on the second. He was much encouraged – to the extent that he had married the girl by special licence! Treatment was terminated at the twenty-third interview, exactly three months after its inception, as the patient regarded his sex life as entirely satisfactory. Follow-ups, ranging over the next six years, testified to maintained excellence of sexual performance.

It may be of interest to have a look at a case rather different from those treated above. It deals with an obsessive-compulsive patient; that is to say, a patient who had some queer and odd compulsion to do a certain thing, an obsession which could not be resisted. This discussion will illustrate that the methods discussed above are of use, not only in the treatment of phobias, but also in the treatment of quite distinct and different neurotic disorders.

THE CASE OF THE AGGRESSIVE HAND-WASHER

This case, which was reported by D. Walton and N. D. Mather, refers to a young man in his early thirties who suffered from compulsive hand-washing which had started some seven months previously. The time he spent washing his hands was so long that it made it impossible for him to keep a job. If ever he cleaned anything he always felt that it was not cleaned adequately. He was of above average intelligence and had entered a university at eighteen, but he left after a few months without giving any reason and took a labouring job. There he became involved in an argument with another labourer and the latter punched him on the mouth. This revived a fear he had always had that damage might be done to his teeth and that he might need false teeth. He experienced intense feelings of aggression towards the man who, he felt, might be responsible for such damage. The next day he took a hammer and sharpening steel to work, for the purpose of battering the man. When he realized that he was capable of such hatred and violence, he felt considerable guilt. He considered that the intention to do harm was as bad as actually doing it, although in fact he never carried out his intention. For a period of several months, this fear of his own aggressive and sadistic tendencies grew and his aggression generalized from one man to other people of the same social class, and even to his own relatives and family. One year after the incident he developed the hand-washing ritual. He attended a psychiatric day hospital for a short time, before he was eventually referred to another hospital for full in-patient treatment.

Walton and Mather put forward the hypothesis that the emotional drive in this patient had been conditioned to the expression of aggressive urges and that environmental conditions had been such as to increase the intensity of these socially undesirable urges, thus increasing the anxiety associated with them. The obsessive-compulsive habit of hand-washing was instrumental in reducing this anxiety, and might be eliminated if the anxiety itself was reduced to manageable proportions. They adopted the method of reciprocal inhibition by self-assertion, which we have considered previously, the assumption being that the anxiety associated with aggressive behaviour would thereby decrease. This would then dissipate the suppressed aggressive tendency and reduce the probability of 'explosive' and impulsive outbursts. Reduction in the intensity of both anxiety and aggressiveness and, therefore, a lowering of the general level of emotionality of the patient might be expected. This would then remove the necessity for the hand-washing, which acted as an anxiety-reducing compulsion. This treatment was carried out over a period of three months. During this time the patient was given periodic encouragement to be more self-assertive. There was a corresponding improvement in his compulsion and by the end of the three months it had completely disappeared; one month later he left hospital 'relieved'.

This case illustrates the importance of attacking not only what appears to be the main symptom, but also all others which are present at the same time. If we deal only with the hand-washing in a case like this, we may easily leave the much more important emotional anxieties (autonomic reactions) intact which, in turn, have given rise to the hand-washing. It is equally important to get rid of these other, rather less obvious symptoms before we can consider the patient as cured. The notion that neurosis is nothing but the sum of the symptoms is often criticized as leaving out important components, but those who make such criticism usually fail to realize that under the term 'symptom' are included not only the most obvious motor and skeletal actions of the patient, but also autonomic and other emotional reactions which may be slightly less obvious. This erroneous interpretation of the term 'symptom' has led to many criticisms of psychologists mainly concerned with the curing of symptoms, rather than the uncovering of hypothetical unconscious complexes; the criticism that behaviour therapists *only* cure symptoms comes rather oddly from those who cannot *even* cure symptoms!

Experimental psychologists sometimes look upon all clinical investigations with suspicion, even when an attempt has been made to conduct what is sometimes called a clinical trial, i.e. compare two groups of patients allocated at random to an experimental and a control procedure. Their scepticism is due to the fact that so many factors are left uncontrolled even in the best clinical trial that these cannot compare with a laboratory demonstration. It is of interest, therefore, that a strict laboratory demonstration of the experimental desensitization of a phobia has, in fact, been conducted, in an attempt to evaluate the success of this method. The study was done at the University of Pittsburg, by Peter Lang and David Lazovik. They made use of students who were suffering from snake phobia and they say that they chose this fear because it is frequent in a college population, where approximately three students in a hundred are afraid of snakes, and also because of the symbolic sexual significance which is attributed to this fear by psychoanalysts. 'The fact that snake phobias are held to reflect conflict in more fundamental systems of the personality suggests that this is good ground for a stringent test of behaviour therapy.' Twenty-four subjects in all were used, and these were selected on the basis of their very strong fear of harmless snakes. They rated this fear as 'intense' and reported various disturbances associated with the fear – 'I feel sick to my stomach when I see one.' 'My palms get sweaty; I'm tense.' These students would become upset at seeing snakes in motion pictures or on the television screen and would leave, close their eyes, or turn off the set. 'Even pictures in magazines or artifacts such as a snakeskin belt were capable of evoking discomfort in many of these subjects.'

An estimate of the degree of fear of each subject was

made on the basis of his verbal reactions, but he was also taken to an experimental situation where a large but harmless snake was exhibited in a glass case, at a point fifteen feet from the entrance to the room. The experimenter would enter the room with the student and then walk to the case, remove a wire grill at the top, and assure the subject that the snake was harmless. He would then ask the student to come over and look down at the snake, as he was doing. A measure was taken of the actual distance the subject would come, as a behavioural measure of the fear felt. Tape-recordings were made of the subjective feelings of the subjects, who were interviewed extensively concerning their fear. On the basis of these procedures, the total group was then divided into two: those who were to receive behaviour therapy and those who were not. Behaviour therapy was conducted for a period of eleven sessions regardless of whether the patients were sufficiently improved by the end of that time or not. At the end of that period, both groups, the experimental and the control groups, were again submitted to the experience of being shown the snake and being invited to go towards it and handle it, and another extensive interview was held with each student.

The results of the experiment were as follows. In the first place, it was found that the control group did not overcome their fears, but were just as afraid of the snakes at the end of the experiment as they were at the beginning. There was no spontaneous remission during this period of a few months. The experimental group, however, showed a significant improvement and demonstrated much less fear of the snakes on the second occasion than they had done on the first. Several were able to touch or hold the snakes at their final avoidance test. In spite of the very small number of sessions, therefore, there was a very marked improvement in the condition of the subjects who underwent behaviour therapy. Interestingly enough, the amount of improvement seemed to be a function of their general lack of anxiety; those patients – if patients we may call them – who, in the interview, showed anxieties on a large number of subjects benefited strikingly less from the treatment than those for whom the snakes constituted almost the only type of irrational fear. There seems to be every reason to believe that it would have required a longer experimental session to cure the more anxious subjects as well as the generally less anxious ones.

Lang and Lazovik come to three main conclusions on the basis of their experiment. The first is, 'It is not necessary to explore with the subject the factors contributing to the learning of the phobia or its "unconscious meaning" in order to eliminate the fear behaviour.' The second conclusion is that, 'The form of treatment employed here does not lead to symptom-substitution or create new disturbances of behaviour.' Their last conclusion is that, 'In reducing phobic behaviour it is not necessary to change basic attitudes, values, or attempt to modify the "personality as a whole". The unlearning of phobic behaviour appears to be analogous to the elimination of other responses from the subject's behaviour repertoire.' This interesting and well-planned experiment, therefore, appears to substantiate on every point the results achieved in the more clinical studies mentioned elsewhere in this chapter.

These, then, are some of the more widely used techniques for inducing reciprocal inhibition of anxiety and fear responses. There are many others, but they are of a more technical nature and would not fit well into the pattern of a popular book like the present one.

The reader may wish to go beyond the simple recital of case histories and find out whether the technique described here is, in fact, generally efficacious in treating neurotic disorders. In particular, he may wish to know whether it is more successful than, say, psychoanalysis, and he may also want to know whether it is successful in 'beating bogey', i.e. in showing a greater rate of success than that produced by spontaneous remission. As is well known, the rate of spontaneous remission in severe neurotic disorders is such that some 45 per cent recover after one year and over 70 per cent after two years, without any form of psychiatric treatment. Within five years, about 90 per cent of all cases recover. Orthodox psychiatric and psychoanalytic treatment produces effects which are not in advance of these figures and, in many cases, may even be below them. No treatment can be accepted as being worth its salt if it does not produce recovery figures in advance of these figures.

Wolpe himself, Lazarus, and several other people have now reported long series of patients with severe neurotic disorders who have been treated by means of behaviour therapy, as this type of treatment is usually called. Wolpe's claim is that in about thirty treatment sessions there is a complete cure, or a very marked recovery, on the part of about 90 per cent of his patients. As thirty sessions will usually take not more than three or four months, if that, this is clearly a rate of improvement which is very much superior to the rate of spontaneous remission, and which is also well in advance of anything reported by psychoanalysts or orthodox psychiatrists. Other psychiatrists and psychologists, properly trained in the methods of behaviour therapy, have reported similar figures, and there seems little doubt that the methods advocated by Wolpe are, indeed, superior to any others current at the moment. We even have available now experimental studies in which neurotic patients were matched for the type and severity of the symptoms, and were then allocated, on a random basis, to either a psychotherapy or a behaviour therapy group. Their progress was then watched, and it was found that the cases receiving behaviour therapy were significantly superior in their adjustment to those who were treated by psychotherapy. My own evaluation of the evidence which is available now would be that a very strong case has been made out for the power of behaviour therapy in neurotic disorders, and that there is no other method currently practised in our hospitals which bids fair to rival it in its curative powers.

This conclusion is sometimes criticized on the following grounds. In the first place, it is said, actuarial comparisons of this type are not strictly admissible. The type of patient treated by Wolpe may have been different from the type of patient treated by psychoanalysts, or taking part in the experiments establishing the rate of spontaneous remission. If the patients treated by him were less seriously ill, or were highly motivated to get better, or different in other ways, then one might argue that the case was not proven. This, of course, is true and must be admitted as a powerful and reasonable argument. However, on the whole, I am not particularly impressed with it. The kind of person who goes to the psychiatrist is not usually very knowledgeable about the kind of methods the psychiatrist is likely to use in curing him, and the cases treated by Wolpe, Lazarus, and other people are simply a series of patients coming for treatment in the ordinary way, just as they might have gone to a psychoanalyst or an orthodox psychiatrist. It seems unlikely that any great selection had taken place through choice of a particular psychiatrist, and the description of cases given by Wolpe does not differ very much from the type of case described by psychoanalysts and others. In any case, the matching experiment, mentioned above, fairly effectively shows that this argument does not, in general, apply with any great force.

More powerful, perhaps, is another argument which has become fairly popular in recent years. When it was first pointed out, in the early 1950s, that there was no evidence for the success of psychoanalytic treatment, as compared with spontaneous remission, there was an outcry among psychoanalysts and psychiatrists denouncing this conclusion. However, in recent years, it has become quite widely accepted, even among leading psychoanalysts, and indeed the evidence is pretty well conclusive now that this is nothing but a simple statement of fact. Several studies, however, have since produced evidence that, while the general level of recovery of the neurotic is not affected by the therapy he receives, there is a tendency for patients treated by psychoanalysis to show a greater scatter; in other words, as compared with a non-treated, control group, they show both a greater number of patients who recover, and a greater number of patients who get much worse, and it has been suggested that possibly this is due to differences in ability among the psychiatrists concerned. On this argument, the theories and methods of psychiatrists are quite irrelevant to their success, which depends exclusively on some mystical ability which they either do or do not possess. This is an argument where, too, it might be said that possibly Wolpe, Lazarus, and some of the other people concerned, were simply very good psychiatrists who happened to succeed in their treatment by virtue of this particular ability, and that this was quite irrelevant to the judgement of the theory on which they were working. Well, again, there is undoubtedly something to be said for this argument. Individuals differ considerably in their ability to get on with other people, to have empathy with their troubles, to be sympathetic towards them, and to think of different ways of helping them. Personal acquaintance with the people concerned leaves little doubt in my mind that Wolpe and some of the others concerned have a very special ability to understand the difficulties and troubles of the neurotic, and to devise ways and means of getting them out of these difficulties. As one completely lacking in this ability, I have often felt that although my knowledge of learning theory is probably not much inferior to theirs, it would never, by itself, suffice to enable me to duplicate the splendid work that they are doing. To say this is not to admit that learning theory is irrelevant to the success which behaviour therapists have achieved; Wolpe himself, for instance, was a confirmed psychoanalyst before his lack of success turned him in the direction of behaviour therapy and led him to elaborate the system of treatment which he originated. If the same person is successful with one system and unsuccessful with another, it is difficult to attribute his success to personality features, because these would be equally relevant to his work with the unsuccessful system. Indeed, this has been a fairly universal tendency. Albert Ellis, another behaviour therapist, has compared his successes when using psychoanalysis and his successes when using a rational system of therapy, and has come to the conclusion that the latter has undoubtedly been very much more efficient. Again, the same person is concerned with both systems, and we can hardly suggest that the system which he was using was irrelevant, when we find that when using the one a great deal of success was achieved, while when using the other success was almost completely lacking.

A third argument, which is sometimes related to the other two, maintains that other people have been very much less successful in using the methods of behaviour therapy, and that we should pay attention to the failures as well as to the successes. In a general sort of way, this is undoubtedly true, but as an argument it has certain serious weaknesses. Psychoanalysts insist that no one should be allowed to use their method of treatment who has not himself been subjected to a very prolonged and time-consuming process of training. They would not regard it as the failure of their method if someone who had not, in fact, been trained along these lines but who claimed to be using psychoanalytic method, were to be found to fail in his task of curing neurotic patients. Similarly, behaviour therapy is firmly based on modern learning theory, and no one can regard himself as seriously experimenting with the methods of behaviour therapy who is not fully conversant with these laws, and who has not been trained, in turn, by an expert in behaviour therapy. Amateur experimentation may be all very well, but it cannot be taken very seriously. Many published reports show quite clearly that the authors were, at best, beginners in this field, with very little knowledge of learning theory to back them up, and with very little in the way of training. Reports of their work may be interesting, but they cannot be used in any reasonable way to suggest the inefficacy of the method. Failure only becomes meaningful when it is set in a context of competence.

Another point which should be considered in this connexion is the following. Fair comparisons can only be made when there is no distorting feature in the selection of cases. However, there is, very frequently, such a distorting feature when a new method is being tried out. I have often noted that cases are only sent for treatment by behaviour therapy when all other methods have been tried and found not to work. In other words, it is not a random selection of cases which is being treated by behaviour therapists and compared with other types of treatment, but only the most difficult and recalcitrant ones. Other cases which are easier to treat, or which may remit spontaneously, never reach the stage where they are referred for treatment by behaviour therapy. Great care is necessary, in assessing the literature, in making sure that this kind of bias does not enter into the comparison.

No doubt all these troubles and difficulties will be ironed out in due course. Several experiments are now under way in an attempt to study the precise degree of success which behaviour therapy may claim in relation to other types of therapy, and to establish which type of case is particularly responsive to each type of treatment. In the next ten years we shall undoubtedly know a great deal more than we do now about the relative efficiency of these new methods. It might be the part of wisdom to wait until then before coming to any kind of conclusion. However, I would like to state that, in my view, the evidence now available is already sufficient to establish behaviour therapy as one of the most promising treatments to come to light in recent years, and as one which has very great promise indeed to solve finally the theoretical and practical problems associated with the neurotic paradox. It differs from all other methods that have been used, by having a rational basis in scientific theory and being derived from laboratory experimentation. It is, to a much greater degree than any other method, an essay in applied science, in the way that these words are understood in the exact sciences. Instead of basing itself on *ad hoc* procedures and fortuitous and empirical evidence, it is derived from widely accepted theories and experimental practices.

It is one characteristic of scientific theories that they can explain phenomena other than those they were originally called upon to put into a coherent framework. Is that possible in relation to the theory of conditioning, as applied to neurotic behaviour patterns? I shall give one example of such an application, and then proceed to illustrate another aspect of applied science to which the possibility of making predictions from scientific theories on to phenomena is not yet known.

The phenomenon which I wish to explain, in terms of our general theory, is that of spontaneous remission. Perhaps no other fact in the whole field of neurotic behaviour is as important, as well-substantiated, and as ill-understood as is that of spontaneous remission. No one doubts any longer that neurotics, without any form of psychotherapeutic treatment, get better, and I have given some figures to illustrate how quickly and how thoroughly recovery proceeds under these conditions; yet, obviously, the process is a mysterious one. We can say that spontaneous remission is a function of time: the longer the time elapsing, the greater the amount of spontaneous remission that takes place. Yet to say this is, obviously, not saying very much. Clearly, it is not time itself which is the active factor producing the remission; it must be something which happens during this time, and what precisely it is that happens to produce a remission is still very much of a mystery. Indeed, according to the most widely-popular psychiatric theories, those of psychoanalysis, spontaneous remission should be completely impossible. According to the analysts, neurotic disorders are, in fact, a kind of breakthrough of unconscious libidinal wishes and fears which have been repressed during the very early life of the infant, and which have lain dormant in that repressed and unconscious state; something happens to reactivate them, and they erupt in the form of neurotic symptoms. According to psychoanalytic belief, only a process of uncovering, that is to say a process which makes the individual conscious of these early libidinal strivings and their relation to the symptom, can be effective in banishing the symptom once and for all, and curing the neurotic disorder. All other methods, whether they be those of hypnosis, suggestion, behaviour therapy, or anything else, can only be palliatives and cannot be effective for any length of time. They may indeed succeed in banishing the symptom, but it will recur again in a very short period of time, or another one, even worse, will take its place. On this hypothesis, spontaneous remission is clearly impossible, particularly if it is, as it usually is, a permanent effect without any recurrence of the same symptom and without the growth of any other symptom in its stead. One might argue that the very occurrence of spontaneous remission is a very powerful argument against the theory of psychoanalysis.

The theory which is being advocated in these pages is, of course, quite different from the psychoanalytic one. It is maintained that neurotic symptoms are conditioned emotional and motor responses, and it is further argued that these have no underlying complex of infantile origin which gives them their strength. The symptom, as it were, *is* the illness and the disappearance of the symptom means the disappearance of the illness. Furthermore, it is argued that the disappearance of the symptom can be produced by orthodox processes of extinction, very much in the same way as conditioned responses are extinguished every day in the psychological laboratory, whether they be conditioned responses of humans or animals. We are not surprised, therefore, to find spontaneous remission, once it has been achieved, is a relatively permanent cure; the symptom having disappeared, there is no reason to expect its return. But can we explain this spontaneous remission itself?

The explanation of this phenomenon is a very easy one indeed; it follows directly from the general theory. What we will find more difficult to explain is the fact that, in a certain proportion of cases, there is no spontaneous remission, and although this task is not beyond the power of modern learning theory, it will be found that these cases complicate the rather simple picture which we have painted so far. Let us first of all explain the occurrence of spontaneous remission. Supposing we have conditioned a particular response in an animal: what is the usual way of extinguishing it? The reader may remember, from Chapter 1, that it is simply the production of the conditioned stimulus in front of the animal a number of times, without this conditioned stimulus being followed by reinforcement, i.e.

without production of the unconditioned stimulus. Once a dog has been conditioned to salivate to the sound of a bell, we can easily extinguish this response, by ringing the bell a large number of times without following it with food. Gradually, the number of drops of saliva secreted by the dog will diminish, and finally no more saliva is produced at all; the response has become extinguished because it has never been reinforced. Now let us apply this paradigm to a typical neurotic, say, to that of a woman who has developed a very strong phobia for cats. Once this fear has originated, through some process of conditioning, the patient will undoubtedly encounter cats in the course of her life. Now, on such occasions, the cat, which is the conditioned stimulus, is present, but there is no reinforcement because the traumatic consequences which originally produced the conditioned fear response are not likely to be present as well. If the reader will cast his mind back to the case of the cat woman, whose fear of cats originated when a little kitten was drowned in front of her by her father, he will also realize that the next time this woman saw a cat, the traumatic circumstances of its being drowned in front of her would not, in all likelihood, be present. Therefore, in the course of her lifetime, the patient would encounter the conditioned stimulus a large number of times, without this being followed by the unconditioned stimulus. According to learning theory, what should happen now, of course, is extinction of the conditioned response; in other words, gradually the fear should fade, until finally it has completely disappeared. This undoubtedly happens in a very large majority of cases, and, indeed, it is possible, in many individual case histories, to trace the development of the spontaneous remission to precisely such a process of extinction. There is no difficulty in explaining spontaneous remission, therefore; the difficulty is rather in explaining why our cat woman, for instance, did *not* show spontaneous remission, but developed a very strong phobia which required special treatment.

The answer probably lies in a certain very important difference between the experimental laboratory animal which is being deconditioned and the human being. Pavlov's dogs were tethered to their stand; they could not leave the room, and were, therefore, forced to encounter the conditioned stimuli in the extinction experiment. However, a human being is not in that position; the patient, for instance, when she encountered a cat, had an alternative mode of response – namely, that of turning and running away. Now what would be the consequences of such a reaction pattern? Seeing the cat, in the first instance, even at a considerable distance, would produce a very strong sympathetic reaction in the autonomic system of the patient, thus causing her a considerable degree of fear, and hence a very unpleasant emotional response. Turning away from the cat and walking away in the opposite direction would eliminate the cat from her line of vision and would also put a greater distance between her and the cat; both these factors would lead to a considerable reduction in the autonomic upset, and, therefore, would act as a reward, or reinforcement, for avoiding the cat and running away. Thus we have now a secondary process of conditioning, a conditioning namely of an avoidance response. Once this process has set in, we would expect it to continue to occur and continue to be reinforced, gradually producing a very strong habit of avoiding the conditioned stimulus altogether, thus making it impossible for extinction to take place. The patient thus avoids what is sometimes, in psychiatric parlance, called 'reality testing'; in other words, she makes it impossible for herself to encounter the conditions making for spontaneous remission. This is undoubtedly what happened to our cat woman, and it explains why spontaneous remission fails in a certain proportion of cases.

This explanation also covers certain other facts with which the reader may be familiar. It is well known, for instance, that if a pilot crashes a plane, he will express a wish to go up again immediately, because he knows that if he runs away, as it were, from the task, then a secondary process of conditioning will supervene, rewarding his running away and making it impossible for him ever to overcome this particular conditioned fear again. In a similar way, it was found during the war that neurotic patients suffering from shell-shock could be treated in the front line and be sent back to active duty very soon; if, however, they were sent back to a base hospital, it was almost impossible for them ever to be sent back to the front line. The reason, of course, is exactly the same as discussed above. Sending the patient to the base line meant that he was effectively reinforced, or rewarded, for running away from danger, and this reinforcement produced a conditioned avoidance response to danger which was so strong that no amount of therapy could get over it. Thus we have here a whole series of phenomena, all related to spontaneous remission, which find a relatively easy and obvious explanation, in terms of our conditioning theory of neurotic responses.

How about our prediction now? It will be remembered that psychoanalysts predict confidently that, in terms of their theory, only a process of psychoanalytic 'uncovering' of the underlying complexes which are the putative cause of neurotic behaviour can lead to a lasting solution of the neurotic's problems; anything else will only lead to a recrudescence and an exacerbation of his condition. Our own theory would predict exactly the opposite. If all neurotic symptoms are merely conditioned responses, then their extinction, whether through spontaneous remission or through a process of reciprocal inhibition, should be final. There should be no recrudescence, there should be no exacerbation; on the contrary, if anything, there should be a quite general improvement in the patient's condition, even independent of his symptoms, because, through getting rid of these symptoms, he would now be in a very much better position to cope with all his difficulties and problems, however real these might be.

Behaviour therapists have, of course, been on the alert right from the beginning, to discover to what extent any rational objections could be based on the recurrence of symptoms, and have tried to follow up their patients over long periods of time. The literature is quite unambiguous in asserting that the recurrence of symptoms, or the occurrence of new ones in place of the old ones, is practically non-existent; indeed, it is curious to note that the psychoanalytic literature shows more examples of patients showing recurrence of symptoms after apparent cure by means of psychoanalytic methods than does the behaviour-therapy literature. It is interesting that the first attempts to apply methods of behaviour therapy to neurotic symptoms were made by a well-known adherent of the psychoanalytic tradition, Professor O. H. Mowrer, who originated the 'bell and blanket' method of treating enuresis. He claimed 100 per cent success in the treatment, and also followed up his patients, because he firmly believed psychoanalytic theories which predicted a recurrence of the symptoms. He found no such recurrence, and this possibly is one of the reasons why he has turned away from psychoanalytic techniques in recent years to become one of their foremost critics. However that may be, there is no doubt that this particular objection cannot be made to behaviour therapy, and indeed it could be argued that the failure of the psychoanalytic prediction of recurrence of symptoms is one of the most crucial arguments against their theory. The reason for regarding this particular fact as of the utmost importance is this. As has often been pointed out by its critics, psychoanalysis is a theoretical system which is inherently inconsistent and which makes very little contact with external reality. It is almost impossible to make clear-cut predictions from psychoanalysis which can, in fact, be tested experimentally, or clinically. Popper, the famous philosopher and historian of science, has pointed out that the essential criterion of a scientific theory is its falsifiability; in other words, there must be ways of empirically disproving a theory, if a theory wants to aspire to the status of being scientific. He also points out that Marxism and Freudianism are more like two religious beliefs than two scientific theories, because they are almost completely invulnerable to empirical falsification. They can explain, after a fashion, everything that happens, but they can predict nothing, and where prediction is lacking, obviously falsifiability is lacking too. There are, however, one or two points on which psychoanalysts are agreed, and where they all make a consistent empirical prediction: the recurrence of symptoms after treatment other than that of 'uncovering' is one of these points where contact is made with empirical reality and where we can indeed falsify the psychoanalytic theory, if in truth it should be incorrect. Now the facts, quite clearly and incontrovertibly, do falsify the theory, and show that Freud's prediction, in fact, is not borne out. In view of the central position that this prediction holds in the Freudian system, one would perhaps have expected that psychoanalysts would take heed of this fact and renounce their general theory, particularly in view of the large-scale evidence now available to show the relative lack of success of methods based on psychoanalytic theory in alleviating neurotic suffering.

It is interesting to see that this is not what has happened. Instead of disowning the theory, psychoanalysts have rather tended to dissociate themselves from the original deduction, and to argue now that it does not follow from Freud's theory that symptoms should indeed recur after any but psychoanalytic treatment. This is a curious reacsion, because Freud, and all the great names in the history of psychoanalysis, clearly maintained this point of view, and it is difficult to see how one can go on believing in the general theory of psychoanalysis and throw this particular prediction overboard. It may be expected that gradually, as the evidence in favour of behaviour therapy increases, so psychoanalysts will modify their beliefs more and more until, finally, the two are indeed indistinguishable. By that time, no doubt, psychoanalysts will still trace back their theories and their beliefs to Freud, although nothing but an empty shell will remain of his grandiose scheme. Such tendencies are indeed already noticeable, and many psychoanalysts have maintained that the differences between psychoanalysis and behaviour therapy are largely semantic ones; in other words, that the differences are apparent rather than real, and derive simply from the use of a different vocabulary.

Up to a point, this is perhaps not completely untrue. We may look upon a conditioned autonomic reaction as being, in some ways, equivalent to an unconscious complex, giving rise to a variety of behaviour patterns, which cannot be understood except by reference to this underlying causal factor. However, while there are some similarities, there are also considerable differences. The complex is supposed to be almost universal and to have originated in certain, quite definite, life-experiences during the first few years of life. The conditioned autonomic reaction, however, is believed to have occurred in the life history of any particular individual through a particular concatenation of circumstances; it may have happened at any stage of his life, not only in the first few years, and, furthermore, it is believed to occur with much greater probability in the life history of certain people constitutionally predisposed to form conditioned responses of this kind; that is to say, in people who condition easily and whose autonomic responses are particularly labile and strong. To suggest that these two hypotheses are identical is merely to make a state of confusion worse confounded; the slight similarities between them fade into nothingness, as compared with the very great differences which are apparent. These differences relate particularly to the mode of treatment which is suggested by the two theories, and it is here that there is no similarity. The Freudians insist on an emotional 'uncovering' which is achieved, if it is indeed achieved at all, through a process of talking and interpretation. The behaviour therapist insists rather that the treatment must consist in a process of desensitization and deconditioning, involving, as it does, active participation and work on the part of the patient. This activity on the part of the patient is not concerned with 'uncovering', or the patient elaboration of symbols in dreams and other fantasy productions; it is rather concerned directly with the kind of behaviour concerned in his neurotic symptom. No argument can bridge the gap between these two entirely disparate types of therapy.

This is not to say that one cannot explain part, at least,

of any success that psychotherapy may have in terms of the principles of behaviour therapy enunciated above. In the typical psychotherapeutic session, the patient will often discuss his problems, his fears, and his anxieties in the presence of an observer, the psychotherapist, who is usually encouraging, who accepts without criticism some statements which would normally appear quite outrageous; and who, in general, has a calming, reassuring kind of influence. In other words, we have here the beginnings of a process of reciprocal inhibition. The anxieties and the fears and the situations giving rise to them are mentioned by the patient, and parasympathetic stimulation is supplied by the calm and reassuring behaviour of the therapist. Under these conditions, it is not impossible that reciprocal inhibition may occur and may generalize sufficiently to outside life situations to produce a certain amount of amelioration. Why is this amelioration not greater than that found under conditions of spontaneous remission? The answer is possibly to be looked for along two lines. The sufferer who does not go to a psychoanalyst will undoubtedly discuss his troubles with other people whom he considers to be likely to listen to him sympathetically and calmly; in other words, he will get the same kind of reciprocal inhibition as the psychoanalytic patient, but he will get it in a non-therapeutic situation from lay people. There is no reason to assume that the reward which he obtains from such discussions will be any the less because the person with whom he is discussing his difficulties is not, in fact, a trained psychoanalyst. Quite the opposite may, in fact, be true. The psychoanalyst was trained to raise certain points and to discuss certain issues such as those of early infantile sexuality, feelings towards the parents, and so on, which may themselves be anxiety-arousing and, therefore, lead to a failure of the reciprocal inhibition which, as we insist, is the cause of any improvement in the condition of the patient.

Rather than postulate, as some psychoanalysts do, that there are essential similarities between psychoanalytic doctrine and behaviour therapy, we would rather claim that whatever success may be achieved in psychotherapy was due to the haphazard and unplanned use of the fundamental paradigm of behaviour therapy: that is to say, that of reciprocal inhibition. We would also further claim that reciprocal inhibition quite frequently occurs in ordinary-life situations and thus further helps in the process of spontaneous remission.

It is, of course, difficult to substantiate views of this type, but occasionally it becomes clear, from the writings of psychoanalysts, that in fact they are making use of treatment methods which derive from behaviour therapy and that it is these, rather than the putative psychoanalytic 'uncovering' techniques, which are effective in producing changes. Here is an amusing quotation from Wolpe's book, *Psychotherapy by Reciprocal Inhibition*, in which he is discussing the use of assertion training as a technique of behaviour therapy.

There can be little doubt that even though the analysts (and therapists of other convictions) who do not explicitly encourage assertion (and perhaps even oppose it), nevertheless owe some of their favourable therapeutic results to their patients' behaving assertively, either because this seems to be a logical implication of some of the discussions with the therapist, or because of a feeling of support which the therapeutic relationship gives. Some illuminating examples of therapeutically effective assertiveness manifested in the face of strong prohibitions from the therapist are to be found in a paper by Seitz, on the treatment of twenty-five patients with psychocutaneous excoriation syndromes. He encouraged his patients to express, *during interviews,* their hostile feeling towards other people. At the same time, he discouraged them from expressing aggression in their life situations, i.e. 'acting out', but eleven out of the twenty-five did so to some extent. *In these eleven alone the skin became clear;* in the remainder it was unimproved. It was of particular interest that when patients who had 'acted out' were rapped on the knuckles for doing so and, in consequence, became more restrained outside the consulting room, there was a tendency to relapse. Expression of aggression during the therapy hour was not an effective substitute. Clearly, declaiming to the therapist, however vigorously, about one's friends and relations can scarcely inhibit the anxiety they arouse as effectively as opposing these people in the flesh. It is indeed lamentable that Seitz should have been so preoccupied with psychoanalytic dogmas that the lessons of his excellent study escaped him.

We have now shown that modern learning theory can explain many of the facts of neurotic disorders and that it can make predictions of previously unknown facts which can be verified. Several further examples of this fact will be given in later chapters. To close the present one, however, I would like to discuss one further point which I believe is a very important one. It is often suggested in criticism that behaviour therapists, very much like psychoanalysts, quote single cases to illustrate their theories, and that while these may be good illustrations and may sound quite convincing to the reader, nevertheless they are only illustrations and have no power of proof. We have already pointed out that there are now large collections of cases showing a very high rate of recovery, and that there are also controlled studies, in which different methods of therapy have been compared, to the advantage of the methods of behaviour therapy. But it would be quite wrong to assume that nothing of scientific value can be learned from the individual case. In science it is usually considered that we have achieved a considerable advance when we can bring a particular phenomenon under experimental control; that is to say, that we can cause the phenomenon to vary concomitantly with certain variations in the external conditions over which we have some control. Consider now the following case reported first by the East German psychologist, Katsch. One of his patients had regular attacks of a severe kind of asthma whenever he went to bed at night with his wife. Long periods of orthodox psychotherapy provided no relief for this condition. Katsch finally arrived at the hypothesis that the patient's mother-in-law, with whom he had many conflicts, constituted the source of the emotional trouble producing the asthmatic attacks and that a very large picture of her which hung in the bedroom of the patient was a conditioned stimulus for these attacks.

Such a theory can obviously be tested by making predictions from it which can be falsified or verified. Accordingly, Katsch turned the mother-in-law's face to the wall, as it were, and immediately the asthmatic attacks ceased. They could be brought back at will, by turning the picture round again, and they could again be terminated by turning it to the wall once more; in other words, Katsch had achieved complete control over the asthmatic attacks of his patient. To say that this is merely a single case report, signifying very little if anything at all, is a complete misunderstanding of the scientific method. If Katsch had merely reported that on the basis of a conditioning type of theory he had cured a particular patient of a particular disorder, then indeed we would be justified in saying that nothing very interesting or important had been achieved, because patients have been cured by all sorts of methods ranging from the sublime to the ridiculous. Thus, there are reports in the literature of complete cures of neurotic patients due to electric shocks, sleep, cold baths, hot baths, elimination of septic foci by the extraction of all the patient's teeth, flogging, hanging up in chains, encouraging the patient to eat more or to eat less, to drink or not to drink, explaining his symptoms in terms of Freudian symbols or Jungian symbols, or indeed, in any of a large number of other ways. Reports of cures, therefore, simply as such, are treated with the utmost reserve by experts in the field, and are indeed no proof of the accuracy of the theory on which the treatment was based. However, within a particular therapeutic session we may attempt to bring the phenomena we are dealing with under strict experimental control, as, for instance, in the case of the experiment by Katsch just mentioned; and when we achieve such a measure of control, we may quite reasonably say that we have gone beyond the simple stage of curing or not curing a neurotic, and have come to the point where very much more detailed predictions are possible and where, therefore, a much better way has been achieved of testing the general theories under which we are working. Further examples of this technique will be adduced in later chapters; here I wish merely to draw attention to this point, which is a very important one, but which is often overlooked.

There are one or two points which may prove puzzling to the reader. For instance, how is it that when the behaviour therapist presents fear-producing stimuli it is the parasympathetic responses produced by the therapist which inhibit the sympathetic stimuli produced by the fear-producing object? Why is it not exactly the other way round, that the patient should come to fear and hate the therapist because of his association with the fear-producing stimuli? This is not as unreasonable an objection as it may at first appear, but the answer may be found in a very famous experiment conducted by Pavlov many years ago. He used as the unconditioned stimulus, food, and as the conditioned stimulus, an electric shock to the leg of the dog. Now the conditioned stimulus, in this case, is, of course, also, in one way, an unconditioned stimulus; the shock will normally lead to a sympathetic reaction, a cessation of digestion and salivation, and therefore will be antagonistic to the feeding response which constitutes, in this experiment, the proper unconditioned stimulus. Pavlov managed to use the electric shock as a conditioned stimulus by reducing its strength to such an extent that it was hardly felt as painful by the dog. Gradually, by associating it with feeding, time and time again, he managed to build up the strength of the shock to the point where it was almost paralysing. Even then, however, because of the continued association with feeding, the dog continued to regard it, as it were, as a conditioned stimulus, and to respond with salivation. Now we know, from a great deal of work which has been done along these lines, that if a very much less powerful shock is given before feeding the dog, under conditions where no training has preceded the application of the shock, then not only would the dog not show any kind of salivation, but he would refuse the food and indeed reverse the process of conditioning; that is to say, he would now regard the whole feeding situation with suspicion and produce sympathetic reactions towards it. The experiment proves, therefore, that the direction in which conditioning takes place – from A to B, or from B to A – can be controlled quite powerfully by manipulating the strength of the respective reactions, and by being very careful to build up the strength of the conditioned stimulus, if it is indeed an aversive one, only very slowly.

Exactly the same is true in behaviour therapy. If the behaviour therapist started his system of treatment by immediately confronting the patient with stimuli which were particularly strong and anxiety-provoking, then indeed it is quite likely that the patient would take an immediate dislike to the therapist, would begin to feel fear and anxiety in his presence, and indeed would reverse the proper process of conditioning. It is necessary, therefore, to make sure that the amount of anxiety which is provoked in the therapeutic situation is relatively small and no greater than can be handled in terms of the amount of relaxation, assurance, and so on, which can be given under the circumstances. Usually, the therapist will judge this as best he can in terms of his experience, and by observation of the patient's behaviour, or even by getting the patient to rate the amount of anxiety present and lift his hand when it becomes too large to be borne. It is possible, however, to get a more accurate report of this by making use of electronic recordings of the responses in the autonomic nervous system, for instance, the galvanic skin response (G.S.R.) which we have discussed before; in other words, the tendency for the electric conductivity of the skin to increase with increasing emotion. As an example of this, we may perhaps quote our next case which is that of the bird woman.

THE CASE OF THE BIRD WOMAN

This case, which has been reported by D. F. Clark, concerns a woman of thirty-one years of age who had a specific phobia for feathers and birds which was of socially crippling proportions. It was impossible for her to walk out-of-doors, in parks, to go to zoos with her two-year-old boy, or to the seaside on holiday with her husband,

because of the possibility of having birds near her, or, worse
still, swoop over her. She used Dunlopillo pillows and
cushions in her house so as to have no feathers in the
building. She had anxiety dreams of people throwing
feathers, and of birds swooping down upon her. This
phobia was of more than twenty-five years' standing, the
first memory of it being at the age of six, when she did not
want to look at some farm chickens, felt frightened, cried,
and had to be picked up. Apart from this phobia, her
personality seemed relatively normal.

The psychologist made an attempt to list all the items
and situations producing the anxiety response. The psychologist and the patient together ranked the hierarchy in
order of importance and then proceeded to systematic
desensitization. The patient sat in the psychologist's office,
and the electrodes of the G.S.R. apparatus were fixed to
her left hand. After some words of reassurance, the patient
was then, on the first occasion, shown a single feather at
some twelve feet distance.

If any subjective feelings of apprehension were felt, she was to
say so immediately and the stimulus, i.e. feather, would be withdrawn. The galvanometer needle was also watched closely for
drops in resistance reflecting sympathetic system nervous changes
below the threshold of subjective appreciation. This was of some
importance, since autonomic reactions were to be deconditioned as
much as subjective feelings. If no adverse signs were noted, the
feather was brought closer to the patient, until it was no more than
a foot away. The stimulus was then removed and further efforts at
relaxation and calmness were suggested to the patient hypnotically.
One session consisted of three or four such trials. At the slightest
sign of apprehension, the stimulus was immediately removed, and
reiterations of instructions were soothingly made until P.G.R.
readings returned to normal. If the patient, after these trials
showed objectively or subjectively no apprehension or anxiety,
then the next item in the stimulus hierarchy was proceeded with at
the next session. The material used as stimuli included feathers,
large and small, stiff and downy, a polythene bag full of feathers, a
bundle of feathers about four inches by one and a half inches bound
with black thread and having a solid feel, a stuffed blackbird
perched with folded wings, a stuffed pigeon with wings outstretched

forward in a landing position, a (caged) budgerigar, and many farm chickens, park ducks, and pheasants, etc.

By the time the sessions with stuffed birds had been reached the patient was urged to combine her visits to the hospital with visits, first to a museum where many stuffed birds, large and small, were available, and second to an aviary where living birds were behind the wire screen. Later, when a live budgerigar was used during treatment, she went to a public park where ducks and other birds were tame enough to walk up to visitors to be fed. The patient made all these visits in the company of her husband and small son and was instructed that she should immediately retreat from the situation as soon as any apprehension was felt. By the time twenty sessions of treatment had been completed it was considered that the patient was well enough to be discharged, with instructions to continue her exercises in relaxation whenever she felt stress, and to make as much contact with birds as she was now able to. She had long since declared herself to be completely undisturbed by sleeping on feather pillows, could have handfuls of feathers flung at her, could plunge her hands into a bag of down, and no longer feared going out-of-doors or birds in the garden or hedgerows.

Clark comments on the value of the P.G.R. in connexion with the point that one of the important aspects of this type of therapy is that in having increasing stimuli in the gradient presented to him the subject must never be induced to break down the reciprocally inhibiting set. He must never be allowed to cross the threshold of apprehension while the stimulus is presented. In this connexion, it is important accurately to assess and maintain the stimulus hierarchy.

An incident early in treatment demonstrated this rather well. In talking soothingly to the patient while reintroducing relaxation after the presentation to the subject of the stimulus low in the hierarchy (single stiff feather), the psychologist accidently mentioned a sparrow which chirped outside the office. The patient's P.G.R. immediately dropped sharply and she became tense and agitated, necessitating a re-starting of the session with the very first and most innocuous stimulus and working through the ones she had successfully coped with. This procedure was always followed if there was any question of stress having been produced. In this instance, the notion of a live, small bird had unwittingly been introduced too soon in the stimulus hierarchy.

This fact produces a difficulty in therapy which will immediately be obvious to the reader. If the bird accidentally chirping outside the office can produce such a disastrous consequence, what then would happen to the woman, if, on her way home, she were to encounter some large bird swooping down on her? Would this upset the whole process of conditioning? In answer to this kind of problem, a rather different kind of method of treatment has been elaborated which may be used concomitantly with the others discussed so far. It is, as it were, a built-in, conditioned tranquillizer, which can be brought into action whenever required. Essentially, the procedure is something like this. The patient is fitted with two electrodes and is administered an electric shock which starts from being mild and gradually increases in severity until he can hardly bear it; at that point, he cries, 'Stop!' and the current is immediately turned off. In terms of conditioning, we have the conditioned stimulus which is the awareness on the part of the patient of the muscle movements and the sounds involved in shouting, 'Stop', the unconditioned stimulus which is the turning off of the shock, and the response which is a feeling of relief and the cessation of the sympathetic pain response. This conditioning process is repeated a number of times, the hypothesis being that, in due course, the conditioned stimulus by itself, i.e. the patient saying, 'Stop!' to himself will be sufficient to produce feelings of relaxation, of relief, and a cessation in sympathetic arousal. If now the patient, in his ordinary life situation, encounters a stimulus which in the normal run of things would set off a neurotic anxiety or fear response, he would simply have to say to himself, 'Stop!' in order to reduce very much, or even eliminate the sympathetic innervation produced by this neurotic stimulus. This method of control has been shown to work well in a number of situations, particularly of course with people who condition easily and strongly. As these constitute the majority of people who are liable to neurotic disorders in the first place, it can be seen that this method has, perhaps, a good deal to be said for it, and will undoubtedly in the future be used much more widely than it is now. It may be regarded, in a way, as a counterpart to the concept of 'conscience' which is a kind of anxiety reaction conditioned to anti-social and socially disapproved actions, as we shall see in a later chapter.

Before closing our account of behaviour therapy, there are two more things which need saying. In the first instance, the method has been used, not only with cases of phobic disorders but, with even greater success, with cases of severe anxiety, depression, sexual disorders of various kinds, obsessional and compulsive disorders, and so forth. The reason why the cases quoted have usually been of rather simple, phobic reactions is essentially that more complex cases require a great deal of space. One single case discussed in sufficient detail to make it intelligible may run to the length of this whole chapter, and readers interested in the method will find such cases in some of the books mentioned in the list of further reading at the end of this book. My attempt has not been to give a thorough review of the field, but merely to introduce the reader to these new methods of treatment and to give him some appreciation of the problems arising in connexion with it.

The other point is that the dysthymic conditions: that is to say, anxieties, phobias, reactive depressions, obsessional and compulsive disorders, which have been discussed in this chapter are not the only types of disorders which arise among neurotics and they are not the only types of disorders which can be treated by means of behaviour therapy. They do, however, constitute a fairly coherent group and have, therefore, been discussed together in this chapter. Other disorders also make up a fairly coherent and comprehensive group and will be discussed in the next chapter.

The dysthymic disorders we have been discussing so far are, of course, not the only ones which are commonly grouped under the heading 'neuroses'. They have been treated together for two reasons. In the first place, they tend to occur in certain personality types, namely, in those people who are both introverted and highly emotional; and, in the second place, they appear to have pretty much the same kind of causal background: that is to say, they appear to arise from conditioned autonomic reactions and give rise to all the consequences which flow from this. In addition to disorders of this first kind, however, there are disorders of a second kind. These, too, are characterized by occurring in persons having similar personality patterns, although this time they are perhaps more likely to be extraverted than introverted, as well as being emotional. In addition, there is also a common cause, but this time it is not derived from some kind of traumatic conditioning which is responsible for the occurrence of symptoms which are painful and which the individual would like to get rid of. On the contrary, disorders of this second kind are characterized by symptoms which the individual may find quite enjoyable, but which run counter to the interests of society at large, or at least which society at large believes to run counter to its interests. I am thinking here of such deviations as homosexuality, or fetishism, transvestism, i.e. the habit of dressing in the clothes appropriate to the other sex, alcoholism, drug addiction, bed-wetting, and perhaps even criminality. Society may punish by law some of these activities but the pressure exerted is often indirect and may induce a great deal of anxiety, guilt, and self-disgust in people. These feelings may provide motivation for seeking help every bit as strong as is the threat of prison.

What is common to all these disorders? Persons suffering from them show unusual and perverted behaviour patterns which, as pointed out above, are disapproved of by society, but which, apart from disapproval, are not necessarily experienced as painful, disgusting, or generally obnoxious by the person himself. These habits may be innate, or they may have been acquired through a previous process of conditioning; it is often very difficult to know which of these two hypotheses is true. Take homosexuality, for instance. If we make use of our experimental paradigm of twin studies, we find that in the largest series that has been reported to date there is 100 per cent concordance among identical twins, but only 12 per cent concordance among fraternal twins; this would seem to suggest a very strong hereditary component. On the other hand, it is well known that certain environmental circumstances very much exacerbate any possibly inherited tendencies; thus, for instance, public schools are known to be a breeding ground for homosexuality, as is the army, the navy, or life in prisons. In other words, whenever men are thrown together with other men to the almost complete exclusion of female company, then there we find a great burgeoning forth of homosexual practices. Quite likely, this is due to some form of generalization from the female to the male; after all, both are human and share many attributes in common; given a strong sex drive and deprivation of the company of the other sex, it is not inconceivable that a process of conditioning should be initiated which would receive the usual reinforcement and, in the long run, lead to almost complete homosexual dependence.

However, we are not, at the moment, concerned with the question of how these aberrant behaviour patterns originate; we are merely concerned with the fact that they do exist and that there may be a strong pressure, on the part of society, for their elimination. Neither are we concerned, however, either with defending this attitude of society, or with arguing against it. It has often been said that homosexual and other perverted sex patterns are signs of decadence, and that their growth is likely to lead to the ultimate dissolution of the society in which they occur. Others have held the opposite view and, pointing to ancient Greece for instance, have held that private morality is unrelated to the fate of nations in this particular connexion, and that the state and society have no right to interfere in the practices of adult people, as long as these do not interfere with the rights and privileges of the rest of society. The ethical problems involved are known to be very thorny ones and they also arise, of course, in relation to transvestism, fetishism, and other sexual perversions. I shall come back to these questions a little later on.

The whole group of disorders which we are discussing now, and which we may perhaps call disorders of the second kind, can be split into two. On the one hand, we have those disorders where, clearly, a positive response has been acquired, or where at least a positive response has been manifested which may be due largely to hereditary factors, or which may be due to a process of conditioning; in this category would be such disorders as fetishism, homosexuality, and so on. On the other hand, there are disorders where one might argue that there has been a failure on the part of the organism to acquire socially desirable responses; this category, for instance, might be exemplified by enuresis, or the habit of wetting one's bed at night, and possibly also by criminality, where there has been a failure to acquire what is often called a 'conscience'. This distinction is perhaps, on the whole, less important than it might appear at first, and, in any case, it is obviously rather blurred. The acquisition of the homosexual habit implies a failure to acquire the heterosexual habit, and one can look upon the homosexual with equal ease from either point of view. Similarly, the failure to have acquired the habit of waking up and going to the toilet when the urge to urinate is present may equally well be termed a habit of bed-wetting which has been acquired on the part of the person indulging in it. Similarly, criminality may be looked upon as a habit of evil-doing acquired during the course of life, or a failure to acquire the socially-approved habits and mores. While there is probably a genuine difference between the two groups we have posited above, there is no doubt also some truth in the criticism, and we shall not differentiate between them to any great extent in what follows, for the simple reason that the method of treatment appropriate to one is also, in most cases, appropriate to the other. However, we have separated out criminality from the other disorders mentioned and will be devoting a whole chapter to a discussion of its origin and the appropriate methods of treatment.

In principle, how would we set about the treating of antisocial habits, perverse conditioned responses, and other undesirable traits of this type? The answer, of course, lies in an exact reversal of the principle of reciprocal inhibition we have been discussing in the last chapter. There we were dealing with conditioned anxiety responses which had to be inhibited by conditioning certain parasympathetic, pleasant, relaxing responses to the same stimuli. In this chapter, we are dealing with undesirable behaviour patterns which, when carried out by the patient, produce pleasant, parasympathetic, relaxing stimulation, and the only way to eliminate and extinguish these behaviour patterns, is of course, to associate them with strong, sympathetic stimulation. This procedure is sometimes called aversion therapy, and it resembles, to some degree, the ancient methods by means of which mankind has always tried to restrain evil-doers, perverts, and others, from carrying out their wishes, by punishing them through imprisonment, flogging, and various other ways of inducing deterrence.

Now it is well-known that punishment is not an efficient way of doing this. As we shall see in Chapter 7, there is no evidence that any sort of punishment, however severe, makes very much difference to the behaviour of the criminal, and the whole history of mankind is evidence that sexual and other perversions are not banished by means of punishment. All that happens is that these perversions are driven underground, that those who are under threat of punishment now become liable to blackmail and other forms of persecution, and that a great deal of unhappiness is generated. Punishment has always failed and always will fail, for reasons which we will discuss later.

Reciprocal inhibition, although its application may, at first sight, look like a form of punishment, in actual fact is something quite different, resembling it neither in its underlying philosophy nor in the effects which it produces. An example may make clear just what precisely is involved in the kind of reciprocal inhibition we have in mind here.

THE CASE OF THE PRAMS AND HANDBAGS

The patient was a married man, aged thirty-three, from the out-patient department of a mental hospital, for consideration of a prefrontal leucotomy after he had attacked a perambulator. (Prefrontal leucotomy is, of course, an operation by means of which the frontal lobes are severed from the rest of the brain; it is a very severe operation which has many very undesirable after-effects and it is usually only carried out on psychotic patients who are so ill that almost any change will be a change for the better. It is now going very much out of fashion and is only attempted in a very small minority of cases.) This attack was the twelfth known to the police, and because of the previous incidents, they took a very serious view of the patient's recent actions in which he had followed a woman with a perambulator and had smeared it with oil. He had been charged previously by the police, the first time on account of six incidents. In one of these he slashed two empty prams on a railway station before setting them on fire and completely destroying them. He had also admitted five other incidents involving cutting or scratching prams, and he was convicted of causing malicious damage and put on probation to accept medical treatment. He was sent to a mental hospital, and was then transferred to a neurosis unit. The view was there expressed that he was unsuitable for psychotherapy, was potentially dangerous, and should remain in a mental hospital. He left the hospital, however, and proceeded with his career of damaging prams. He was not charged this time, but was admitted to a mental hospital where he stayed for eighteen months. After his discharge, he deliberately rode his motor-cycle combination into a perambulator with a baby in it. He swerved at the last moment, but hit the perambulator and damaged it. He was convicted of careless driving and was fined. Later on, he damaged a pram and a woman's stockings and skirt, squirting oil on them. He was convicted of causing malicious damage and fined. A fourth charge arose out of incidents in which he rode his motor cycle through muddy puddles, splashing a pram and its coverings and the woman who pushed it. He was charged with driving without due care and attention.

The next incident, the twelfth known to the police, has already been mentioned, and he was charged and convicted of causing wilful damage, and was also put on probation to accept medical treatment. The prosecuting counsel stressed that the accused deserved sympathy, but added that he was still a menace to any woman with a pram. He also spoke of 'a real fear that he may cause serious injury to a baby or mother unless he is put under some form of restraint'. The patient was treated by Dr M. J. Raymond, who wrote up his case in the British Medical Journal. Apparently the patient had

had impulses to damage perambulators and handbags since about the age of ten, and although the police only knew of twelve peram-bulators he had attacked, the number of times he had so indulged was legion. He had sometimes made several attempts in one day, but he estimated the average at about two or three a week, fairly consistently. With the handbags, he was usually satisfied if he could scratch them with his thumb-nail, and as this could be done unobtrusively, a handbag had only once led him into trouble with the police. He had received many hours of analytical treatment and had been enabled to trace his abnormality back to two incidents in his childhood. The first was when he had been taken to the park to sail his boat and had been impressed by the feminine consternation manifest when he struck the keel of his yacht against a passing perambulator. The second was when he became sexually roused in the presence of his sister's handbag. He had been led to see the significance of these events and to understand that perambulators and handbags were, for him, 'symbolic sexual containers', but the attacks continued.

Apparently he had masturbated from the age of ten onwards, with fantasies of prams and handbags and particularly of damage being caused to them by their owners.
Intercourse, he said, was only possible with the aid of fantasies of handbags and prams.

There were two children, and his wife said that he was a good
husband and father. The domestic perambulator and his wife's
handbag, however, were not immune from attack, and the handbag, filled to capacity and bulging, often provided piquancy to his
masturbation. While it was true that handbags and perambulators
roused him sexually, his attacks upon them were never accompanied
by emission, although he was usually conscious of release of tension.

At the beginning of the treatment it was explained to the
patient that it was the aim of the treatment to alter his
attitude to handbags and perambulators, by teaching him
to associate them with an unpleasant sensation, instead of
with the pleasurable erotic one. He was quite sceptical about
the treatment, but said he was willing to try anything, for
his despair had been deepened by recent sexual arousals
when handbags appeared in the ward on visiting day, and
by illustrated advertisements in newspapers.

The treatment was based on the injection of a drug called
apomorphine, which produces nausea. According to the
conditioning paradigm, the conditioned stimuli, prams,
handbags, or pictures thereof, were produced just
before the nausea occurred, thus constituting the conditioned stimuli; the nausea, of course, constitutes the
unpleasant response with which the conditioned stimulus is
to be associated.

The treatment was given two-hourly, day and night, no food was
allowed, and at night amphetamine was used to keep him awake.
At the end of the first week treatment was temporarily suspended,
and the patient was allowed home to attend to his affairs. He
returned after eight days to continue the treatment, and he
reported jubilantly that he had, for the first time, been able to
have intercourse with his wife without use of the old fantasies.
His wife said that she had noticed a change in his attitude to her,
but was unable to define it. Treatment was re-commenced and

continued as before, save that emetine hydrochloride was used whenever the emetic effect of apomorphine became less pronounced than its sedative effect. After five days he said that the mere sight of the objects made him sick. He was now confined to bed and the prams and handbags were continually with him, the treatment being given at irregular intervals. On the evening of the ninth day, he rang his bell and was found to be sobbing uncontrollably. He kept repeating, 'Take them away,' and appeared to be impervious to anything which was said to him. The sobbing continued unabated until the objects were removed with ceremony and he was given a glass of milk and a sedative. The following day he handed over a number of photographic negatives of perambulators, saying that he had carried them about for years but would need them no longer. He left hospital but continued to attend as an out-patient. After a further six months it was decided empirically to re-admit him for a booster course of treatment. He agreed to this, although he did not consider it at all necessary. A coloured cinematic film was made of women carrying handbags, pushing prams in the careless provoking way which he had described previously. The film was started each time just before the onset of nausea produced by an emetic, and was continued throughout the period of nausea. He was also given handbags to handle.

The patient was followed up over a period of years and appeared to be doing well. He maintained that he no longer required the old fantasies to enable him to have sexual intercourse and he did not masturbate with these fantasies. The wife said that she was no longer constantly worrying about him, and about the possible imminence of police action against him. She also said that their sexual relations had greatly improved. The probation officer reported that the patient had made very noticeable progress, and that his general attitude to life, his conversation, and his appearance had all shown a marked improvement. The police reported no further trouble, and at work he had been promoted to a more responsible job.

This case, which is typical of many, raises many problems, only some of which we shall be able to discuss now. The first problem is raised by the extremely mechanical way in which this patient's difficulties have been attacked and solved. This very much offends many people who feel that this is a kind of brain-washing, and that it is degrading to treat human beings in such a mechanical fashion, as if they were nothing but boxes of conditioned reflexes. Such stress on the value of individuality and on the sanctity of each person's private life is all too rare in our more and more bureaucratic and autocratic type of society, and I would be the last person in the world to decry it as unworthy or irrational. Nevertheless, one must look at the problem from more than one point of view, and one's feelings must be controlled by a consideration of the alternatives which are possible at the moment. The first alternative, of course, might be some form of psychotherapy, either psycho-analytic or otherwise. There is a great deal of evidence in the literature and much of it outside the literature to show that, for cases of this type, psychotherapy is quite useless. Successes, where they have been reported at all, are extremely rare and, quite frequently, short-lived. Neither can we rely, to any extent, on spontaneous remission; neurotic disorders of the second type, as it were, do not show the high rate of spontaneous remission manifested by neurotic disorders of the first kind, and indeed, remission is very rare, with or without treatment. We may, therefore, dismiss, however reluctantly, the notion that our patient would have improved over the course of years, either with or without psychiatric treatment; indeed, he had already received a good deal of psychiatric treatment without any success whatsoever.

The second alternative would have been to send the patient to prison. If he had not agreed to undergo therapy he would have undoubtedly been sent to prison, even on this occasion, and if he had ever again committed misdemeanours of a similar kind – as undoubtedly he would have – the prison sentence would have been very severe indeed. Futhermore, while it would have amounted to a punishment meted out to him, it would not have had any kind of beneficial effect on his future actions. The evidence again is fairly conclusive that to take a sexual pervert of this type and send him to prison has no lasting effect on his behaviour. He may be a little more careful in the future, but the odds are very much against his making any kind of social adjustment, and are very much in favour of his falling foul of the law again. Prison, therefore, would have been most cruel and inefficient as a way of treating this particular aberration.

On the other hand, we must also dismiss the next possibility, which is that of letting him go free or putting him on probation. Society has the right to be protected, and there is no doubt that, in due course, if the patient had been left to himself, he would have committed a serious injury, possibly amounting to manslaughter. Even in his past life he avoided this quite narrowly on at least one or two occasions, when he might have killed a woman and a baby with his motor cycle; the probability is quite high that, at some time in his life, fate would not have been so kind and he would have committed a very serious offence indeed and have injured irreparably some members of society, who are surely entitled to protection. Sympathy for perverts or criminals should not lead us too far in the direction of disregarding the rights of those people who are neither perverts nor criminals.

Looked at from this point of view, then, we must make a rational choice between asking the patient to submit to a method of treatment which is reasonably uncomfortable but not very long continued (the whole treatment amounted to little more than two weeks or so), sending him to prison, allowing him to go free, to the constant danger of society, or asking him to submit to a very lengthy and most likely ineffective psychotherapeutic treatment in a hospital. These are the only practical alternatives which present themselves and, given the circumstances, I find it difficult to say that behaviour therapy should be excluded from consideration, because it makes use of certain well-known principles of conditioning and learning. Indeed, these principles are perhaps not quite as novel as we sometimes think. The philosopher, Descartes, for instance, who was himself a squint fetishist, wrote in 1649, 'From whence come those extraordinary passions which are peculiar to certain men? There is so close a union between mind and body that once we have combined a certain action with a certain thought,

the one never subsequently presents itself without the other.'
And he finally concluded that these strange passions may
well have formed in early infancy to 'remain imprisoned in
the brain until the end of life'. Descartes, in other words,
already anticipated the association theory of fetishism, but
he failed to see the possibility of deconditioning, or dis-
associating, that which had once been conditioned or
associated. There is, indeed, no reason why these associa-
tions should remain imprisoned in the brain until the end
of life; we now have ways and means of dissolving the bond
and of freeing the individual from these mechanical fetters
forged in infancy, or during adolescence.

Even before the elaboration of the conditioning paradigm
to explain the origin of fetishism, it had been noted that
these perversions tended to arise from a specific event. Thus,
the well-known French psychologist, Binet, who produced
the first intelligence test and gave us the notion of mental
age, maintained that fetishism arose from an accident acting
on a predisposed subject, and believed that the form taken
by any sexual perversion was determined quite fortui-
tously by an external event. Similarly, Krafft-Ebing, the
famous sexologist, stated his belief that fetishism arose with
the first awakening of the fetishist's sexual life, when some
event determined the association of lustful feelings with a
single impression. These views may be contrasted with those
of Freud, which are summarized in this form by Raymond.
'A fetish object is a substitute for the woman's (mother's)
phallus in which the boy once believed. It remained as a
triumph over the castration threat and saved the fetishist
from becoming homosexual by endowing women with the
attribute which makes them sexually acceptable. The object may, however, symbolize the boy's last impression
before the traumatic discovery which it screens from his
conscious memory.' It need hardly be said that there is as
little support for this theory as there was for Freud's views
in the case of little Hans, whom we encountered in a previous chapter.

It may be useful now to look at another case, this time of
transvestism.

THE CASE OF THE CROSS-DRESSING TRUCK DRIVER

The patient in this case was the twenty-two-year-old son of a coal miner, who had been a truck driver since the age of eighteen, and who indulged in such masculine sports as weight-lifting and physical culture. He complained of a recurrent desire to dress in female clothing. This had begun at the age of eight, when he found his sister's dress on a bed, put it on, and admired the effect in a mirror. Subsequently he wore her clothes to relieve tension whenever an opportunity arose, but only derived erotic satisfaction from the activity when he was over fifteen. Since puberty he had masturbated infrequently, but this had always been accompanied by transvestite fantasies. He served for two years with the overseas service of the Royal Air Force, and even there continued to practise transvestism, using clothing bought specially for that purpose.

The patient was married and sexual relations were satisfactory, taking place about three times per week. The patient confessed that he had married his wife in the hope that the abnormal behaviour would cease. Shortly after marriage, however, he resumed his transvestism, using his wife's cosmetics and dressing in her clothes. He also had appeared in public in her clothes, on two occasions. C. B. Blakemore and the other authors of the report on his case, state that, 'He was strongly motivated to seek psychiatric advice, both by his fear of being detected in this behaviour and by the encouragement of his wife who had only recently learned of his abnormality.' Treatment was planned very carefully, according to the following lines of thought.

We consider that it is of the utmost importance to prepare the conditioned stimulus carefully, so that it will correspond exactly to the patient's perversion and does not include any material without significance to the behaviour under modification. The stimulus is, therefore, a highly individual affair and will naturally vary from one transvestite patient to another according to the precise nature of his behaviour. Our patient was not excited by the texture or feel of women's clothes, but only by the total effect of dressing in them and viewing himself in a mirror. We therefore decided that he need not wear or handle the clothing during treatment. Prior to treatment, twelve 35 mm. camera transparencies were taken of the patient in various stages of female dress; they ranged from panties only to fully clothed; six were full-face, six were profile.

A tape-recording was also made of the patient reading from a script, as follows: 'I am ... (name). I have now put on and am wearing a pair of ladies' panties. I am ... I have now put on and am wearing a pair of ladies' panties and a suspender belt ...' etc., until all items of clothing were mentioned. The object of this was to reinforce the conditioned stimulus and to ensure the presence of the stimulus even when the patient's eyes were closed during vomiting. It was also designed to facilitate generalization of whatever learning might take place.

The patient was put into bed in a darkened room with a film projector mounted behind the head of the bed, and a 48-inch screen set up at the foot. A close watch was kept on his physical condition throughout treatment, and temperature, pulse, and blood pressure readings were taken every two hours. Aversion therapy was continued every two hours for six days and six nights; the mainstay of treatment was apomorphine. As soon as the injection was acting – the patient usually reporting a headache followed by nausea – a slide was projected on to the screen and the tape-recording played back. While the stimuli were being presented, the patient was strongly encouraged to watch the screen. His cooperation was excellent. The stimuli were continued until he either vomited or became intensely nauseated. During the greater part of the treatment, the patient's physical and mental condition remained excellent. Some idea of his condition can be gained from the fact that after five days and nights of this régime he insisted on cleaning his room and washing the walls, maintaining that he wanted some 'occupational therapy'. Several visits from his wife boosted his morale during treatment and he also had frequent discussions with doctors, psychologists, and nurses between injections. Care was taken to avoid any possible effects of suggestion during these informal talks. After trials, he admitted feeling a deep sense of humiliation every time he saw himself on the screen.

Seventy-two emetic trials had been planned originally, but the last four were abandoned because the patient became irritable and confused. His feeling on viewing the slides now was that the female attire was a 'disfigurement' which he had now grown to resent. Eventually he found it difficult to imagine that the sensation which he had obtained from cross-dressing could ever have been pleasurable. 'The patient and his wife were interviewed on three occasions during the three months following treatment. Each time they stated that recovery was complete and expressed their relief at the removal of this obstacle to the happiness of their marriage. During the last interview the patient report-ed that, at his wife's request, he had recently put on her green skirt, a garment which had previously excited him, and had felt completely indifferent to it.' Several years have now elapsed since the treatment, and there has been no relapse, so confidently expected by psychoanalysts.

Here again, we have a case treated by a method some-times referred to in pejorative terms as 'brain-washing'. Clearly, it is a very rigorous and unpleasant type of treat-ment, producing a certain amount of discomfort and even pain. Again, however, we must compare the choice of treatment with the possible alternatives. Here indeed there is no question, as yet, of any police prosecution because, although the patient had in fact paraded in the street in his wife's clothes, he had never been found out. However, appetite grows by what it feeds on, and he would have very likely indulged more and more in this habit until finally charged and sent to prison. The main motivation for treatment, in this case, however, derives not only from his fear of being found out, but also from a desire to preserve his marriage, which would very likely have foundered, with-out successful treatment. Given, then, that treatment was necessary and indeed, very strongly desired by the patient, what alternatives were there? Psychotherapy has been used in the past, but its record is very poor indeed. Electro-convulsive treatment and surgical procedures, such as castration, have been used in the past, but it is doubtful whether these would be any more pleasant and any less 'mechanical', and indeed the evidence does not suggest that they would have been anything like as effective as the pro-cedure actually employed. Objections to the method used, therefore, if they were to be effective, would have to consist in denying the patient the right to choose this particular method of treatment, and therefore, of being cured of his particular disorder; it is doubtful whether those people who are opposed to aversion therapy would, in fact, wish to carry their opposition to this extreme.

Similar methods to these have been applied also to the treatment of homosexuality. Here the pictures of nude males have usually constituted the conditioned stimuli, although in one or two cases actual films have also been used. It may be supposed that the latter, being more lifelike, are more likely to provoke strong conditioned responses, but no actual comparison of the efficacy of these different stimuli has been made. In these experiments, too, apomorphine has been used, and occasionally some investigators have reported the use of electric shock, which of course has many advantages over apomorphine. The strength of the shock can be regulated much more accurately and its timing is also much more accurate than that of the nausea and vomiting which supervene after an injection of apomorphine, but which cannot be timed at all accurately, or even predicted within as much as several minutes.

The effects of aversion therapy with homosexuals has been variable; very much seems to depend on whether the patient comes of his own volition and is highly motivated, for reasons of his own, to overcome this particular perversity and become 'normal' again, or whether he has no real desire to change, but is told to go for treatment by magistrates, on pain of being sent to prison otherwise. Where motivation is provided from the outside, as it were, the evidence seems to suggest that the effects of treatment, although they may be fairly obvious at first, are not very lasting. Where motivation is, as it were, internal, and comes from the subject himself rather than from outside pressure, there is some evidence that the treatment may have lasting effects. Too few patients have been treated along these lines to make it possible to be at all dogmatic, but even so, the evidence suggests that behaviour therapy is likely to be more successful in cases of this kind than is psychotherapy or psychoanalysis. Certain reservations regarding this statement will be noted later on.

Many questions will immediately come to mind regarding this treatment of homosexuality. One of them relates to the possibility of changing a person's sexual behaviour by means of a process of this type. We have already mentioned the fact that homosexual tendencies may have a very strong innate component, and it might be thought that, having extinguished the sexual desire for members of the same sex, the patient would then be left without any sexual desire at all. This, however, does not seem to be so. In the great majority of cases, there seems to have been a direct increase of interest in members of the opposite sex concomitant with the decline in interest in members of the same sex. Most probably, we are all ambisexual up to a point, some being more directed in their interest towards members of the same sex, others towards members of the other sex. Given, however, that one source of satisfaction is denied us, we are quite likely to make use of the other source. There appears thus little justification for any fears on this point. A homosexual cured along these lines is not likely to remain a-sexual, but will, in the great majority of cases at least, adjust perfectly well to a heterosexual type of life.

The powers of conditioning and training in the field of sexual adjustment are indeed quite remarkable. We take it for granted, in our society, that the proper way of making love involves kissing and fondling of breasts. Yet in other societies, as pointed out before, kissing is unknown and breasts are of only functional importance; South Sea Islanders simply could not understand the interest shown by white sailors, who landed on these islands, in the parts of the female figure so prominently displayed without cover by South Sea Island girls. Even in our own society it is well-known that 'the cult of the bosom', which is so notable nowadays, makes a sexual fetish of a part of the body which, only thirty years ago during the nineteen twenties, was flattened out as much as possible and almost completely denied by its owners. Cultural anthropologists have given many other examples of the marked changes which can take place in a particular culture, and the extreme differences from one culture to another. These can hardly be considered to be innate, and exemplify, therefore, the very remarkable power of conditioning over sexual reactions of this type.

The treatment of homosexuals raises some rather awkward ethical problems, to which I cannot pretend to know the answer. What right, it may be said, has society, through its magistrates and its police force, to face the homosexual with the alternative of going to prison or of having his personality changed to the very marked degree involved in shifting his total sexual life from one sex to another? Wolfenden, and other reformers, have suggested that society does not have this right and that, at least between consenting adults, homosexual behaviour should not be punishable by law, and that, therefore, treatment, if it is sought, should be sought only in terms of the individual's private volition. On the other hand, of course, we have all the well-known arguments about national decadence and the decline of the moral stature of a nation consequent upon the toleration of homosexual practices.

I cannot pretend to be devoid of feelings of revulsion for homosexual practices, but equally I cannot feel that these feelings of mine should necessarily form the basis for other people's conduct. As long as no public harm is done, it does not indeed seem right to punish people for deviations from the normal sexual pattern, which are either inherited and, therefore, outside their control, or initiated in public schools, in the army, or in prison, under conditions for which the homosexual himself can hardly be held responsible. Indeed, it would seem quite wrong for society to condemn the homosexual but to do nothing about the breeding grounds of homosexual practices. Until society makes all schools co-educational, allows prisoners' wives to come and cohabit with them in prison, and makes provision in the army, the navy, and elsewhere for sexual outlets of a proper kind for the armed forces, so long will homosexuality be not only rife but actually encouraged in practice. If society really wanted to get rid of these practices, it would certainly set about it in quite a different way; instead of using the remarkably inefficient, punitive methods employed at the moment, it would make every effort to make ordinary heterosexual contacts easier, and encourage the type of sexual behaviour which is acknowledged by our society to be a desirable one. Neither am I very much impressed by the arguments about national decadence. From the reign of Queen Elizabeth I, to the reign of Queen Victoria, the English were a byword on the Continent for their strong homosexual tendencies. At the same time, however, England was becoming the most powerful country in the world. There seems to be no reason to see any causal relation between the two, but neither can it be denied that the very widespread homosexual practices failed to have any detrimental effect on the national weal. Exactly the same argument seems to apply to ancient Greece, where also a period of national glory was accompanied by a large increase in homosexual practices. Quite clearly, these are entirely different things and should not be mixed up in the argument.

Where does this leave the behaviour therapist, from the ethical point of view? There is no problem, clearly, when he is called in by a person acting on his own free will, a person who is desperately unhappy with his present state, and who will do anything to be, as it were, 'normal' in his sexual relations. The problem arises when a patient is referred to the therapist by a magistrate, who threatens to send him to prison unless he goes for treatment. Under these conditions, the patient is clearly acting under duress, and the therapist will have to decide whether he will undertake to treat him or not. Up to a point, we may say that the responsibility, in truth, lies with society, and is expressed, in this case, through the magistrate. Does this fact make it unnecessary for the therapist himself to consider the ethical implications of the case? The feeling would be that nothing can take away the need for an ethical decision from the individual, and that, in a case of this kind, the therapist would have to make up his mind whether he regarded the treatment, or the refusal to undertake treatment, as being more in line with his ethical beliefs. I would not pretend to give any guidance on a point of this type.

How successful are therapeutic methods of conditioning in disorders of the second kind? On the whole, it is often said that they are much less successful than behaviour therapy undertaken with disorders of the first kind. How far is this assertion true? There are two points to be considered; in the first place, we will see that, from the theoretical point of view, we would expect that disorders of the second kind would be the more difficult to treat than disorders of the first kind, and would be more susceptible to relapses. This is perfectly understandable, and there are a good many things which learning theory suggests could be done about it. There is also, however, a second point which we shall also have to discuss in some detail, and this relates to the fact that many people who have undertaken aversion therapy of one kind or another, have done so without due regard to the teaching of learning theory, and have, therefore, committed errors in their proceedings which make failure inevitable. These failures should certainly not be laid at the door of behaviour therapy and indeed, the fact that these failures can be predicted from learning theory makes them support, rather than contradict, the theory involved. Let us consider, first of all, the reasons why behaviour therapy applied to these disorders would be expected to be less successful than when applied to disorders of the first kind.

We have essentially postulated three different types of neurotic disorder. The first type in our system consists of conditioned emotional responses of an unadaptive kind, probably acquired as a consequence of some traumatic event, or perhaps, in many cases, as a consequence of several sub-traumatic happenings. These unpleasant emotional responses constitute our disorders of the first kind, and we have postulated that they would be subject to spontaneous remission in most cases, and that, in any case, once they had been eliminated – whether by behaviour therapy or by spontaneous remission – there was no reason why any relapse should occur. We have also noted that in fact relapses are extremely rare in conditions of this type. Disorders of the second kind may be broken down into two varieties, which are distinct in many ways. The first kind would be constituted of conditioned emotional responses of an unadaptive kind, which are not unpleasant but which are unacceptable to society; in this group we might include the homosexual disorders, fetishism, transvestism, alcoholism, and so forth. The second category would be constituted of a failure to condition emotional and skeletal responses of an adaptive kind; here we might include such disorders as enuresis (or bed-wetting), and perhaps criminal behaviour. Disorders of the first kind are characterized by the fact that the patient requires desensitization of stimuli which he finds anxiety-provoking, painful, and unpleasant. Disorders of the second kind are characterized by the fact that we are required to produce a strong, unpleasant, conditioned response in connexion with stimuli which either have been conditioned to pleasurable consequences, or have never been conditioned in socially approved ways at all. In some cases, of course, it is difficult to know which of these two hypotheses is true; homosexuality, as we have seen, may either be innate, or the consequence of faulty conditioning. However, it does not matter very much which of these causal factors is the operative one; the important point about disorders of the second kind is that they require a very active process of aversion conditioning.

Aversion conditioning, undertaken in the laboratory, has, of course, to contend with many disadvantages. In the first place, as we have already pointed out, the motivation of the patient is often less strong than in the case of disorders of the first kind, where the suffering is acute and the patient will do almost anything to escape from it. There is much less such individual suffering in the case of perversions and other disorders of the second kind, and what suffering there is emanates usually from society rather than from the individual. Leaving aside for the moment the question we have already discussed, of whether society has a right to provide motivation for cure in the individual, we may nevertheless assume that it will, on the whole, be less strong than in the case of disorders of the first kind.

There is one further difficulty, however, which is very much greater even than this. We have noted, several times before, that conditioned responses are subject to extinction when they are not reinforced. This, of course, applies equally to the aversion conditioning which we have recommended for disorders of the second kind. Take the person who has been conditioned to associate the naked bodies of other males with being sick and with nausea. This conditioned response, like all conditioned responses, is subject to considerable oscillation in its strength; that is to say, it varies from day to day, and almost from hour to hour, in the degree of strength which it exhibits. This oscillation is a well-known laboratory phenomenon. Even the dog which has been conditioned to salivate will not give precisely the same number of drops every time you put him into the experimental room. This oscillation is dependent on a great variety of circumstances, among which undoubtedly are variations in drive. The hungrier the dog, the greater the number of drops of saliva is likely to be. Now take your homosexual who has been conditioned to respond with aversion to other males. Let us assume that he is happily married and that, therefore, his sex drives never reach a very high level. Let us also assume that his wife is ill, or has a prolonged menstrual period. During this time, his sex drive will mount up and there will be no appropriate way of reducing it. Assume now that in this condition he meets an old homosexual friend who invites him to go back to his old practices. If, at a particular moment when temptation is beckoning, drive is strong and the conditioned aversion happens to be at a relatively low level, it is quite possible that he may succumb. This will inevitably produce a certain amount of extinction in the conditioned response, and we will find that the next time that temptation comes along it will be resisted less strongly. Exactly the same type of story could, of course, be told about alcoholics, or fetishists, or other people suffering from disorders of the second kind. In other words, what I am saying is that in this type of disorder there is not likely to be any kind of spontaneous remission, but quite the opposite; the principle of extinction will now work against the therapy and in favour of the 'spontaneous remission' of the conditioned response which we have tried to inculcate in the patient. In other words, relapses will be much more likely under these conditions than they are in disorders of the first kind. Our theoretical analysis would, therefore, lead us to assume that relapses will be more pronounced here, and the facts amply justify this conclusion. There is no doubt that for all types of therapy relapses are much more frequent in disorders of the second kind·

To say that this is so, however, does not necessarily mean that we must for ever be pessimistic about the success of these methods. Modern learning theory gives us many suggestions as to how we could improve our methods and make sure that relapse should not occur. Two of these suggestions are fairly obvious ones, and will perhaps have occurred to the reader already. The first of these is simply that we should continue our process of conditioning well beyond the point where it has begun to take effect. This is sometimes called 'over-conditioning', and the way it works can be described most simply in connexion with a laboratory experiment. Suppose that we have conditioned a P.G.R. reaction to the word 'cow' by pairing the word with an electric shock; and suppose that a particular individual gives a P.G.R. reaction after three pairings. If we stop there and begin to extinguish this reaction by simply showing the word 'cow' without reinforcement, we will find that the extinction period will be relatively short: say, five repetitions of the word. If, however, we went on and on reinforcing the word 'cow' well beyond the point where the conditioned response had been established, say, by pairing the response thirty or fifty times, we would then find that extinction would take a great deal longer. In other words, to eliminate the possibility of extinction and reduce the influence of oscillation in this situation, we must over-condition.

This is not usually done, for a variety of reasons. In the first place, it is, of course, time-consuming, and time is precious, both for the therapist and for the patient. In the second place, experimental investigations using vomiting are inevitably messy and expensive in terms of nursing time and the efforts involved in cleaning the room and making it presentable again. In the third place, the procedure is relatively strenuous and unpleasant, both for the experimenter and for the patient and, consequently, an attempt is usually made to cut it down as much as possible. Any suggestion that it should be prolonged will be vigorously fought by the therapist, but also by the patient, who is quite likely to discharge himself when *he* feels that conditioning has been achieved. Many of these reasons are associated with the use of apomorphine and other nausea-producing and sick-making drugs, and I have always argued that, in any case, these are unsuitable for the purpose of aversion therapy, because they make it so difficult – if not impossible – to achieve a proper time-relation between the presentation of the unconditioned stimulus and the conditioned stimulus. It is well-known that this time relationship is quite vital in the formation of conditioned responses; it has been shown in the laboratory that conditioning is optimal when about half a second elapses between the conditioned and the unconditioned stimulus, and that with even such a very short prolongation of this period as two and a half seconds, no conditioning whatsoever takes place. It will be seen that drugs are not a very good method of producing such finely-regulated time intervals and, consequently, something else, such as the use of electric shock, or loud noise delivered over earphones, would seem much more reasonable. These also have the advantage of being relatively clean, very much less unpleasant for either doctor or patient, and of being much easier to regulate as far as severity is concerned. An example of the use of electric shock in aversion therapy is given below; it illustrates that it is by no means impossible to use a relatively mild shock in this connexion, and it suggests that the difficulties attendant on 'over-conditioning' are not really insuperable.

THE CASE OF THE CORSETTED ENGINEER

In this experiment, the patient was a thirty-three-year-old engineer who had been married for four years and had one son. He had had an unsettled childhood, due to the fact that his father was neurotic, and an older sister very highly-strung. He had indulged in transvestism, as far as he could

recollect, at least since the age of four years. During childhood he often derived pleasure from dressing in his mother's
or his sister's clothing. At the age of twelve he experienced an
emission while wearing a corset and thereafter cross-dressing
was usually, but not invariably, accompanied by masturbation. National Service interfered with this practice, although
even then he frequently masturbated with transvestist fantasies. When he came back to civilian life he regularly
practised transvestism, and finally developed a compulsion
to appear in public at night dressed as a woman, complete
with make-up and a wig. During the early part of his marriage he found it necessary to cross-dress in order to obtain
an erection during intercourse; his wife objected to this,
but although he gave up this practice, he still indulged frequently in his older patterns of cross-dressing behaviour.
Six years of supportive psychotherapy had done little to
modify his symptom, but he had, during this time, become
addicted to sodium amytal which was initially prescribed to
reduce tension.

C. Blakemore, who published this case, described the
procedure which was followed, along these lines.

The patient derived little pleasure from the handling of female
clothes, and while he enjoyed admiring himself in his cross-
dressed state in front of a mirror, his main source of stimulation
and satisfaction came from the actual act of dressing up and feeling
these clothes next to his skin. Treatment was carried out in a small
room which was screened off in the middle. Behind the screen
were a chair, a full-length mirror, and an electric floor grid. This
grid was made of a corrugated rubber mat to which were stapled
strips of copper wire. Alternate wires of this grid were then connected to the two poles of a hand-operated electric current
generator. This was capable of giving a sharp, unpleasant shock
to the feet and ankles of anyone standing on the grid at the time of
the generator being operated.

At the start of each of the trials into which the treatment was
divided, the patient stood naked on the grid, and when instructed,
began to dress in his own 'favourite outfit' of female clothing. This
had been only slightly modified for use during the treatment, in
that slits had been cut out in the feet of nylon stockings and a thin
metal plate to act as a conductor had been fitted into the sole of

each shoe. At some point during his dressing in these female clothes, the patient either received an electric shock or heard a buzzer. Each of these was a signal to begin undressing and the signal, either shock or buzzer, was repeated at irregular intervals until he was completely undressed.

Four hundred trials in all were given, coming in batches of five with one-minute rest intervals between any two, at half-hourly intervals from nine a.m. until late afternoon, over a six-day period. In order to avoid the same number of garments being put on during each trial and stereotyped undressing behaviour, both the amount of time before the signal to undress and the interval between repetitions of this signal during undressing were varied from trial to trial. The progress of the case has been followed up over the years, and it was found that the patient had no desire to indulge in transvestism any more, and that during this period his relationship with his wife had improved. He was also taking less sodium amytal than at any time for a number of years. It appears from this that electric shock may, with advantage, take the place of the rather messy procedures of vomiting and nausea. It is superior, not only from the point of view of the person conducting the therapy, but also from the point of view of the subject, who much prefers a slight electric shock to the much grosser inconvenience involved in nausea and vomiting.

There is an interesting sequel to this case, which illustrates the point made previously in relation to oscillation and the building up of drive. When this patient's wife conceived, the general practitioner forbade all further intercourse, due to a history of recurrent spontaneous abortion. The patient now began to feel a state of tension building up, becoming irritable, feeling frustrated, and making increasing demands for amytal. After three months of this, he felt that he was approaching a crisis; there was no anxious desire to cross-dress, but he was unable to obtain complete sexual relief from masturbation. The crisis was reached on the day before the birth of his child. He became drunk whilst attending an office party and, under the influence of alcohol, made an appointment by telephone with a prostitute catering for transvestites. He kept the appointment and cross-dressed once, apparently obtaining some, but he maintains, not complete, sexual relief. He then returned home, still under the influence of alcohol. This episode caused him a considerable degree of self-reproach, and though medical reasons had precluded intercourse with his wife since her return from hospital, there has been no repetition of transvestism nor has there been any desire to do so. Strong sexual attraction to females in his office still persists, and he experiences considerable satisfaction from sex-play with his wife. He is still deeply concerned over his apparent relapse and feels at a loss to explain it, in view of his normal sexual feelings towards members of the opposite sex.

The second method which may be suggested for overcoming the difficulties involved in relapses is that of giving booster doses. This, of course, is a standard medical practice in a variety of disorders; patients, for instance, who have been desensitized against certain allergies often receive booster doses once a year, in order to make sure that the immunity will last; and, of course, in a similar way, everyone who has had injections against various disorders will know that these gradually lose their force and booster doses have to be given. It is standard practice, therefore, in some clinics for alcoholics, homosexuals, and others who have been treated in this manner, to be called back once a year, or once every two years, and to receive a short booster treatment. Here again, difficulties arise because of the unpleasantness of treatment by apomorphine, but there is no reason to assume that this unpleasantness could not be eliminated in this case also, by the use of other unconditioned stimuli than this particularly unpleasant drug.

These two methods do not go beyond common sense and are just the kind of thing which the man in the street would have been able to think of without the help of learning theory. The third method, however, which is suggested is one which may, at first sight seem to be paradoxical because we would expect it to have the opposite effect to that intended. In the normal run of things when we condition a person, we do this on the basis of what is sometimes called total, or one hundred per cent, reinforcement; in other words, we show the dog the meat every time that the bell is sounded, or we give the person a shock every time that he is shown the word 'cow'. However, there is no reason why reinforcement should be one hundred per cent: it could be partial instead. In other words, we could reinforce the conditioned stimulus in fifty per cent of all trials, or in sixty-five per cent, or in twenty per cent. What would be the effect of this on extinction? There is a great deal of evidence, accumulated during the last thirty years or more, showing that, without any doubt at all, both for animals and humans, the effect of partial reinforcement is to make extinction less likely and slower than does one hundred per cent reinforcement. There are many theoretical reasons given for this effect, but, truth to tell, it is still doubtful why precisely partial reinforcement has this particular effect upon extinction. However, there is no need for us to worry about the theoretical explanation of the effect; it is sufficient to know that it is so, in order to make use of it for the purpose of making extinction less likely in the patients we treat by means of aversion therapy. The Australian psychologist, S. H. Lovibond, has used this principle in an experiment in which he treated two groups of children suffering from enuresis. Both groups were given the 'bell and blanket' treatment already described, but in one group the treatment was one hundred per cent – in other words, the bell rang every time the child wet his bed – whereas in the other group treatment was partial – in other words, the bell rang only two times out of three. It was predicted that when the children were followed up there would be a greater number of relapses among those who had received the total reinforcement, as compared with those who had received the partial reinforcement, and Lovibond was indeed able to show that this was so. Here, then, we have a third way of making extinction less likely, by using the method of partial reinforcement. No doubt there are many other ways in which we can overcome this particular difficulty, but this is not the time or place to discuss at great length the well-known principles of extinction. Suffice it to say that a combination of the three methods already mentioned should be quite sufficient to overcome the tendency to relapse so often noticed in the past when no use was made of these improvements.

We have now discussed the genuine and scientifically valid reasons for believing that aversion therapy is less successful than therapy by reciprocal inhibition of disorders of the first kind. We must now turn to another type of argument which is often advanced against this type of treatment, and which is based more on ignorance than on genuine reasons. It may be illustrated by an experience I once had when I heard a lecture given by a behaviour therapist who had spent a good many years on using and perfecting the 'bell and blanket' method, and who showed, on the basis of very extensive statistical analyses and case material, that this method was vastly superior to any alternative method available or practised in child guidance clinics. At the end of this lecture, a well-known child psychiatrist got up and said, in effect, that he also had used the 'bell and blanket' method and that he had found that it did not in fact work. This criticism made a considerable impression on the listeners, and I decided to investigate the exact position, as it seemed unlikely, on theoretical grounds, that the method should fail.

To cut a long story short, I found out the following. This particular psychiatrist – let us call him Dr X. – only advocated the use of the 'bell and blanket' method as a last resort; in other words, it was not used on a random sample of the enuretic population, but only on the most severe and desperate cases. This in itself would make it impossible to compare figures derived from this small group with those obtained from other groups less severely selected. In the second place, the actual blankets used by him were of a very antiquated construction and were not up to modern standards. It is quite clear that in this method a crucial point is the length of time elapsing between the beginning of urination and the ringing of the bell, and every effort must be made to make this time as short as possible. With the particular blankets used by this doctor, however, the time was

something like two or three times as long as would be possible with more modern constructions. This militates very
strongly against any conditioning taking place. Furthermore, as he had not available to him any technicians, the
blankets and the rest of the apparatus were in very poor
condition, and often failed to function outright. This of
course, would again interfere very much with success. In the
third place, Dr X. would not give any detailed instructions
to the parents, but simply handed over the bell and blanket,
saying something like this: 'Well, here is one last way of
trying to cure your son, or daughter, as the case might be.
Some people believe it works; I don't think much of it my-
self, but you may as well try it.' Such an uninspired introduction to the method would not be likely to call forth any
great efforts on the part of the parents, particularly as they
would not know exactly how to use the apparatus. Indeed
some parents were found to put in a very thick sheet between the child and the blanket, rather than a thin one,
thus again prolonging the time unduly between urination
and the ringing of the bell. Others failed to connect up the
electric parts of the apparatus in the proper manner, thus
never achieving any kind of ring at all. Many parents did
not know that the child was required to turn off the bell
when he woke up, and let it go on ringing. Indeed, the
number of mistakes made in the use of the bell and blanket
was legion, and undoubtedly much of the lack of success of
the method could be laid at the door of this failure to give
adequate instructions. In the fourth place, Dr X. seldom
left the bell and blanket apparatus long enough for it to
have any very pronounced effect. It usually takes a month
or more before the requisite period of seven dry nights is
achieved, and of course, if the conditioning is interrupted
half-way through, you are not likely to get a very successful
outcome. In the fifth place, it was found when his data were
re-analysed, that in spite of all these difficulties and draw-
backs the bell and blanket method had, in fact, proved to
be more successful than any alternative: he had simply
added up his figures wrongly. It need hardly be said that
criticism of this kind, based on this type of investigation, is

not a serious indication of any fault in the method. As was pointed out in relation to behaviour therapy of disorders of the first kind, we can only judge the effect of the treatment if it is carried out properly by people who have been trained in it. Where this training is lacking and where the procedures are not properly carried out, there we can hardly speak of a test of the value of the methods in question.

Even with the best will in the world, of course, it is often found that odd and unexpected things happen in the treatment of enuretic disorders by means of the bell and blanket. To take a single example to illustrate this point, let us look at the case of the Lambert family. Here it was a little boy who was enuretic and he was duly given the bell and blanket. He did not seem to recover very quickly, however, and it was noted that the battery of the appparatus seemed to burn out rather fast (usually the apparatus is plugged into the electric light circuit, but where no electric light is available, battery-operated apparatus is necessarily employed). Furthermore, the metal blankets themselves seemed to suffer some rather odd, and unexpected and inexplicable damage. An investigation of the case showed that the Lambert family were very fond of animals. Thus, the little boy had several cats sleeping on the same bed with him, as well as a tortoise which seemed to take a liking to the taste of the metal blanket and proceeded to chew it up during most of the night. Futhermore, one of the cats was also enuretic and thus would suddenly start the bell ringing in the middle of the night, even when the little boy himself was quite innocent of any offence. This frequent ringing of the bell ran down the battery much more quickly than would have been possible for the little boy himself, because cats, when they are enuretic, can produce a very much greater number of bell-ringings than even the most enuretic child! It was, incidentally, easier to diagnose these difficulties than to remedy them, because, when it was suggested to the Lambert family that perhaps the cats could sleep on the beds of the other children, and the tortoise too, they pointed out, quite reasonably, that the other children already had several cats and tortoises sleeping on their beds, and could not possibly add any more to that number! However, even these difficulties were overcome, and the little Lambert boy recovered and is now happily rejoicing in clean beds; indeed, even the cat seems to have benefited from the procedure!

All this is rather anecdotal, of course, and the reader may like to see a rather better documented example of the way in which the teachings of learning theory may be neglected in the actual form of the treatment. The best example of this is perhaps the treatment of alcoholism, where aversion therapy has been used for a good many years; indeed, of all types of aversion therapy, that of alcoholism has probably the longest history. The most determined efforts to cure alcoholics along these lines have been those of Voegtlin and his associates. Their method is rather complicated, but has proved much more successful than any short-cuts attempted by other people. The conditioning takes place in a quiet, bare room which is kept dark except for a spotlight which plays on the alcohol bottles on a table in front of the patient. The only person present, apart from the alcoholic, is the doctor. He injects hypodermically a mixture of emetine, which is preferred by Voegtlin to apomorphine, ephedrine which is a stimulant drug to improve conditioning, and pilocarpine which adds profuse sweating and salivation to the other symptoms of the patient produced by the emetine. At the same time, the patient is also given an oral dose of emetine and thus brought almost to the verge of nausea and vomiting. At this point the additional gastric irritation of even a small drink is then sufficient to produce nausea and vomiting almost immediately. It is, of course, quite difficult to obtain and maintain this 'steady state' on the verge of nausea, and considerable experience in general is required, as well as some knowledge of the patient's individual reaction-pattern. Between sessions, soft drinks are given freely in order to avoid the development of any kind of aversion to the handling of glasses or the act of drinking itself.

Over 4,000 patients who were treated and followed up for at least one year, and many for ten years or more have been reported on by Voegtlin and his associates. Of these, more than half remained abstinent for two to five years after treatment and about a quarter abstinent for ten to thirteen years. Some required further help and were treated a second time and of these, thirty-nine per cent remained abstinent subsequently. An overall abstinence rate is given of fifty-one per cent of all patients, both those who were treated only once and those who were re-treated after relapse, since the start of the treatment thirteen years previously; this is an astonishingly high figure compared with those given by adherents of any other method that has been tried in relation to this particular syndrome. These patients, we must hasten to add, probably came from a relatively wealthy, middle-class background, as is shown by the fact that the treatment was fairly expensive, costing between 450 and 750 dollars, and that opportunities were available to the patients to back out of treatment between entering hospital and the actual start of therapy. Of his patients, Voegtlin pointed out that inadequate, psychopathic, and highly neurotic personalities were the poorest responders.

Many other attempts have been made to replicate this work, and it is interesting to note that the degree of success achieved varied directly with the degree of fidelity with which these methods were reproduced. One would have thought that in any scientific attempt to study the value of a method it would be taken for granted that the actual method itself would be used, rather than some variant differing in important details from the original. This, however, is not so. Almost everyone who has tried to duplicate Voegtlin's work has added ideas of his own and has left out important parts of the original procedure, either for theoretical reasons, or because he found them time-consuming and difficult. This being so, of course, it is impossible to conclude, as some writers have done, that Voegtlin's method, when tried out by other people, does not work anything like as well as it does in his hands; it is rather that other people have not in fact tried his method at all, but variants of their own which do not give his claims a fair trial.

Consider just one example, a well-known study carried out by Wallerstein and his associates. Wallerstein had four matched groups treated by various methods. The first was treated by antabuse which is a drug producing nausea whenever the patient drinks alcohol after having ingested the drug. The patient is given conscious knowledge of this fact by the doctor, who will also give him a few trial drinks to demonstrate the truth of his warnings. This is not intended as a conditioning process and probably does not work as such. The second type of treatment was that of conditioning according to Voegtlin's method, so Wallerstein claimed. The third method used was one of group hypnotherapy and the fourth group was a simple control group. Now let us look at the way in which the investigator administered the alcohol. 'A strong wave of nausea developed and before actual emesis began, the patient was given $1\frac{1}{2}$ ounces of whisky and told to swallow it directly or briefly smell it first and then swallow it. If the administration of whisky was properly timed, emesis occurred less than 30 seconds after the ingestion of whisky.' It is obvious that Wallerstein considers the act of vomiting as the conditioned response and that the conditioned stimulus, the whisky, is administered a few seconds after the onset of nausea. This, however, is quite different from the approach of Voegtlin, where the onset of nausea is regarded as the conditioned response, and the conditioned stimulus administered just before the patient becomes nauseated. Thus Voegtlin would regard aversion therapy as an attempt to attach nausea and possibly vomiting to a stimulus, whereas Wallerstein takes the second and more variable stage only; it is well-known that vomiting is much less predictable than nausea and may not take place at all. Indeed, we might say that what Wallerstein tried to do was to induce what is sometimes called 'backward conditioning'; that is to say, he gave the unconditioned stimulus before the conditioned stimulus. In the laboratory, for instance, we might try to make the dog salivate by first giving him food and then sounding the bell; this kind of backward conditioning is known not to work. Wallerstein did the same thing by first inducing nausea, the desired response, and thereafter administering the alcohol. It is not surprising that under these conditions the experimental group was no better than the control group. However, this clearly does not demonstrate that Voegtlin's method is useless; it simply demonstrates that Wallerstein used a method of his own which, on theoretical grounds, one would have predicted not to work. The finding that it did not in fact work is of no great importance and merely substantiates the prediction made from general learning theory. Even so, it is rather interesting to find that what appeared to have been the more introverted patients did very much better in this type of therapy than did the extraverted ones, which we may interpret perhaps as indicating that the greater conditionability of the introvert may have benefited from the vestiges of proper conditioning inherent in this procedure better than did the unconditionable extraverts.

Wallerstein, unfortunately, is not the only one who has made the elementary error of using backward conditioning in relation to alcoholism. Many other therapists have made the same mistake, and others of equal gravity, probably because the principles of learning theory are not adequately taught or understood in medical schools. It will hardly be necessary to repeat that negative results of attempts to apply behaviour therapy are meaningless unless the methods used are properly derived from the principles of learning theory and are not such as to go directly counter to such principles. Evaluation of so-called 'failures' should always bear in mind the possibility that what was at fault was not the theory but rather the particular method used by a particular practitioner, who might not be as knowledgeable in this field as he ought to be.

How does aversion therapy strike the intelligent layman? An interesting reaction to a symposium on behaviour therapy was published recently in the correspondence columns of *Mensa*, the journal of a society which recruits its members entirely on the basis of their having a high score on intelligence tests. This is what Ivan Robinson, the writer of the letter, had to say. 'The first macabre illustration of aversion therapy came from Wolpe. He mentioned in passing the use on patients of a mixture of sixty per cent carbon dioxide and forty per cent air to produce a traumatic experience. It was a true throw-away line. From then on I listened with a growing but terrorized fascination.' (Carbon dioxide therapy is not intended to produce a traumatic experience of any kind, and is indeed, if anything, rather pleasant. Further emotional distortions of this kind will be found throughout this letter.)

Morgenstern detailed the use of apomorphine in treating transvestism. He sounded gloomy at being unable to control the erratic operation of the drug. Some patients vomited suddenly and unfairly, when donning conventional clothing at the end of the session. This tended merely to reinforce the original perversion. In other cases, so violent was the drug's effect that considerable and forceful persuasion was required to prevent patients from discontinuing treatment.

A cheering note was struck by Blakemore. He had discovered the electric grid. At the climax of their cross-dressing, patients standing on the grid received severe and unexpected shocks. They continued to experience shocks which diminished in strength in ratio to the rapidity with which the patients resumed socially acceptable garments. It appeared, however, that this treatment was insufficiently shattering. A Canadian was referred to. He injected patients with scoline, a curare derivative. This produced massive respiratory failure; there occurred a sensation of dying, or of death even. It was a highly satisfactory method.

The writer of the letter then describes how he discussed, with several other people, the details of aversion therapy. He commented on the deliberate use of therapeutic violence.

Did then the behaviour therapist advocate the savagery of planned thrashing to break children of bad habits? Analysis might pinpoint a patient's possible masochism but what safeguards existed against the flare-up of latent sadistic tendencies in the therapist? What of the patient who was subjected to treatment under the authority of a third party?

The reply was a reproachful duet. Children? Psychologists eschewed violence! And surely it was better for a patient to be an integrated personality within a conventional society... Above all, the behaviour therapist achieved in a matter of months what the psychoanalyst failed to over a period of years. It concluded with an intellectually admirable, but morally unconvincing defence which confirmed my suspicion that when the behaviour therapist walks into the treatment room, ethics fly out through the air-conditioning duct. Kill or cure, the end justifies the means. And that has been heard before, under grimmer circumstances, to the counterpoint of rubber truncheons twenty years ago.

The title of the letter, appropriately enough was, 'Behaviour Therapy and Knuckle Dusters'.

In the next issue, a reply was forthcoming by a behaviour therapist, who, being a medical practitioner, could not give his name. It ran as follows.

Because of the emotional colouring of the original writer's vocabulary, I had believed his letter to be a personal and beneficial catharsis or abreaction, rather than a serious criticism of behaviour therapy. However, even his piquant humour cannot alleviate the seriousness of his imputation of medical ethics, and I have been invited to comment on this.

His principal fear seems to be for the freedom of the individual. It should, therefore, be made quite clear that patients receive behaviour therapy only after having the nature of the treatment explained to them in detail, agreeing to receive the treatment, and signing a legal document to this effect. Neither the therapist nor any third party has authority to give such treatment without the consent of the patient, who is adequately protected against trespass to the person, under common and statute law in both the civil and criminal courts. Since the Legal Aid Act (1949) came into effect, the therapist has a healthy respect for the litigious potential of the N.H.S. patient.

The techniques of behaviour therapy are admittedly sometimes crude: so was surgery before the advent of anaesthetics. All methods require development and refinement; is one ethically entitled to eschew an effective treatment because it offends aesthetic susceptibilities? More revolting procedures will be found in medicine if they are looked for.

The patients, after all, are not complaining. Many of them go to considerable time, trouble, and expense to seek out a behaviour therapist; would your correspondent deny them the right to obtain the treatment of their choice? Apart from the hypothetical 'latent sadistic tendencies' he believes therapists to possess, the latter have no vested interest in the treatment. Mental hospitals are overcrowded and psychiatric waiting lists are already too long.

No one would be more pleased than the therapist if his patients refused treatment and returned home to cope with life in their own individual ways.

In its short life, behaviour therapy has proved itself to be a safe, swift, and effective treatment for many conditions which have proved resistant to protracted courses of alternative forms of therapy. Like all therapeutic methods, it will one day be replaced by something better; until then it will continue to be used on patients who want it and for whom the therapist believes it will be effective. Those of us who see happy and useful lives newly created out of misery and frustration will have little sympathy with some persons' misplaced concern for our future Sturm Abteilung.

This reply deals in an admirable fashion with the emotional misconceptions of the original critic, but it does not, of course, deal with the problem we noted before. The desire of the patient for treatment of a homosexual condition is likely to be due to social disapproval and social action. This may take the form of committal by the magistrate for treatment, with the alternative of going to prison, or it may take the form of an almost intolerable pressure on the part of parents and other relatives, friends, and so on, all of whom show the patient disapproval and hostility if he continues in his homosexual ways. Even if society were to change its laws and refuse to treat homosexual behaviour among consenting adults as a crime, nevertheless it is unlikely that social pressure would be very much less in many other ways, and it would still be a powerful force in making the homosexual prefer to come for treatment rather than continue on his deviant ways. We may feel that such pressure is unjustified and undemocratic but, on the other hand, we cannot deny the objectors their right to feel as they do and to react appropriately. We should not legislate against sin (if we agree to call homosexuality a sin), but, on the other hand, we cannot force other people to condone a sin and to treat it as if it had never happened. The same considerations, of course, apply in a rather lesser way to adultery. This also is treated as a crime in some countries; it is not treated as a crime in England, but it is regarded, by many people, as a sin. Each person must resolve the question in his own mind of whether he should regard it in this light, and he must be left to decide for himself whether he wishes to mix socially with adulterers and homosexuals or not. The resulting pressures may be regarded as unfair by the homosexual and the adulterer, but they constitute the matrix of social opinion in which we all live and which we cannot eradicate by any kind of legislative fiat, even if we should regard this as desirable.

The ultimate decision, therefore, must always be left to the sufferer. If he prefers to give up his old ways, to receive behaviour therapy, and to experience the changes which this method brings about in his personality, in his behaviour and his adjustment, then it does not seem right on *a priori* grounds to withhold the possibility of receiving this treatment from him. On the other hand, if he decides, after mature reflection and a full understanding of what is implied, that he would rather stay as he was and not be treated in this manner, then it would certainly be completely unjustified and unethical to force this type of treatment – or, indeed, any other type of treatment – upon him. As far as children are concerned, there is, of course, the additional problem that they are not in a proper state to give or withhold consent, because they are too young to understand the consequences of their actions or of their words. Fortunately, the problem is not as insoluble as it may appear at first. Behaviour therapy in children, in the vast majority of cases, implies disorders of the first kind and, therefore, a simple process of desensitization, against which surely no complaint can be made on any grounds. (Even with adults there are at least a hundred cases of behaviour disturbances of the first kind which are being treated by behaviour therapy, as against one case of disorders of the second kind. This proportion should always be borne in mind by those who criticize behaviour therapy as a form of brainwashing.) Children, precisely because they are not mature physically, do not show fetishistic, transvestite, or homosexual impulses, and, therefore, the question of aversion therapy for them does not arise. The only possible exception is enuresis, and there, of course, no degree of suffering is in fact involved, unless we call being woken up in the middle of the night by the ringing of the bell a severe punishment; it is certainly a kind of punishment to which most adults have to submit if they want to catch the early morning train to the office!

The reader may still be left with some niggling doubts on these ethical questions; there would be little point in trying to resolve these here. In a later chapter we shall again encounter this whole question of social values, brain-washing, therapy, and the various social and ethical implications of these methods in connexion with our discussion of crime; the reader must make up his own mind on these questions.

6   Accidents and Personality

During the war I was working at an emergency neurosis hospital for the armed forces and was concerned, among other things, with research into personality correlates of body build. Some of the results of this are discussed elsewhere in this book. We found that it is possible to look upon body build, in a rough-and-ready way, as a kind of rectangle, in which the ratio of height to width gives a notion of the type of body build, and the product of height and width gives an idea of the total size of the body we are considering. It was also found, however, that this simple formula did not work too well with women, for the obvious reason that they seemed to protrude both fore and aft from the simple rectangular framework; clearly, a much more complex formula was needed and it was decided that we needed a greater amount of knowledge of the female form than we possessed.

We obtained some help from nurses and other casual collaborators, but we decided that it might be more parsimonious to go and watch some burlesque shows in which we could, in the course of one evening, observe large numbers of female bodies, without any of the difficulties normally attending such inquisitiveness. Whilst undergoing this rigorous form of self-discipline, my friends and I remembered the old saying that you could always tell a psychologist from other people because he was the one who, at a burlesque show, watched the audience rather than the stage. From my knowledge of psychologists and psychiatrists, this had never seemed a very likely hypothesis, but, in glancing round the audience, I did notice one thing which seemed to me rather interesting; that was that the audience was made up almost entirely of men. This, of course, is not an original finding, but I decided to

make an actual count on each occasion of the number of
women present, and later I decided to plot these on a sheet
of graph paper. I noted that the resulting distribution was
very far from the normal bell-shaped type of distribution
which one usually gets in relation to biological phenomena,
and I also noticed that the distribution had certain rather
interesting statistical properties. With the help of several
friends, I collected a much larger number of cases, always
plotting the number of women present at a given show,
until finally I ended up with a diagram showing the
results of several hundred such observations. The resulting
curve was clearly J-shaped; that is to say, on the largest
number of performances there were no women present at
all. On a rather smaller number, there was one woman
present. On a much smaller number there were two women
present, and so on, constantly decreasing in number.

Having collected sufficient information for my purpose,
I then turned to the largest textbook on statistics I could
find, in order to see how I could set about turning my ideas
into proper statistical formulae. Alas, the first thing I found
was a diagram looking exactly like the one I had produced,
depicting not the number of women present at burlesque
performances but the number of soldiers killed by horse
kicks in certain Prussian army units during the years 1875
to 1894. This was given as an illustration of a very famous
distribution, the so-called Poisson distribution, which had
long ago been derived by a French statistician from certain
theoretical assumptions: to wit, that if a group is homo-
geneous with respect to both personal and external factors,
and if it has been exposed to the risk of accident for a given
period of time, then the plot of these accidents would give a
J-shaped distribution rather like the one I had observed.
This aroused my interest in the Poisson distribution and
also in the study of accidents, to which it has been most
frequently applied. This chapter is one result of the interest
aroused in those far-off days.

There are, of course, better reasons for studying accidents
than this odd display of ignorance. Accidents take a
tremendous toll in all civilized countries. In Great Britain,

for example, 19,000 people died and 200,000 received serious injuries as a result of accidents in 1958, which is the latest year for which full figures are available. This means that accidents kill twice as many people each year as do infectious diseases. Most people, of course, are familiar with the large number of those dying in road accidents, which accounted for 6,000 deaths, but these were easily outnumbered by accidents in the home, which killed 8,000; in addition to these, we have industrial accidents in which 1,200 people were killed. It is estimated that in this country someone is killed or injured in road accidents approximately every ninety seconds throughout the year. Over a third of a million people were killed or injured in road accidents in 1962, and in the same year almost two children were killed every day of the year. During the Second World War, 244,723 servicemen were killed; on the roads of Britain since the beginning of this century, 275,000 have died.

In the United States accidents are the biggest cause of death from birth to middle age, and even in people over seventy years of age they still constitute the fifth most frequent cause of death. The number of deaths and injuries caused by traffic accidents during the Second World War was more than three times as large as the number of war casualties! (Traffic deaths and injuries totalled 3.4 million, while the total number of war casualties was 0.95 million.) Figures such as these far outstrip those for most of the killer diseases of which we are afraid and for the investigation of which we spend a great deal of money. As Professor G. C. Drew, in his presidential address to the British Psychological Society pointed out recently: 'The discrepancy between the research money invested, the prestige attaching to research workers, public alarm at any temporary failure in control of poliomyelitis, for example, and of accidents, is a problem worthy of attention in itself.' (The number of people who died from poliomyelitis in England and Wales in 1958, for instance, amounted to 129!)

Many accidents, of course, are in part due to poor roads, poor lighting, bad weather, mechanical failures, and so forth. As Drew pointed out in the address mentioned above, 'The railways were fortunate in that at the opening of the Manchester and Liverpool Railway in 1830, they managed to run over and kill a former President of the Board of Trade just after he had declared the line open. This resulted in the segregation of rail from other traffic. Perhaps if an early motor car had been fortunate enough to "bag" a Prime Minister, we might now take motorways for granted.' However, while changes of this type might reduce the total incidence of accidents, it has usually been found that the proportion of accidents due to human failures of a psychological kind remains pretty constant, between 80 and 90 per cent. In other words, the vast majority of accidents are caused by human beings, and one would expect that psychology should be able to make some contribution to this problem.

What sort of a contribution can we expect? Perhaps the most consistent efforts of psychologists have been devoted to an attempt to give scientific backing to a commonsense notion which most people accept almost without thinking: that is, the notion of accident proneness. We, almost naturally, believe that some people are more likely to have accidents than others; they may be careless, slow, stupid, clumsy, or handicapped in some way or other, that predisposes them to have accidents. This popular belief is often backed by quoting evidence such as, for instance, that 4 per cent of all drivers are responsible for 36 per cent of all accidents, the assumption being that this 4 per cent are the accident-prone. The assumptions on which such an argument is based, however, are not statistically sound. Let us suppose that we are dealing with a thousand people working in a factory under identical conditions, and that the work they are doing exposes them to certain risks. Let us further suppose that these thousand people are all identical twins; in other words, they all are exactly alike in every possible way. Now we cannot assume that, under these conditions, the accidents will be spread out exactly uniformly among these identical twins. The distribution of accidents will, in fact, resemble the Poisson curve; that is to say, it will look rather

J-shaped, with the largest number having no accidents and a very small number having a relatively large number of accidents. Why should this be so? The answer is that the popular notion involves an untrue assumption which is identical with that involved in the old saying that lightning never strikes twice in the same place. Once lightning has struck in a particular place there is no reason why it should not strike there again; the fact of one accident does not make another accident less likely. Lightning is indeed unlikely to strike the same place twice, but only in so far as lightning is a very rare occurrence and the probability of its striking any particular place is very small. This probability does not become any smaller because lightning has struck before. The accidents are, from the causal point of view, quite independent. In the same way, the fact that red has come up on the Monte Carlo roulette wheel for thirty times running does not make it any less likely for it to come up on the next round. The next round is causally quite independent of all the previous ones, and the laws of probability apply to it in the same way as if the previous runs had all been black or had been half black and half red. What happened before simply makes no difference at all to the coming event. In the same way, the fact that Smith has had one accident does not make him any less likely to have the next accident, and thus reduces the probability that the distribution of accidents would be perfectly even over the whole group.

Strictly speaking, what I have said just now is not perfectly true. If we look at the lightning which strikes a particular place and consider that there must have been some particular physical cause for the lightning's striking that particular place – such as, for instance, that the object struck was rather isolated and standing out from the rest of the landscape, thus producing a particular concentration of negative electricity at a lesser distance from the cloud than the rest of the landscape – then I think that we must conclude that this place is rather more likely to be struck again on a second occasion than any other place, simply because the physical configuration which produced the first stroke of lightning would still remain the same. Similarly, with respect to people having accidents. An accident might have certain consequences upon the behaviour of the person; thus it might make him more cautious and careful and thus decrease the probability of further accidents, or it might make him more fearful and worried, thus increasing the probability of further accidents. In any case, of course, the problem of having accidents would have to be seen against the fact that people become more used to a particular type of work and, through experience, learning, etc., become more adaptive and probably have a lower rate of accidents altogether. There is a good deal of evidence for the general lowering of accident rates with age and experience, but there is no evidence that having had an accident makes one more cautious and less likely to have another one afterwards. Nor is there very much evidence for the alternative hypothesis that having had an accident makes one more likely to have another later on as the result of fear, anxiety, or worry induced by the original accident.

This leaves us strictly with two main alternative hypotheses. One is that all men, as it were, start out equal and that accidents happen strictly at random. The other alternative is that, from the beginning, some people are predisposed to suffer accidents and will, therefore, in due course accumulate a larger number of these accidents than other people who are not so predisposed. On the first of these hypotheses we will get a distribution of accidents which is identical with the Poisson curve. On the second hypothesis we will get a departure, more or less striking, from the Poisson curve. The degree of departure will depend on the importance of accident proneness in the total situation; where chance plays a large part, accident proneness a relatively small one, the departure will be relatively minor; where accident proneness plays a large part and chance only a small one, the departure will be considerable. Thus statisticians have used the Poisson distribution as a measure, as it were, of the presence or absence of accident proneness in a particular situation.

Some fifty years ago, Greenwood and Woods carried out

an examination of accidents happening to women munition workers who were engaged in manufacturing shells. The Table below shows the actual number of accidents per individual, between the dates of 13 February 1918 and

Number of accidents per individual	Number of individuals having given number of accidents	Chance (Poisson)	Accident proneness
0	447	406	442
1	132	189	140
2	42	45	45
3	21	7	14
4	3	1	5
5	2	0	2
Total	648	648	648

Number of accidents suffered by women working on six-inch high-explosive shells in 1918 together with figures showing expected numbers of accidents on the basis of a chance hypothesis (Poisson distribution) and of accident proneness. (From M. Greenwood and H. M. Woods, *Industrial Fatigue Research Board Report*, No. 4.)

20 March 1918, the number of individuals having a given number of accidents, and the number of individuals who should have had a given number of accidents according to chance (Poisson distribution), or according to the hypothesis of accident proneness. It will be seen that the accident proneness figures fit the situation very much better than does the Poisson curve.

There has been an enormous amount of work using this type of approach. The results have not, on the whole, been terribly impressive. Many people have found great deviations from the Poisson type of distribution, while many others have found that the Poissonian distribution fitted their data quite well. There has been a good deal of academic skirmishing and in-fighting regarding the interpretation of all these data, each side proving to its satisfaction that there was, or was not, a certain amount of evidence for the concept of accident proneness. These arguments are not very enlightening. The fact that investigator A, studying a particular type of worker carrying out a particular type of activity, finds a particular type of distribution of accidents over a certain range of times, while investigator B, studying quite different people doing quite different things over quite a different range of times, fails to get similar data obviously proves nothing other than that these two people studied different groups working under different conditions. To imagine that the results of the one contradict the results of the other is like saying that because I like cheese and you like strawberries, it means that we disagree on some objective fact. Yet obviously we both agree on the facts, which are that I like cheese and you like strawberries!

The sad truth, of course, is that this statistical method, while very elegant, is quite inappropriate to the study of accident proneness. Departures from a Poissonian distribution are often assumed to be due to accident proneness, but such a conclusion does not by any means follow. Let us return to our thousand uniovular twins working away at their machines. Let us assume that we have observed a very significant departure in their accident rates from a Poissonian distribution; is that necessarily due to differences in accident proneness? By no means; it might just as well be due to the fact that the machines they are working on are not equally well adjusted, so that some in fact represent a much greater safety hazard than do others. This might be due to the fact that some machines are older, others are newer, or that they are serviced in different ways and by different people, or to any of a large number of different causes. Similarly, if we find that some taxi drivers have more accidents than others, in excess of what would be permitted by the Poissonian distribution, this might indeed be due to differences in accident proneness, but it might also be due to differences in the age of their cars, to differences in the parts of the town to which their journeys take them, to differences in the number of hours which they drive, or the times of day during which they are driving, according to the roster put up by the owners of the company, or to any of a million different causes. Thus, a statistical examination of accidents cannot give us any very good evidence about accident proneness, and the main reason why this is so is simply that it is completely non-specific. Science, in general, works along the lines of the hypothetico-deductive method; in other words, we put forward a specific hypothesis, then collect some evidence for or against this hypothesis, and finally, either throw it overboard, or improve it, or accept it as being provisionally in accordance with the facts. No such precise, detailed, and psychological hypothesis is being examined by looking at overall distributions of the kind dealt with by the statisticians and, consequently, we cannot expect any very sensible answer to what is not a very sensible question. Let us try again, therefore, and start this time from a more psychological consideration of the possible factors in the situation.

There are two main ways in which the psychologist approaches this problem experimentally. In the first place, he may take two groups, one made up of people who have had many accidents, the other made up of people who have had few accidents, care being taken, of course, that both groups have had pretty much the same exposure, and are similar in other ways. The psychologist will then formulate hypotheses regarding the causes of accident proneness in the one group and its lack in the other, and he will then incorporate these hypotheses in the form of a variety of tests, making up a battery which is administered to the two groups. If the hypotheses are correct, then the two groups will be sharply differentiated in their responses to the various tests in the battery.

The other method, which is sometimes combined with the first, is a selection method. A psychologist formulates his hypothesis about the likely personality attributes of accident-prone people, constructs tests to measure these attributes, and then selects applicants for the particular job in question in line with their performance on the tests, rejecting those who do poorly and accepting those who do well. If his hypotheses are correct, then there should be a decided decrease in the number of accidents experienced by the people he has selected compared with unselected groups. Sometimes the selection tests will be given and applicants accepted, regardless of their scores, so that it is possible to follow up people who do well and people who do poorly in their later work, to see whether in fact those who score well have fewer accidents than those who score poorly. In many cases there is a three-stage process. In the first stage, we have the method we described first of all, in which people having many and having few accidents are compared with respect to a battery of tests; those which distinguish successfully between the groups are retained and others are thrown out. The second stage, then, is one in which the remaining tests are applied to candidates for the job, all of whom are accepted and all of whom are then followed up, to see whether the tests do in fact give correct predictions about their accident proneness. Having found out which tests do this most successfully, these are again retained and the remainder dropped. Now the third stage is approached, in which the psychologist actually uses the remaining tests for the purpose of selection, rejecting the less successful and accepting those who do well on the tests.

This psychological approach is obviously much more relevant than is the purely statistical one, because, in the first place, we have quite specific hypotheses regarding the personality traits of accident-prone and non-accident-prone people; in the second place, we can incorporate these hypotheses in a proper experimental design; and, in the third place, we have a clear-cut decision as to the accuracy or falsity of our hypotheses in the follow-up figures which we obtain from our study. What are the results of experiments of this kind?

Our first example is a study conducted by L. Shaw and H. S. Sichel into accidents among bus drivers in South Africa. The work was carried out in Johannesburg and Pretoria, two cities which have the unenviable record of having among the highest accident rates in the Western world; the death rate per vehicle registered in Johannesburg is four times that of New York! A ten-year period was selected for investigation, from 1951 to 1960, and covering an analysis of the accident records of 898 bus drivers. During this period 30,452 accidents had been reported, although many of them, of course, were quite trivial.

In order to characterize the driving ability of each driver, Shaw and Sichel made use of a new statistic, namely the average time interval between accidents. This they found to be very constant indeed for individual drivers, thus giving them an excellent method of classification, which retained its reliability over many years. They found that, for new drivers, there was a definite learning period, as one might indeed have expected, but that after a year or so their accident rate settled down to a fairly steady figure, as expressed in terms of the number of days elapsing between accidents. It was found that fully 90 per cent of the drivers displayed accident patterns which were so consistent in themselves that, on the basis of a man's past history, it was possible to predict what his future record would be like. For the remaining 10 per cent most of the changes in accident pattern had occurred because of some definite explainable circumstances. There was, in addition, a small percentage of drivers whose driving showed no particular pattern and which fluctuated in a manner which made prediction of future behaviour difficult, if not impossible. It was found that the very fact that these people did fluctuate meant that they were not good risks; in many cases it was found that these men were heavy drinkers. It was also found that major, or serious accidents occurred mostly in the records of drivers with the short-time intervals, even where these were based, in the first place, on relatively minor accidents. Over a period of six years, during which time only 20 per cent of the drivers displayed patterns of short-time intervals, 60 per cent of the serious accidents – that is to say, accidents which were due to recklessness and dangerous driving – were caused by drivers in this category. Shaw and Sichel concluded, 'The most significant aspect of the whole investigation was the proof it provided of the individuality of each driver's accident liability, and of the fact that this liability was so consistent that it was possible to predict what sort of an accident risk a man was likely to be in the future on the basis of his past behaviour.'

Practical steps were taken by the company to make use of this information. Drivers with poor records, according to this system, were dismissed and new drivers were taken on after a special psychological selection procedure making use of a variety of psychological personality tests. The results were fairly dramatic. In the Johannesburg area alone, where greater traffic density has been accompanied by an increase of 25 per cent in the accident rate of the motoring public over the last eight years, the company's accident rate was shown to decrease by 38 per cent. Figure 20 below shows the trend of accidents for the company drivers over an eight-year period. It will be seen that there is a constant decrease from a mean accident rate of about $2\frac{1}{2}$ down to almost 1. The only break in this sequence will be seen to have occurred between 1956 and 1957, when a boycott of buses was declared by the native population; this increased the general emotional temperature in the cities concerned so much that there was an upswing in the number of accidents, which is faithfully mirrored by the graph. However, after one year the accident rate returned to the fairly regular downward sweep which is indicated in the graph, and has now continued to an all-time low. This investigation is of particular interest because it has succeeded in establishing two facts. In the first place, it has established that accident liability is a very reliable feature of the individual, ranging from very high to very low over quite lengthy periods of time. This discovery, of course, was only possible because of the conditions under which the investigation was carried out; that is to say, there was a complete and accurate recording of all accidents, however minor, and there was a complete and accurate knowledge of the exact number of miles driven by each driver and the precise neighbourhood in which the driving was carried out. In this way it was possible to correct for differences in exposure to traffic and various other factors, which are relevant to the number of accidents which a person might suffer.

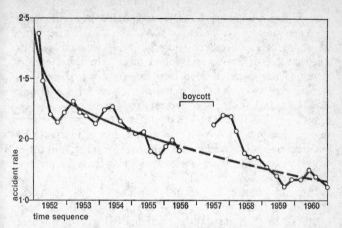

Figure 20. This diagram shows a decline in the accident rate among bus drivers in South Africa as a proper scheme of selection is being brought into operation. Note the regularity of the drop, as indicated by the curved line; this is upset during the 1956–7 period by the well-known boycott of buses by the native population, which produced a considerable emotional disturbance and led to an increase in the number of accidents. As will be seen, however, the rate has returned to its regular decline by the end of 1958 (from an article by L. Shaw and N. S. Sichel).

The other important finding of this investigation was that it is possible, by a suitable process of elimination and testing, to reduce the number of accidents suffered by the company's employees by a very substantial margin. There is no doubt that improvements can still be made, but the level of accidents is now so low that one must expect progress to be very much more difficult and very much slower than it has been in the past. Altogether, the data reported by Shaw and Sichel firmly support the notion of accident proneness, i.e. of some people being much more likely than others to suffer accidents of a certain type.

The notion that the probability that an individual will experience an accident can be determined from the number which he has already sustained is not, of course, a new one. It is sometimes called 'the law of recurrence', or 'Marbe's Law' – after the German psychologist, K. Marbe, who carried out a whole series of investigations on accidents in the early nineteen twenties. In one of these studies he made a record of the accidents suffered by 3,000 active commissioned and non-commissioned officers in the German Army. These were divided into three groups: those who during five years had no accidents; those who had one accident; and those who had multiple accidents. Marbe found that those in the no accident group had 0.52 accidents in a subsequent five-year period. Those who had one accident had 0.91 accidents in the next five years, and those who had multiple accidents had 1.34 accidents during the second five-year period. There is, thus, considerable consistency in the accident records of these officers. He compared the predictive accuracy of his findings with a system adopted by the insurance company with which these officers had been insured. The company, as is usually done by companies of this type, varied the insurance rate according to the risk of the particular occupation the person was engaged in. Marbe found that while it was true that accident rates varied somewhat according to the risk of the occupation, this variability was much less and was much less predictable than that due to personal factors of accident proneness, as shown over the two five-year periods he studied. Marbe, therefore, questioned the ordinary classification according to risk, which is adopted by most insurance companies, and pointed to the importance of a supplementary classification by susceptibility as a basis for a graded scale of insurance rates. He was also one of the first to point out the significance of differences in accident proneness for vocational selection. He stressed the importance of not only selecting workers with respect to their capacity for the job, but suggested that, in addition, considerable attention should be paid to accident susceptibility in the task, as an aid in reducing the mounting cost of accidents to industry.

Marbe's Law was also verified in a recent report by Sauli Häkkinen, a Finnish investigator who studied the accident proneness of tram and bus drivers. He found that they, too, showed the tendency noted above of having fairly constant accident records over the years, some having many, some having few accidents in given periods of time. In addition, he applied a very large battery of psychological tests to these subjects, demonstrating that those with many accidents differed considerably from those with few accidents. Curiously enough, the differences were very similar for both tram and bus drivers, in spite of the rather different nature of the tasks which these two groups of people have to perform, suggesting that the accident proneness of a person is more fundamental than the highly specific duties which he may be called upon to undertake. Having established a successful battery for the discrimination of accident-prone and non-accident-prone drivers, Häkkinen was asked to apply this to new intakes, and showed that the battery was very useful indeed in predicting future performance by these new recruits.

What types of test, therefore, have been used in this sort of investigation, and how do they relate to accident proneness? Let us start with measures of intelligence, mechanical aptitude, and various other abilities. By and large, intelligence does not have very much to do with accident proneness. Usually, the more intelligent are very slightly less prone to accidents, but, from the point of view of prediction, the differences are so small as not to be worthy of consideration. The picture changes a little when we get to drivers considerably below the average in intelligence. When we get down to I.Q.s of 80 or thereabouts, we find a very marked increase in the number of accidents suffered by drivers with such low I.Q.s. Thus there may be good arguments for giving intelligence tests to applicant drivers, and making particularly sure that those with very low I.Q.s undergo a more stringent examination and test than those of average and above average intelligence. Unfortunately, investigators have usually left the problem at this point and have not tried to investigate further into the reasons why poor intelligence is accompanied by a bad accident record. It is by no means obvious why there should be such a relationship, and it would be most interesting to find out in what precise ways the dull differ from the average in respect to their patterns of behaviour. A hypothesis which is sometimes expressed is that perhaps mechanical aptitude might be the factor mediating the relationship between low ability and accidents, but this is hardly likely; tests of mechanical aptitude do not show any greater relationship with driving accidents, or industrial accidents, than do other tests of intelligence.

Other abilities which have often been tested might be thought, on theoretical grounds, to be more closely related to a tendency to have accidents. They include the ability to estimate speeds and distances. However, results on the whole have not been encouraging. There is little reason, apparently, to believe that people are accident prone because of an inability to estimate speeds and distances in laboratory situations; such mistakes as they make in the course of their driving or of their industrial performances must be due rather to personal attitudes and other judgemental features superimposed upon the sheer ability to discriminate between one speed and another, or to assess accurately distances.

Reaction times have frequently been measured for both accident-prone and safe drivers, and indeed, for the public at large, the measurement of reaction times may often appear to be the be-all and end-all of all psychological experimentation in this field. In actual fact, this is far from being true, particularly as the usual assumption that fast reaction times are a help in safe driving has not been verified on the whole. There are numerous investigations, all tending to show that the relationship between reaction times and the number of accidents suffered is practically non-existent. This may, at first sight, seem surprising, as one would expect that a person who can react quickly to a dangerous situation would be at an advantage, as compared with another one who was rather slower. There are many reasons why such an assumption would be unlikely to be true. In the first place, of course, the driver is seldom confronted with a situation such as that represented by the typical reaction-time experiment. In the experiment, a lamp suddenly lights up and he has to press a bell-push as quickly as he can in response to this signal. He knows exactly what is going to happen and what kind of response is required of him, and, therefore, the actual reaction time is minimal, of the nature of about a fifth of a second. On the other hand, he does not know the precise moment when the light will light up. In the traffic situation the position is usually exactly the opposite. There is no sudden emergency which cannot be foreseen with any degree of precision, as is the case with the lighting-up of the lamp; the good driver is likely to have anticipated future developments from a general survey of the situation and from his experience of driving in situations of this kind. He will notice children playing with a ball on the sidewalk, and anticipate the possibility of the ball rolling out into the street, with a child running after it. This ability to anticipate events is far more important than the sheer reaction time to the child's actually emerging into the road, and is much more likely to lead to an avoiding reaction than would the simple reaction time, like stepping on the brake once the child had run out into the road. There is no reason to imagine that anticipation and reaction time have any relationship at all, and while undoubtedly in some, usually quite rare, circumstances reaction times might be important, in the great majority of cases anticipation is a factor which is very much more closely related to safe driving.

Another point which also deserves attention is that reaction times must always be related to other factors, such, for instance, as the speed at which the car is being driven. It is quite likely that a person who knows his reactions to be quick will take greater risks, in the knowledge that he can react more quickly than other people. In doing so, he may overstep the safety margin provided by his quicker reactions and, in actual fact, be a less safe driver than the person who has slow reaction times, knows that he is slow, and drives fully within the limitations set by this particular disability. Driving is such a compound skill, set in a pattern of such complexity, that no simple-minded application of rules of thumb or reaction time experiments can be expected to be of very much use in predicting accident proneness.

The situation becomes a little better, although not very

much, when we turn to more complex reaction time experiments, requiring the subject to make discriminations. For instance, we might give him a set of five coloured lights and five coloured keys, the instructions being that he should press the appropriate key when a particular light lights up. His reaction then puts off the light and puts on a new one to which he must react again, and so on. There are many ways in which a typical reaction-time experiment can be complicated and it may indeed be made very similar to the ordinary driving situation by showing the subject a film taken from the driving seat of an actual car going through traffic, and requiring him to react to certain stimuli emerging on the film, such as a child running out from behind a car, and so on. Though tests of this type have greater 'face' validity, that is to say, although they look more like the kind of thing that may be predicted, in actual fact it is doubtful whether much reliance can be placed on results even of tests such as these.

Oddly enough, there is one measure taken from reaction-time experiments which does seem to have predictive validity, although at first sight one might not find it easy to see why this should be so. In going through a series of reaction-time tests, one's main interest is usually in the average speed of reaction. In addition, however, we may note the variability of reaction times. There is all the difference in the world between Mr Smith, whose reaction times on five successive occasions are 210, 195, 190, 200, 205 milliseconds, making up an average of 200 milliseconds, and Mrs Smith, whose times are 290, 200, 250, 110, 150 milliseconds, also having an average of 200 milliseconds. It will be seen that, while the means are the same, Mrs Smith is very much more variable than Mr Smith, her longest reaction time being 290 milliseconds as against his 210, and her shortest being 110 as against his 190. There is some evidence to show that greater variability of performance is related to greater accident proneness, and we shall see later why, on theoretical grounds, we would have expected this to be so. Even on commonsense grounds, however, one might perhaps find a clue to an explanation in the following consideration. If there are, in traffic, occasions when quick reactions are called for, then, of any two people having on the average equally quick reactions, those with the greater variability will be, on a larger number of occasions, in a state when they give relatively long reaction times and, under those conditions, they would be more likely to be involved in accidents. That this is only a clue to a true explanation and not the explanation itself will be suggested later on.

The next group of tests to be discussed are the so-called psychomotor ability tests. Tests of this kind involve the learning and control of various movements, in which different movement complexes have to be initiated in response to a specified series of stimuli. Such tests may make use of simple tapping tasks, or dotting tests in which the subject has to make dots with a pencil in a series of small circles on a roll of paper which is being drawn along over a series of rollers in front of him, or he may be asked to perform on the pursuit rotor we have described in the first chapter, or some other similar apparatus which requires the following of a target in some way or other, either with a stylus (as in the case of the pursuit rotor), or by the turning of steering wheels which move a stylus in various directions by being geared with these wheels. Such tests can become very complex indeed, as, for example, in the Link trainer which was used during the war to give practice to pilot candidates in flying. In this trainer, the whole process of flying was simulated by means of dials, rudders, controls, and so forth, and responses could be monitored very accurately. Thus tests of psychomotor ability constitute an enormously large class of tests, ranging from the simplest to the most complex. They are often further complicated by making use of additional stimuli, the purpose of which is to tap certain personality reactions such as frustration, concentration, and so on. Thus ability to concentrate may be measured by introducing distracting stimuli such as flashing lights, noises, verbal comments by the experimenter, and so on. Frustration may be measured by interfering in some way with the execution of the task without the knowledge of the subject, who suddenly finds that he is doing much worse than before. Once frustration has thus been induced, it is then possible to remove the disturbing stimuli again, also without the subject's knowledge, and see whether he regains his emotional balance quickly and gets back his original scoring rate, or whether the frustration rankles and interferes with his future performance. Obviously, the ingenuity of the experimenter is the only limitation to the number of variations which can be played on these themes.

It is tests of these types which have proved most diagnostic in relation to accident proneness, and it has been a fairly universal finding that the best predictors tend to be those tests which are most complex and complicated. It is not always easy to know which particular test would, in a particular situation, give the best results, but certain general trends have been discovered. Thus, it has been found that it is better to use tests the speed of which is controlled by the experimenter, rather than tests the speed of which is controlled by the subject himself. As an example, take a multiple reaction-time experiment, such as the one described before, in which coloured lights light up and the subject has to press an appropriate key, thus re-setting the apparatus and producing a new stimulus for himself. When this is done in the manner described, the test has little predictive accuracy, as we mentioned above. If now we change it in such a way that the lighting up of the lights is controlled by the experimenter, who can speed it up or slow it down, we find that the test becomes rather more discriminative and correlates with various criteria of accident proneness. The reason for this is probably that when the subject himself controls the speed of the test, he can make up for lost time by working a little more quickly later on; thus the variability in his performance, which as we saw before is such an important feature, is lost in the mean, and two people differing very much in variability may yet achieve the same mean performance. This, however, is impossible when the speed of the performance is controlled by the experimenter. If the subject has a long reaction time to a particular stimulus, he cannot make up for this by being particularly quick the next time; the opportunity has gone, never to return, because the experimenter has already put in the next stimulus before the long reaction takes place. Therefore an error is recorded. There are various other such rules which are well-known to psychologists working in this field, which can be used to put together a useful and valid battery of selection tests.

We have already mentioned the fact that psychomotor tests may often be used to measure personality features as well as the simple ability involved in carrying out the test. One specific example of this may illustrate precisely what is meant. There is a test of psychomotor ability which has been frequently used in which the subject has to move a pointer by turning a wheel right or left. The pointer has to be moved in the direction indicated by a lamp which lights up, either to the right or to the left of the subject, and the pointer has to be moved to a specified position indicated by a line. The situation can be complicated in various ways, such as, for instance, by lighting two lamps and requiring the subject to make the movement towards the brighter of the two, or by occasionally introducing a situation where two equally bright lamps light up on both sides and seeing what the subject will do under such conditions of conflict. In studies of accident rates, no consistent differences were found between people high and low in accident proneness when such ability variables were studied as response time, amplitude of responses, number of erroneous responses. On the other hand, when the graphic record was investigated according to the degree of 'organization' of activity, quite considerable correlations were found with accident proneness. The investigators assumed that what was concerned were certain over-emotional and neurotic tendencies in the individual which exerted impairing and paralysing influences on the performance of accident-prone individuals performing in stress situations.

Such indirect investigations of personality characteristics are of great interest and importance, particularly because they are very difficult, if not impossible, to fake. Another source of evidence, of course, comes from inventories and questionnaires, and many studies have been reported in which these have been given to accident-prone and safe groups of drivers and industrial employees. In one such study, B. J. Fine investigated the safety records of 993 male freshmen in the General College of the University of Minnesota. He divided his subjects into three groups on the basis of a personality questionnaire, extreme extraverts, introverts, and intermediates. He discovered that the extraverts had significantly more accidents and also were guilty of more traffic violations than were the other groups. A similar tendency for extraverts to be more likely to be involved in accidents was reported by S. Biesheuvel and M. E. White, who studied the human factor in flying accidents in South Africa. They discovered, in comparing an accident group and a non-accident group of pilots, that the accident-prone members were rather more emotional, panicked more easily, were significantly more extraverted, more easily stimulated and therefore more distractible, that they tended to act more on impulse and were generally less cautious, that their behaviour was more variable and they were apt to be influenced by the mood of the moment. Here, results are fairly typical of many other such investigations. They point up the great importance of extraverted personality patterns, and we will return to this point in our more general discussion of the causes of accidents.

Attitudes and interests are a part of personality which one might think would be obviously of relevance to accident proneness, and there is some evidence that this is indeed so. People with mechanical interests tend to have fewer accidents than people interested in persuasiveness, literary, and computational matters; and also there is some evidence that accident-prone people have less satisfactory attitudes towards problems of safety, of cooperativeness, and so forth, than do people who are not accident prone. Studies of this kind, of course, also suffer from the same defects as questionnaire studies, in that responses are easily fakeable and that one has to rely very much on the honesty and cooperation of the subjects, which may not always be forthcoming. On the whole, we can conclude this survey by saying that there are many different tests and measures which have been found to correlate with accident proneness, that there is a tendency for the more complex of these to give better predictions than the simpler ones, and that personality seems to be implicated as playing a stronger part perhaps than does ability. It may also be concluded that a battery of tests is better than a single test is likely to be, and that the particular relationship between test and accident proneness is very much subject to the precise nature of the task involved. We would not expect tests to be identical when we are trying to predict accident proneness in driving and when we are trying to predict accident proneness in coalmining, or some other industrial operation. Given the wide variety of circumstances, however, in which studies have been carried out, the great differences in populations studied, and the many difficulties under which research of this type labours, it is surprising that the results have been as promising as they have turned out to be. They certainly leave little doubt about the reality of the concept of accident proneness.

In saying this, however, we must realize that the term 'accident proneness' is often used in two different ways, and that it is important to distinguish between these. We may mean by accident proneness – and undoubtedly some people do use the term in this sense – that some people are innately predisposed to suffer accidents under almost any conditions and in relation to almost any type of task. Taken in this way, I think the term must almost certainly be rejected. It is highly unlikely that accidents are quite as generalized as this with respect to their causes, so that a person likely to have driving accidents is also likely to have accidents in respect to every other activity in which he may indulge. Let us take a hypothetical case and say that Johnnie has a high accident proneness for motor driving because he likes to show off to his girl friends, likes being in charge of a powerful vehicle which enables him to express his power drive by going very fast, and that his very competitive nature makes it very difficult for him not to indulge in private racing duels on the Queen's highway. Let us also assume that Johnnie is fond of mountain-climbing. Now, is there any reason to assume that he would be accident prone under those conditions also? Mountain-climbing is not, by and large, a competitive sport; Johnnie is little likely to be accompanied on these occasions by an adoring string of females for whose sake he might be willing to show off and undergo risks, and there is no way in which he can use mountain-climbing to express any power drive he may have, other than by getting safely to the top. Therefore Johnnie may be a perfectly safe climber, but a very dangerous person at the wheel of a motor-car. One must always look at the precise causes of a person's accident proneness in relation to a particular activity, before one can come to any reasonable conclusions, and, to the degree to which activities differ, to that degree will it be very unsafe to generalize.

We come, therefore, to a second conception of accident proneness which is rather more restricted. It says, simply, that for any given activity there are certain abilities, personality patterns and traits, interests, attitudes, and so forth, which are necessary for the safe performance of that task, and that, when these are missing to a greater or lesser extent in that person, then that person is more or less likely to suffer accidents in the pursuit of that activity. It is not suggested that a person who is accident prone, according to this definition, will inevitably suffer an accident because, again by definition, an accident is, in part, controllable and happens in a manner dictated, in part, by chance. Nevertheless, if an accident does occur it is more likely to occur to a person lacking in the requisite personality characteristics, abilities, and so on, and to the degree to which these play a part in the safe performance of the task, to that degree will this predetermination be measurable, be expressed in actual accidents, and be controllable by means of appropriate selection devices. The evidence is practically conclusive that this second meaning of the term expresses a psychological truth of very great importance. It is true, of course, that in this chapter we have laid stress on positive findings and successful investigations, and it is only fair to point out that some people have failed to get positive predictions and correlations between tests and performance, or tests and accident proneness. This fact, however, does not in any way contradict our main conclusion. Many of the investigations which have failed to produce positive results have been characterized by a poor choice of tests, a poor choice of problems, a poor choice of statistical methods of investigation, and a poor control over relevant variables. Clearly, under these conditions, failure was almost a foregone conclusion and does not detract from the positive results achieved under more satisfactory conditions. Consider, for instance, a well-known investigation in which the experimenter tried to substantiate certain Freudian theories about the unconscious determination of accidents. In other words, he tried to show that accidents occur because the person involved in the accident unconsciously wanted an accident to happen. As a measure of the hypothetical unconscious activity, he used a test which has been quite widely used in the United States, and which essentially consists of pictures of dogs, male and female; the subject looks at these pictures and then has to make up stories about them. One of the pictures, for instance, would be of a male dog looking in a rather old-fashioned way at the rear end of a bitch. Other pictures are supposed to produce material relating to family relations, and so forth. In addition to this test, the author also used the so-called Rorschach test, in which the subject's responses to various coloured and mono-chromatographic ink blots are interpreted. In the final analysis, people who had suffered accidents and those who had not were not differentiated in any way by these so-called tests. 'Experiments' such as this are difficult to discuss seriously; they recall Dr Johnson's comment on the plot of Cymbeline – that it is impossible to criticize unresisting imbecility. Their failure can certainly not be used as an argument against the possibility of discovering differences in personality between the accident-prone and those who are not given to accidents.

If, as the evidence seems to suggest pretty conclusively, accident proneness is related to personality traits more closely than it is to abilities, then we should be able to specify with some degree of accuracy the kind of personality patterns expected on theoretical grounds from the accident-prone person, and also the kind of pattern actually observed. We might start out by noting that the kind of behaviour in a motorist which gives rise to accidents can also be the kind of behaviour which is punishable by law. It is not often realized how very large is the number of offences committed by motorists in this country. In 1962, prosecutions of motorists neared the million mark, and of the 989,812 prosecutions, convictions in magistrates' courts totalled 953,600. In addition to these offences, we have about 203,246 parking offences. All in all, motoring cases now account for almost 60 per cent of all offences dealt with by the courts. Figures like these are often brushed aside by people who declare that traffic offences are in an entirely different category from ordinary ways of breaking the law, and that they should not be confused in any way with serious offences like larceny, robbery with violence, murder, and so on.

The actual facts do not bear out such an easy division between what are often considered working-class and middle-class offences. W. A. Tillman and G. E. Hobbs, in Canada, compared groups of accident repeaters with two groups of accident-free drivers. They found that of the accident repeaters, 34 per cent had been before adult courts, whereas only 1 per cent of the accident-free groups had been before courts. Of the repeaters, 17 per cent had been before juvenile courts; of the accident-free groups, only 1.2 per cent, 18 per cent and 1 per cent, respectively, of these two groups were known to social-service agencies, and 14 per cent and 0 per cent, respectively, were known to venereal disease clinics. In this country, Dr Terence Willett studied the criminal records of 653 traffic offenders who appeared in court charged with one or more of the following offences: causing death by dangerous driving, driving recklessly or dangerously, driving under the influence of drink or drugs, driving while disqualified, failing to insure against third-party risks, or failing to stop after or to report an accident. It turned out that over one-fifth of the 653 drivers had criminal records for non-motoring offences. Another sixty individuals had no criminal record, but were 'known to the police' as notorious or suspected persons. On the whole, therefore, about one-third of the total were far from being 'respectable citizens', but had some form of criminal record. Compared to usually accepted estimates of criminality in Britain, the criminal proportion in this sample of drivers who had been charged with driving offences, was about three times as large.

Willett also found that a further 24 per cent of the offenders had previous convictions for motoring offences, making a total of 307 out of 653 who had had previous convictions of some kind. When a further analysis was made of the 151 individuals whose records included convictions for non-motoring offences, it was found that they collectively were responsible for 549 different motoring offences and 610 non-motoring offences, of which only about thirteen could be called trivial. Two-thirds of this group had in fact previously been convicted three or more times. Four out of the five people charged with causing death by dangerous driving had criminal records, as did 78 per cent of those charged with driving while disqualified.

These findings have been duplicated in America and on the Continent, and there can be very little doubt that the usual picture of the driver involved in a traffic accident as being the innocent, accidental victim of chance and circumstance is simply not true. The person who breaks the ordinary laws of society also tends to be the person who breaks traffic laws, particularly when such infringement is considered very serious and likely to lead to grave consequences. We would thus be led to believe that our typical accident-prone driver would be likely to be found in the same quadrant of our personality diagram as were criminals of other kinds, and this is indeed true. We have already noted several studies in which accident-prone drivers and others appear as being strongly extraverted, or in which there is some suspicion of a neurotic or emotional component. Furthermore, the traits which have been discovered in accident-prone people all tend to fall into the same quadrant. Carelessness, aggressiveness, impatience of authority, emotionality, distractibility, impulsiveness, lack of caution, variability, liability to be influenced by the mood of the moment – all these are psychopathic, hysteric, or choleric traits, if you like, and the literature is remarkably unanimous in attributing them to traffic offenders, accident-prone drivers, and indeed people having accidents in industrial and other conditions as well. We must, therefore, conclude that there is considerable evidence to suggest that certain personality patterns go with accident proneness and that these personality patterns are remarkably similar to those exhibited by criminals. Tillman and Hobbs concluded from their study that, 'A man drives as he lives,' and although this is perhaps too epigrammatic a way of expressing the facts, it nevertheless suggests some very important conclusions. Experimental studies in the laboratory suggest that this saying may be extended to read that, 'A man reacts to laboratory situations in the way that he lives;' that is to say, his personality expresses itself as much in the laboratory situation as in driving, and in driving as much as in other situations. Indeed, the very notion of personality would imply something of this kind, because personality, if it means anything at all, means the relatively permanent, firmly-set patterns of behaviour, habits, and tendencies which a person has developed throughout his life, on the basis of his heredity and in response to the rewards and punishments which he has received throughout his life. There is every reason to suspect that these patterns will pervade all his activities and not be restricted just to a few.

Superimposed on the general personality factors, of course, are many others, such as those of age and sex. In heavily industrialized countries at least, there is a very familiar pattern relating accidents to age. For males, deaths from road accidents show a sharp rise from birth to about five years of age, followed by a drop from five to ten; after that there is another steep rise, reaching a maximum at about eighteen, remaining high until the early thirties, and then dropping down to a moderate level by thirty-five or so.

From thirty-five to sixty and over, the rate remains fairly low, almost constant, only to rise again from sixty-five onwards rather steeply. Women deviate a little from this; they share the rise from naught to five and the fall from five to ten, but they show a less conspicuous rise thereafter. In part, this may reflect a lower exposure rate in women, but it has often been suggested that there is a real sex difference in socialization or conformity. This would agree rather well with the frequent finding that women tend to be less extraverted than men and that, therefore, they would be found less frequently in the criminal and accident-prone quadrant. It is well-known that the driving patterns of women are much more socialized and much less aggressive than those of men, but there is much other evidence to suggest that altogether they are perhaps more amenable to rules and regulations.

Drew, in the address referred to at the beginning of this chapter, recalls a road situation which had been studied by the Road Research Laboratory.

In planning the position of pedestrian crossings, they first plotted the position at which every person crossed certain stretches of road, over a period of some weeks. The distributions obtained were roughly rectilinear. A pedestrian crossing was then installed. The effect of this crossing was to draw all pedestrians towards it. Plotting the frequencies of crossings at different points on the road then gave a symmetrical, bell-shaped distribution, but the distribution for women was much steeper than that for men. That is, a higher proportion of women than of men crossed on the crossing, and, those who did not, were drawn nearer to it than were the men. Authority, in the shape of a policeman, was then stationed on the crossing, doing nothing but stand there. The effect was dramatic. Almost all men now conformed, and used the crossing, although they reverted to the no-policeman distribution as soon as he was removed. His presence, however, had absolutely no effect whatever on the behaviour of women. These observations were shown to be repeatable, but whether they are psychologically meaningful or not must wait until some psychologist becomes interested.

Training is another factor which cuts across personality features of one kind or another. There would be few accidents throughout the country if every driver had acquired the skill and competence of the average police driver. It is well known that the accident rate of the London Metropolitan Police fleet is very low compared with the general accident rate. Even at this level, however, improvements are possible through further training, and the accident rate of the fleet as a whole was between $2\frac{1}{2}$ and 3 times that of the Hendon Police Driving School, who may be regarded as the best-trained group of drivers in the country. Similarly, surveys made in the U.S.A. and on the Continent have shown that drivers not trained at school have two or more times as many accidents as those who have been so trained. To take but one example: the traffic histories of 1,100 drivers in the State of Delaware, who had taken formal training, were compared with those of the same number of drivers who had not received such training. The records of the untrained drivers showed almost five times as many arrests for serious traffic offences, four times the number of accidents, and three times the number of police warnings as did those of the trained drivers. Other studies have reported a much smaller incidence of traffic accidents among drivers who were trained at school – that is to say, when they were very young – as compared with drivers not so trained. These results, of course, do no more than confirm common sense. Driving is a skill, and skills tend to be acquired very much better under conditions of proper training than when they are 'picked up' as it were as a person goes along. It seems almost incredible that the actual training in this very difficult and complex skill should still be left to the haphazard administrations of people, many of whom have never been trained themselves. There is little doubt that a great contribution could be made to the reduction of traffic accidents if proper systems of training were introduced for all drivers, and if reliance was not placed exclusively on a very short and not very comprehensive test.

But however important these factors of age, sex, training, and so forth may be, we are always led back again to the personality of the offender. After all, it is the psychopathic type of person who would benefit most from training but who is least likely to accept it or to pay attention to it when he gets it. There is, however, one factor which has been much studied and which is very relevant in this connexion, primarily because it has the highly disadvantageous corollary of making people more extraverted. This is alcohol.* We have already seen, in earlier chapters, how stimulant drugs make people more introverted, while depressant drugs make them more extraverted. Of all the drugs which are consumed nowadays, perhaps none is as widespread and as dangerous in its effect as is alcohol, and as its effects mirror those of extreme extraversion, we would expect to find that drink is a very powerful factor indeed in the causation of accidents. An examination of the evidence leaves very little doubt that this is indeed so.

Now, to most people it is natural to talk about alcohol in the context of just what has been consumed: three pints of beer, or two double whiskies, or whatever it might be. However, what matters from the point of view of behaviour is the amount of alcohol the subject has in his blood, regardless of what he has had to drink, although, of course, the former is to some extent a function of the latter. The relationship, however, is so complex that it would be very difficult to estimate the one from the other in any individual case. Concentrations of alcohol in the blood are usually expressed as the weight of alcohol in a given volume of blood, or, more precisely, as mg. per 100 ml., or mg. per cent. This gives us a scale, and the most important points to note are perhaps the 50, 100, and 150 mg. per cent; 400–500 mg. per cent is a fatal level for about nine people out of ten. Fifty mg. per cent would be the sort of concentration you might find if a man of about eleven stone drank six single whiskies, or three pints of beer, in a relatively short time, an hour or two after an average meal. To reach 150 mg. per cent, he would need twelve to fourteen single whiskies, or about a gallon of beer. These figures may sound too high to be of any practical importance, but H. J. Walls has shown that the average blood-alcohol

*The reader may be familiar with the definition of conscience as that which is soluble in alcohol!

concentration of those alleged by the police to be 'under the influence' is 220 mg. per cent, and he found that with an even higher blood-alcohol level of 300 mg. per cent, three out of twenty-three drivers were in fact acquitted.

Literally thousands of experiments have been done in the laboratory to detect the effects of alcohol on performance. There is no doubt that deterioration is shown even with quite low concentrations of blood-alcohol, and that deterioration increases as concentration increases. Simple responses, like ordinary reaction times and sensory thresholds, are little affected by small doses of alcohol and thus show a threshold effect, but more complex skills do not show any such threshold; deterioration there occurs even with the slightest doses of alcohol. Of particular importance in relation to driving is the very interesting work by G. C. Drew, who made use of a simulated driving task. Reactions on this test seem very closely related to those made in actual driving conditions, and the deteriorating effect of alcohol even in quite small amounts was demonstrated quite dramatically.

When we leave the laboratory we find that the severity of accidents tends to increase with increasing blood-alcohol. While alcohol is involved only in some five per cent of all accidents, high blood-alcohol is found in fifty per cent or more of fatal accidents. In fatal accidents involving only one vehicle, the proportion goes up to nearly ninety per cent. One American study, using United States Air Force personnel, compared blood-alcohol concentrations of drivers involved in accidents, and control drivers drawn from the same place, at the same time, and so forth. It was shown that whereas only five per cent of the control group had had two drinks or more, the corresponding percentage in the accident group was sixty-four per cent. Ninety per cent of these had had three or more drinks, and sixty per cent six or more. Other investigations have shown that seventy-three per cent of the group held responsible for accidents in which they were involved had been drinking, while only twenty-six per cent of a control group had. Of the accident group, forty-six per cent had blood-alcohol concentrations of 250 mg. per cent or more; none of the control group came anywhere near this level. In Bratislava, it was calculated, on the basis of a number of surveys, that the risk of being involved in an accident increases with increasing blood-alcohol, until at levels of 150 mg. per cent and above, the risk is about 130 times as great as with zero blood-alcohol. It has also been found that, of drivers involved in accidents with high blood-alcohols, substantial numbers have been registered as chronic alcoholics. In Sweden, 3.5 per cent of the male population are registered as heavy drinkers, but these accounted for forty-eight per cent of all accidents in which alcohol was a factor.

Another way of demonstrating some of the facts is one adopted by Barbara Preston, who published the diagram given overleaf in the *Observer* newspaper (Figure 21). It shows the percentage of drivers killed and also the amount of traffic for different times on Saturdays. Only six per cent of the day's traffic is on the roads between ten p.m. and midnight, when nearly one quarter of the drivers are killed. The increase in casualties is not mainly due to the onset of darkness, as the ratio of the number of drivers injured between nine and ten p.m. and ten and eleven p.m. is higher in winter, when it is already dark by nine o'clock, than in summer when the onset of darkness might affect safety after ten p.m. The figures speak for themselves.

No one familiar with the facts can doubt for a moment that drink is a killer and that the most drastic ways of reducing drunkenness on the roads should be adopted. In Sweden, if the blood-alcohol concentration is above 150 mg. per cent, the punishment is imprisonment except when there are extenuating circumstances. If the blood-alcohol concentration is less than this but above 50 mg. per cent, a quite heavy fine is imposed. In Norway, too, a driver with more than 50 mg. per cent of blood-alcohol is considered to be 'under the influence'. In Denmark, a driver suspected of being drunk has a clinical medical examination and a blood test; if the blood-alcohol concentration is much over 100 mg. per cent, sentence is passed without clinical evidence, but below this concentration the decision

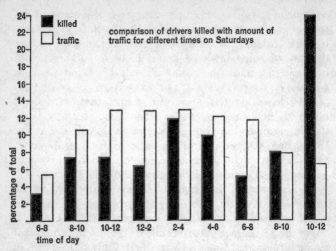

Figure 21. This figure shows the terrible increase in the number of accidents following the closing of pubs on Saturdays. It is also shown that this is not due to the amount of traffic on the roads, because this is the only time when the proportion of accidents greatly exceeds the proportion of traffic on the roads, being about four times as large (from an article by Barbara Preston, in the *Observer*).

is made on the medical evidence. Some such objective standard seems to be required, in order to reduce the undue leniency of juries who seem reluctant to convict even when the medical evidence is completely conclusive. Whether the estimation is done by means of blood test, urine test, or breathalyser – that is to say, by the analysis of alcohol in the breath – is relatively unimportant; the important thing is that an objective standard should be set.

It is often objected to this that some people actually drive better with a certain amount of alcohol under their belts,* and also that the effects of alcohol are different for different people, and that the objective standard does not take this into account. The main answer to the first point is a very simple one; people under the influence of alcohol *believe* that they drive better, whereas in actual fact they do not.

*This, surely, is a case of 'putting the quart before the hearse'!

Professor Cohen, of the University of Manchester, has shown this rather neatly. He presented professional bus drivers with a test in which they had to judge first of all whether they could drive the bus through a gap between two sticks pushed into the ground, and then they had actually to undertake the manoeuvre. He showed that not only was the performance worse as the alcohol increased, but he also found that the driver was more confident that he could do the impossible – drive an eight foot bus through a gap less than eight feet wide. This general increase in confidence and belief in one's own abilities, while in actual fact this ability was decreasing, is quite characteristic of the effects of alcohol and has to be taken into account in coming to any conclusions.

Regarding the differential effect of alcohol on different people, there can be no doubt that this is a perfectly correct observation. Indeed, on theoretical grounds, we would have expected something of this kind. Consider Figure 22 below. It represents a continuum from extreme introversion to extreme extraversion. Let us now consider a person (A) located exactly in the middle. He has equally far to go to either extreme, and he will be shifted in one direction or the other by doses of stimulant or depressant drugs. Compare him now with person B who is already very extraverted. He has very little space left to go to the extraverted end, but a great deal of space to go to the introverted end. Consequently, he should be very tolerant of stimulant drugs, and very intolerant of depressant ones. Exactly the opposite should be true of Mr C., who is located near the introverted end; he should be tolerant of depressant drugs but intolerant of stimulant ones. Much evidence has accumulated to show that this is indeed so. We shall see in a following chapter on crime, that the typical behaviour disordered child and adolescent, with his extraverted personality, benefits from stimulant drugs and is capable of absorbing a great amount of this type of drug, much more than would be possible for the average person or for the introvert. Alcohol has exactly the opposite tendency. The introvert is more tolerant of it than is the extravert, provided that the

two are equated for habituation. Alcohol thus does not only
have extraverting effects, but the shift in the extraverted
direction is more dramatic and brings the extraverted
drinker near the point of no return more quickly. Now, it
has been shown that it is the extravert, who is more a
danger, who also tends to drink more, so that we have a
multiplication of risks. The person predisposed to accident
proneness, in terms of his personality, is also the person
predisposed to increasing his accident proneness by way of
alcohol ingestion.

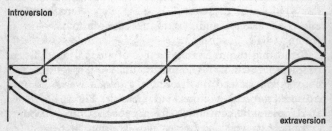

Figure 22. This diagram shows the position of three people, A, B, and C,
on the extraversion/introversion continuum. B is an extravert, C is an
introvert, A is an average person. Depressant drugs, like alcohol, have
extraverting effects and should, therefore, be more dangerous for B,
who is already very near the extraversion extreme, than for A or C. On
the other hand, B should be more tolerant of introverting (stimulant)
drugs, like amphetamine or caffeine, which would be rather more
dangerous for C. A would be expected to be intermediate between the
two for both types of drug.

There are two final points, and the first, I think, is vital.
We have noticed, in earlier chapters, that one characteristic
of extraversion is the quick growth of inhibition and the
resulting decline in vigilance. Now, there is some suggestive
evidence that in a fair number of accidents what is responsible is the decline in vigilance resulting in fairly lengthy
involuntary rest pauses of the kind we have discussed previously. During such an involuntary rest pause the driver is
in fact, for all practical purposes, asleep, and is not paying
any attention to the task at hand; no wonder that he
becomes involved in accidents during such periods. Now,

involuntary rest pauses are much more frequent and much longer in extraverts than they are in introverts, and alcohol, being an extraverting drug, has the effect of increasing the occurrence and prolonging the incidence of such involuntary rest pauses. The individual, of course, is quite unconscious of what is happening and has no idea that he is becoming a danger to himself and to everybody else. Neither are these involuntary rest pauses necessarily related to his ability to walk along a chalk line or to multiply digits in his head, or carry out any of the routine tasks demanded by a medical examiner. Thus, he may feel that he is perfectly fit to drive because he can carry out tasks of this very simple routine nature, whereas in actual fact he is not fit to drive, because of the large number and long duration of involuntary rest pauses which make him a considerable hazard on the road. Even the slightest amount of drinking increases his liability to be involved in an accident because it increases these involuntary rest pauses. No talk of not being susceptible to alcohol will get the driver out of this particular dilemma, because not being conscious of these involuntary rest pauses, he would have no way of assessing their number or duration in his own driving record.

I think it is difficult to disagree with Barbara Preston, who ends her article on the drunken driver thus: 'If new legislation were introduced in this country making it an offence punishable by disqualification to drive with more than, say, 50 mg. per cent in the blood, and if this were strictly enforced by the police taking in the first case breath tests on those driving away from public houses, would this not deter many people from driving after drinking? And would this not be a good thing? The pleasure of driving after drinking does not justify 500 killed and 2000 or 3000 maimed a year.'

One further point: there is ample evidence from laboratory investigations that when people are presented with a task giving them the chance either to go fast and make many errors, or go slow with few errors, under these conditions extraverts elect to go fast, whereas introverts prefer to make few errors. We would, therefore, expect extraverts and people who have been drinking to go fast, at the risk of making errors, where we would expect introverted people and people who have not been drinking to lay more stress on error-free driving, even at the risk of going rather slowly. There is little direct evidence on this point, but many people, particularly motorists, often declare that speed itself is not an important consideration in the number of accidents which occur. What is the empirical evidence? In 1935, the 30 miles per hour speed limit was introduced in London and, at first at least, it was respected by drivers. The annual report of the Commissioner of Metropolitan Police stated that, 'The clearest single item of evidence in regard to the value of a limit on speed can be found by comparing the pedestrian fatalities caused by (1) vehicles of the private-car class which were brought within the 30 miles per hour speed limit on 18 March, and (2) commercial vehicles which were subjected to speed limits before that date. The statistics for the second quarter of the year, when the general speed limit was enforced and generally respected, show that, whereas there was no appreciable change in regard to the pedestrian fatalities caused by vehicles of the commercial class, the corresponding fatalities caused by private cars were brought down by fifty per cent, compared with the previous quarter.'

Some countries have made the opposite experiment; that is to say, they have abolished speed limits. This was done in recent years in Germany, but casualties increased so much that the speed limits had to be re-introduced, being now very similar to the British ones.

Of particular interest is an experiment carried out in Providence, a small town in southern New England, where a 25 miles per hour speed limit was rigidly enforced from 1938 onwards. Statistics are available for the years before and after the enforcement of this speed limit.

The figures for 1937 and 1938 are, respectively, as follows.

Children killed 7, as opposed to 1.

Adult pedestrians 3, as opposed to 12.

Car drivers 9, as opposed to 0.

Total injured, 1,432, as opposed to 713.

Overall, therefore, there is a drop of over 50 per cent in the numbers of killed and injured. These figures, and many similar ones accumulated all over the world, leave little doubt that strict speed limits, properly enforced, are very important in reducing the traffic toll. The arguments brought forward against this view by motoring organizations are not very convincing. What they tend to say is that the good driver knows when it is safe to go fast and he will merely be hindered by rules which force him to go at a slower speed. Even if this were true, it still remains a fact that the good driver is not distinguished in any way from the bad driver, who may also consider himself to be a good driver although, in actual fact, he is not. He will, therefore, go fast when free to do so, under conditions where he constitutes an actual danger. As, unfortunately, the great majority of drivers are bad rather than good, it follows that the truly good must suffer with the truly bad who believe themselves to be good, in the interests of greater overall safety. Being an enthusiastic driver and hopefully belonging to the 'good' class, I regret this conclusion, but I see no logical fallacy in it and, for the sake of the greater good of the community, I cannot but feel that we must give up our undisputed right to go at any speed we like. Theory suggests that extraverts would go fast even when it was not safe, would consider themselves good drivers, and would be impatient of any restrictions on the speed at which they were allowed to drive. This is not a good combination of qualities, and one which is likely to lead to a greater incidence of accidents. Really high speeds should be reserved for special motorways and even there American experience has shown that such high speeds can lead to terrible, multiple accidents.

We may conclude this chapter by saying that a good deal is in fact known about accidents and accident proneness, and that already psychologists can make suggestions, albeit of a rather commonsense variety only, which should, if adopted, lead to a considerable reduction in the terrible toll which accidents take of our national life. What is suggested more strongly by the evidence, however, is the importance of further research guided by psychological theories of the kind discussed here. For the purpose, it would seem most desirable to introduce into this country the traffic courts and traffic clinics so frequently found in Canada, in the United States, and on the Continent. Drivers and pedestrians involved in accidents, and particularly people guilty of motoring offences whether or not these led to accidents, are studied by these clinics in considerable detail, are given psychological tests, and the accidents in which they were involved are studied with great care, to obtain further knowledge on the causes of accidents and personality correlates of accident proneness. A good deal of what we know in this field has been the result of the work of these traffic clinics, and their study of the best way of dealing with the accident repeater has given us much of the little knowledge we have in this particularly difficult field of cure and treatment. It seems eminently desirable that traffic clinics and traffic courts dealing only with motoring offences should be set up as separate units, thus relieving the ordinary courts of an ever-growing burden of cases for which they are not properly prepared and which they cannot deal with in any satisfactory manner. Such courts and clinics, working in intimate cooperation with psychologists, sociologists, and psychiatrists, and being encouraged to carry out and commission special research projects, would seem to carry our best hopes for reducing the terrible number of accidents on the roads.

7 Crime, Conscience, and Conditioning

We have noted in a previous chapter that there is a 'neurotic paradox'; it is interesting to note that there is also a 'criminal paradox'. The nature of the paradox is rather similar. In the case of the neurotic, we notice that he carries out a series of actions which in the end are self-defeating. The neurotic does the thing he does not want to do and fails to do the things he does want to do. He seems to stand outside the general law of hedonism which appears to govern human and animal reactions generally. Much the same is true of the criminal, particularly the recidivist. In spite of being caught, sentenced, and sent to prison many times, the recidivist seems unable to learn that his particular line of conduct does not lead him to greater happiness, satisfaction, and contentment, but rather lands him in eternal trouble and may in the end lead to his spending the greater part of his life in prison.

Like the neurotic paradox, so the criminal paradox has been with us ever since recorded history began, and it is curious that people concerned with the administration of the law and with the maintenance of order have persisted, through thick and thin, in a belief which is patently contradictory to facts, and which has no empirical backing. This belief may be put in the following way. Human beings are, in the main, rational; they make a kind of hedonic calculus of the consequences of their actions, and prefer those which, on the whole, lead to greater happiness to those which, on the whole, lead to unhappiness. If it is desired that a particular line of conduct should be discouraged, then an appropriate punishment should be established which could be made to follow, as invariably as possible, the pursuit of that line of conduct; this would introduce a bias in the hedonic calculus which would dissuade people from going in for this particular line of activity. You don't want people to steal, murder, and rape others; consequently, you establish certain penalties which follow upon stealing, murdering, and raping. In this way, so the theory runs, it should be possible to eliminate conduct of this kind from our society.

Unfortunately, the theory itself is psychologically faulty and would not, on the whole, be expected to work very well. One of the main reasons for this is the existence of a law which we may call the 'law of temporal sequence'. What this law says is, roughly, that if a given action is followed by two consequences, one of which is agreeable or positive, while the other is disagreeable or negative, then the probability of a person's undertaking this action will be proportional not only to the respective size of the positive and negative reactions, but also to their temporal sequence. The nearer a given consequence, whether positive or negative, is to the action itself which produces it, the more powerful will its influence be, whereas the further removed in time the consequence is, the less will it determine the probability of that action being taken. If the positive and negative consequences are roughly equal, then the action will be undertaken if the positive consequences occur prior to the negative ones, and it will not be undertaken if the negative ones occur prior to the positive ones. This law has some similarities with the well-known principle of the lever; if weights are suspended on two sides of a bar pivoted in the centre, then the power of the weights to depress their side of the bar depends not only on the actual weight itself, but also on its distance from the fulcrum; the further away from the fulcrum, the greater the power of the weight to depress its side of the bar.

This principle will be seen to work very strongly *against* the hope that punishment will have any very marked effect on criminal activity. The reward of the criminal activity comes almost at once; the murderer has the immediate satisfaction of seeing his hated victim die, the rapist has the immediate satisfaction which is produced by his sexual relief, and the thief has the immediate satisfaction of possessing the desired object or objects. Thus, the positive rewards produced by the activity are not only large but immediate. The negative results of criminal activity, if they occur at all, occur at a very much later time. Weeks, months, or even years may elapse before the criminal is brought to justice, before a trial can be held, and before a conviction can be secured. Thus, the negative effects of punishment are very much attenuated by the long period of time elapsing between crime and retribution. Further-more, while the positive consequences of a crime are fairly certain, the negatives ones are very much less so. It is impossible to give any kind of accurate statistics regarding the proportion of crimes which are committed and finally brought home to their perpetrators; many crimes, perhaps the majority, are never reported to the police and, there-fore, are not in fact known. Even of those that are reported to the police, however, not more than about a quarter are finally brought home to the criminal; and when it is realized that this figure includes cases which are simply 'taken into account', the number of crimes in which retribution comes as a consequence of that particular crime is probably not much more than ten or fifteen per cent, if that. Under the circumstances, therefore, we would not expect punishment to be very effective, and indeed, throughout the centuries, experts have kept complaining about the sad refusal of human nature to fall in line with their theoretical predilections, and have commented upon the deplorable ineffectiveness of prison, the stocks, or even flogging, as deterrents to criminal behaviour.

Does psychology have any reasonable alternative to offer, as far as the theoretical basis of criminal and law-abiding behaviour is concerned? Curiously enough, the explanation here will be, in effect, similar to that given of neurotic behaviour. In doing so, we shall make use of the notion of 'conscience', which is widely used as an alternative hypo-thesis to the hedonic calculus, in accounting for moral behaviour. Many people would argue that human beings are not in fact motivated entirely, or even mainly, by some form of hedonic calculus; they would argue that behaviour is determined rather by a person's conscience, or inner guiding light, or however we like to express this indefinable moral consciousness, this 'moral law within us' which we find easier to recognize than to describe. The notion of conscience often takes on a religious colour because it is, in the main, the Church which talks in these terms, but there is nothing necessarily religious about it; many famous atheists and agnostics have also appealed to their conscience for justification of their actions, and we can accept the notion of conscience descriptively without necessarily accepting any kind of divine or supernatural origin for it.

How does conscience originate? Our contention will be that conscience is simply a conditioned reflex and that it originates in the same way as do phobic and neurotic responses. What happens is that the young child, as he grows up, is required to learn a number of actions which are not, in themselves, pleasant or pleasurable and which may in fact go counter to his desires and wishes. He has to learn to be clean and not to defaecate and urinate whenever and wherever he pleases; he has to suppress the overt expression of his sexual and aggressive urges; he must not beat other children when they do things he does not like; he must learn not to take things which do not belong to him. In every society there is a long list of prohibitions of acts which are declared to be bad, naughty, and immoral, and which, although they are attractive to him and are self-rewarding, he must nevertheless desist from carrying out. As we have pointed out before, this is not likely to be achieved by any formal process of long-delayed punishment, because what is required to offset the immediate pleasure derived from the activity must be an immediate punishment which is greater than the pleasure and, if possible, occurs in closer proximity to the crime. In childhood it is possible for parents, teachers, and other children to administer such punishment at the right moment of time; the child who does something wrong is immediately slapped, told off, sent upstairs, or whatever the punishment may be. Thus we may regard the evil act itself as the conditioned stimulus and we may regard the punishment –

the slap, the moral shaming, or whatever the punishment may be – as the unconditioned stimulus which produces pain or, at any rate, some form of suffering and, therefore, of sympathetic response. On the principle of conditioning, we would now expect that after a number of repetitions of this kind, the act itself would produce the conditioned response; in other words, when the child is going to carry out one of the many activities which have been prohibited and punished in the past, then the conditioned autonomic response would immediately occur and produce a strong deterrent, being, as it were, unpleasant in itself. Thus the child would be faced with a choice between carrying on, obtaining the desired object but, at the same time (and perhaps even earlier), suffering from the unpleasant punishment administered by its conditioned autonomic system, or desisting from carrying out the act and thus avoiding this punishment. Provided that the conditioning process had been carried out efficiently and well, it is predictable, on psychological principles, that the choice would lie in the direction of desisting rather than carrying out the act. Thus the child acquires, as it were, an 'inner policeman' to help in controlling his atavistic impulses and to supplement the ordinary police force which is likely to be much less efficient and much less omnipresent.

In this process of conditioning, much help would, of course, be forthcoming from the law of generalization which we have encountered previously. Each special undesirable activity would go through this process of conditioning, but conditioning would also generalize to other similar activities, helped in this particularly by the process of verbal identification, or naming, which is involved when the mother calls all the undesirable activities 'naughty' or 'bad' and draws attention, in this way, to their essential similarity. There is much evidence, from laboratory investigations, that generalization follows the rules of our language and thought patterns, so that, as we have pointed out before, when a person is conditioned to give a galvanic skin response to the word 'cow', he will also give one to the words 'goat' or 'sheep', but not to the words 'house', or 'tree', or 'flower'. In this way, then, there is built up in the child a complex, interwoven, generalized autonomic re- action to a great variety of activities which have been punished in the past and which have been linked together through a labelling process by the mother, by the teacher, by his peers, and by anyone who has been in direct contact with him. In this way, so we suppose, does conscience grow, and this is why we believe that it is justifiable to say that conscience is a conditioned reflex.

We may perhaps illustrate this hypothesis by reference to some experiments carried out by R. L. Solomon at Harvard. Using six-month-old puppies, who had been starved for twenty-four hours, he carried out the following set of experiments. He would sit on a chair in a room bare of all furniture except for two feeding dishes which were placed to the right and left of the chair. In one of the dishes was boiled horsemeat which was very much liked by the puppies; in the other dish was a less well-liked commercial dog food. The dishes could easily be changed from side to side and the puppy usually chose the horsemeat a few seconds after he had come into the room. The experimenter carried a rolled-up newspaper, and whenever the puppy touched the horsemeat, the experimenter would swat him over the rump with the newspaper. In this situation, eating the horsemeat is the immoral activity which is to be elimi- nated and which constitutes the conditioned stimulus; swatting the puppy over the rump is the unconditioned stimulus which produces a certain (very slight) degree of pain and displeasure in the animal. By making the swatting coincide temporarily with the touching of the horsemeat, it is hoped to establish a conditioned reflex which would, in due course, evolve into a miniature 'conscience' with regard to eating horsemeat.

After a few days the animals learned to avoid the horse- meat when the experimenter was sitting in his chair and immediately went over to eat the less preferred dog food. Now came the crucial part of the experiment. The puppies were kept without food for two days and then brought to the experimental room, but with the experimenter himself absent. The two dishes of food were there again, horsemeat in one, commercial dog food in the other. All the puppies would gobble up the dog food very soon and then begin to react to the large dish of horsemeat. As Solomon himself describes it: 'Some puppies would circle the dish over and over again. Some puppies walked around the room with their eyes towards the wall, not looking at the dish. Other puppies got down on their bellies and slowly crawled forwards, barking and whining. There was a large range of variability in the emotional behaviour of the puppies in the presence of the tabooed horsemeat. We measured resistance of temptation as the number of seconds or minutes which passed by before the subject ate the tabooed food. Each puppy was only given a half-hour a day in the experimental room in the presence of the horsemeat. If he did not eat the horsemeat at that time, he was brought back to his home cage, was not fed, and a day later was introduced into the experimental room again.'

There was a considerable range of resistance to temptation. One puppy only took six minutes before it went and took the boiled horsemeat, whereas another one kept away for sixteen days, when the experiment had to be terminated because the puppy was in danger of starving. On the whole, the experiment showed very strongly the effects of the conditioning procedure and the fierce 'conscience' built up in these animals through a process of 'punishment' which was very slight indeed. If one can compare the pain produced by starvation with that produced by a light swat on the rump, there is no doubt that the slight pain produced by the swatting was very much less severe than that produced by the hunger which these animals suffered. Yet, in spite of the fact that any rational calculus of pleasure and pain should have led them to eat the boiled horsemeat, nevertheless they did not do so. The conditioned autonomic reactions apparently sufficed to keep them in line for a remarkably long period of time. It is interesting to note that Solomon carried out similar experiments on children with similar effects.

Solomon hypothesized that conscience could be divided

into two parts, which he called *resistance to temptation* and
guilt, and he tried to see whether, in his particular experiments, he could separate out the causal antecedents of
these two states. He provides some evidence to show that
when puppies are walloped just as they *approach* the
tabooed food, high resistance to temptation is built up.
When such puppies, however, do submit to temptation,
they fail to show any emotional upset or guilt following the
'crime'. On the other hand, if puppies are left to eat some
of the horsemeat before they are walloped it is still possible
to establish an avoidance of the meat, but in this case there
is a considerable degree of emotional disturbance following
the 'crime', and this Solomon calls a *guilt reaction.* He found
that the presence of the experimenter was not required to
elicit this guilt reaction, although it seemed to intensify it.
'Therefore, we believe that the conditions for the establish-
ment of strong resistance to temptation as contrasted with
the capacity to experience strong guilt reactions, is a function of both the intensity of punishment and the time during
the approach and consummatory response-sequence at
which the punishment is administered. We feel that
delayed punishment is not very effective in producing a
high level of resistance to temptation, but it is effective in
producing emotional reactions after the commission of the
crime.'

Even lowlier organisms than the dog can be made to act
as if they were obeying the dictates of conscience. A very
famous experiment, dating back to the early 1920s, is that
of the pike and the minnows. The experimenter divided a
very large tank into two parts by putting a glass plate in the
middle. He then put some minnows into the one part and a
very hungry pike in the other. The pike rushed towards the
minnows, which constituted the conditioned stimulus, but
banged its snout against the invisible glass plate (the
unconditioned stimulus), thus producing considerable pain
and frustration. The pike repeated this performance time
and time again, until it finally became conditioned to
ignore the minnows. Now the experimenter removed the
glass plate and the pike continued to ignore the small fish

although it was now swimming right amongst them. It was very much like the fable of the lion lying down with the sheep, having developed a conscience and become a vegetarian. Unfortunately conditioning does not generalize very much in fish, and the pike's conscience only extended to the particular minnows it had been trained to regard as potential sources of blows on the snout; when new minnows were put into the tank with the old, the pike had no compunction in polishing these off. Perhaps with some training in generalizing the pike could have become a more saintly figure than it did, but the experiment shows clearly the need for all possible help in stimulus generalization in the conditioning of 'conscience' which language can give in the human child.

What determines the differences between individual organisms in response to this situation? As we saw, some puppies resist temptation for only six minutes or so, while others may resist for a period of eight hours or more, with temptation constantly arising because of the increasing amount of hunger. Similarly, it is obvious with human subjects that they, too, differ very much in their response to training, upbringing, and moral persuasion, ranging all the way from the saint at the one end to the moral imbecile, or psychopath, at the other: from the person whose whole conduct is permeated and determined by moral and ethical considerations to the person to whom moral and ethical concepts are simply meaningless words, and who is a prey to every passing impulse. What is it that discriminates between these two ends of the scale of morality? One possible hypothesis which may occur to the reader is that the moral imbecile, the psychopath, the criminal are more highly emotional and this emotional instability is reflected in their behaviour. It is often pointed out in courts, for instance, that kleptomaniacs steal when they are in a state of high emotional disturbance, and this is sometimes said to be an extenuating circumstance. There is a good deal of evidence, to which we shall refer later on, showing that criminals as a whole are indeed high on the factor of emotional lability and do not differ very much in this from hospitalized neurotics. But before going on to any discussion of this point, let us consider another experiment, this time dealing with rats. These rats are taught to run to a trough the moment a bell is rung; in that trough they will then find a pellet of rat food. Having so trained them to run to the trough and devour the pellet, the experimenter then introduces a quite arbitrary social rule: to wit, that it is impolite to eat the pellet until three seconds have passed from the beginning of the signal. Any rat that eats before the three seconds are up is punished by a fairly mild electric shock to its feet.

The experiment is carried out on two strains of rats, the emotional and the non-emotional ones; the reader may remember that we have already encountered the rats and the experiment in the first chapter of this book. Each rat has a choice of three ways of behaving. It can either behave in a criminal or psychopathic manner by eating the food immediately it is put into the trough and thus brave the punishment which follows immediately; it can behave in a normal, socialized, integrated manner by waiting a few seconds and then eating the food when it is safe to do so; and it can, lastly, react in a neurotic manner by refusing to eat the food at all, even when it is perfectly safe to do so. Now, among the non-emotional rats, the integrated, normal type of reaction is much the most frequent; the great majority of these animals learn to take the food when it is safe to do so. What about the emotional animals? Here we find that both the non-integrative types of activities are much more pronounced. These animals tend either to behave in a neurotic fashion, not eating the food at all, or they tend to behave in a psychopathic–criminal fashion and eat the food immediately, thus suffering the shock which follows it. The results of this experiment, then, do not seem to support the notion that emotion is the crucial factor which discriminates criminal behaviour from all others; rather, it suggests that there is a link between neurotic and criminal activity on the one hand, as opposed to normal, integrated behaviour on the other. We may put this in terms of our diagram in an earlier chapter, by saying that both neurotics and criminals may be expected to have high scores on neuroticism or emotionality, and that any difference between them must be sought along different lines.

It is not difficult to find a theoretical reason for the difference between these extreme groups, the criminal on the one hand, the neurotics on the other. We have shown that the typical anxiety, phobic, obsessional-compulsive, and other characteristics of the neurotic are, in part, due to his over-readiness to form conditioned responses firmly and strongly. We have also shown that there exist theoretical grounds for believing that conscience is in fact a conditioned response. It would seem to follow, quite logically, that the absence of conscience in criminal and psychopathic persons may be due to the fact that they form conditioned responses very poorly, if at all, and even when these responses are formed, they extinguish quickly. It will also be remembered that we found conditioning to be related to extraversion/introversion in the sense that introverts condition well, extraverts poorly. We may then express our hypothesis by suggesting that just as neurotics of the dysthymic type tend to be introverted in personality, so criminals and psychopaths would be extraverted. Figure 14 (page 87) shows the results of a large number of different studies carried out by means of questionnaires on various groups of neurotic, normal, criminal, and psychopathic groups. It will be seen that, on the whole, our hypothesis is borne out. The neurotic groups tend to be strongly introverted, the criminal groups strongly extraverted, and both types of personality tend to have a strong emotional component which we have labelled 'neuroticism' in the diagram.

There is, fortunately, also some direct evidence available to show that psychopaths and at least certain types of criminals do in fact condition very poorly. Various different types of conditioning have been tried out on these groups, and the general consensus seems to be that just as dysthymic neurotics condition very much better than normals, so psychopaths and criminals condition decisively less well than do normals. On the whole, therefore, it seems reasonable to conclude that this particular hypothesis has some predictive value, and may serve to explain a good deal of criminal conduct.

The picture we have painted so far is probably rather one-sided, because we have concentrated entirely on what we may call negative conditioning; that is to say, the build-up of 'conscience' by means of punishment. There is, of course, the other side of the medal which is the build-up of systems of behaviour and conduct through immediate reward. We must stress here, as before, the 'immediate' aspects of reward, just as previously we stressed the 'immediate' aspects of punishment; in so far as we are concerned with conditioning, delays of even quite a short duration are fatal to the build-up of conditioned responses; it is the immediacy which counts. Unfortunately, there is very little experimental work along these lines which would be directly relevant, and consequently we cannot go much farther than mentioning this very important way of investigating our general hypothesis.

As an illustration, however, and a possibly useful analogue, we may discuss briefly the treatment of encopresis in children. Encopresis is to faeces as enuresis is to urine; in other words, encopresis is a disorder in children in which they cannot control their bowel movements and soil their clothes during the daytime instead of going to the toilet. We have shown, in the treatment of enuresis, which may be regarded, in a sense, as typical of the building-up of a new conditioned response through a process of 'punishment', that this particular 'crime' can be eliminated quite easily; what can we do with a child who soils his pants? In theory, perhaps, we could rig up an apparatus which would also produce the kind of result which our 'bell and blanket' does in the case of enuresis. In practice, however, there are too many difficulties in the way to make this a feasible proposition. What was done in fact was an attempt to use conditioning by reward. Nurses were instructed to observe how soon after eating the child would defaecate. They were then instructed to put him on the toilet before this moment had come, to praise him very much to give him sweets and other rewards the moment he had defaecated in the toilet. Thus a process of conditioning was set up, and it was soon noticeable how quickly the child learned to go to the toilet when the need arose, even without the nurse being required as an extra stimulus.

We must now return to our discussion of personality. There is additional evidence which strongly suggests that there is indeed a connexion between criminality and extraversion. As an example of an additional type of evidence, consider the so-called Porteus maze test. This test consists of a series of printed mazes which have to be traced by the subject who is given a pencil and certain instructions, such as that he is not to lift his pencil to cross lines, or cut corners. Originally, this was intended as an intelligence test and it is still widely used in that manner. However, Porteus also advocates the use of a qualitative score or Q score, in which he scores various types of misdemeanour, i.e. of behaviour which goes counter to the test instructions. Thus, if the subject lifts his pencil, crosses a line, or cuts a corner, these errors will be summed and weighted, to constitute finally a global qualitative score. Extraverts have been found to have higher scores on this test when attention is paid only to the Q score, and much work has been done recently to show that delinquents also have much higher scores than non-delinquents. In America, the average score of delinquents, in a number of investigations, has been found to be about fifty, that of non-delinquents in the neighbourhood of twenty. In England, the figures are thirty-five for delinquents, and fourteen for non-delinquents. In both countries, therefore, the delinquents incur over twice as many penalties as do the non-delinquents, thus aligning them with the extraverts in studies on normal people; but it is also interesting to note that Americans, as a whole, tend to score more highly in the 'delinquent' or extraverted direction than do English people, a result which, in view of the much higher rate of criminality in the United States and their often-remarked-on extraversion, is not perhaps very surprising. On this test, then, there is no doubt that again we find a relationship between

extraversion and criminality, much as was hypothesized in
our original theory, and found in work with questionnaires,
ratings, and with conditioning techniques. There are
various other tests of an objective nature which have been
used in a similar manner and the outcome seems to be
always in the same direction, linking extraversion and
criminal conduct.

A quite different line of evidence, which may be of considerable importance, however, for various reasons which
we will discuss later on, is that deriving from an analysis of
physique, or body build. The belief that there is a relationship between physique on the one hand and personality,
mental and physical disorders, on the other, is very old
indeed; Hippocrates, who lived about 430 b.c., already
discriminated the two main types of body build, the long,
lean, linear type which is often referred to as 'leptosomatic',
and the thickset, stocky type, sometimes referred to as
'pyknic'. He taught that the leptosomatic type was more
liable to tubercular disorders, whereas the pyknic type was
more liable to apoplexy and coronary disorders. Many
other writers have followed him in this distinction between
these two body types, some adding a third, more or less
intermediate, type, but little was in fact added to Hippocrates' original teaching until Kretschmer, in Germany, put
forward the hypothesis that these body types showed a close
and probably causal relationship with the two main forms
of psychotic disorder. Schizophrenics, he taught, tended to
be leptosomatic in body build, whereas manic-depressive
patients tended to be pyknic. There is some truth in this
hypothesis, although the relationship is not close enough to
be of any very great use diagnostically or psychiatrically.
However, Kretschmer inspired many other people to take a
closer look at body build, in the first place, and the relationship between body build and personality, in the second, and
much work has since been done on normal people to show
that there is a distinct relationship between leptosomatic
body build and introversion, and pyknic body build and
extraversion. The reader might like, in this connexion, to
think of Sir Winston Churchill, who is both typically

extraverted in many ways, and also a pyknic, and of Neville Chamberlain, who was rather introverted in personality and leptosomatic.

If extraverts are, on the whole, pyknic in body build, and if criminals, on the whole, tend to be extraverted, then we would expect that delinquents and criminals would have pyknic body build as compared with the normal population. Is this true? There have been many studies in the United States, carried out particularly by Sheldon and by the Gluecks, in which they found very dramatically that there was indeed a relationship of the predicted kind. Similarly, in this country, there have been several studies, notably one by T. C. N. Gibbens, in which a similar relationship was established. The reader may like to have a look at Figure 23 in which are given distributions of scores obtained by tubercular patients, American students, American delinquents, and patients suffering from cancer of the breast and cancer of the uterus. Low scores in this context denote pyknic body build: high scores denote leptosomatic body build. It will be quite clear that tubercular patients tend to have scores which stretch farther in the direction of leptosomatic body build than any other group. American students make a fairly reasonable control group, showing the kind of distribution to be expected on the average from an unselected population. The American group of delinquents, it will be seen, is very much more pyknic than either the tubercular group of patients or the American students. Most pyknic of all will be seen to be the two cancer groups; they are cut off at a score of six, which is only about the average score for the American student group, some of the members of which have scores ranging up to sixteen. The delinquents will be seen to cut off at a score of ten. The mean score for the delinquents is between three and four, but for the total American student group, is around six. There is thus no doubt that our prediction is in fact verified. (The reader may be interested to know that some recent work on cancer has shown conclusively a marked relationship between cancer and extraversion, just as we would expect from the figures on body build in the Table.

Similarly, a relationship has been established between coronary disorders and extraversion. The reasons for these relationships are obscure, but it is interesting to see how the early theories of Hippocrates, of almost 2,500 years ago, can now be seen to have had a strong element of truth in them.)

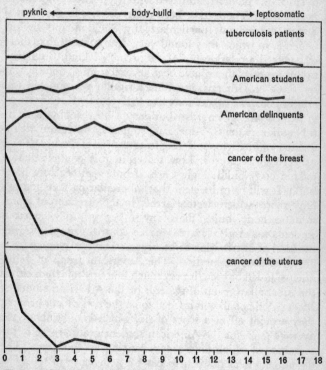

Figure 23. This diagram shows body build of various groups from the pyknic (broad, thickset) to the leptosomatic (lean, thin), and it will be seen that cancer patients and delinquents tend to be pyknic on the whole, tuberculosis patients leptosomatic. The original figures on which these diagrams are based were reported by W. H. Sheldon.

It has often been suggested that the correlation between body build, on the one hand, and personality and disease, on the other, may be interpreted as giving some grounds for believing in the physiological and biological determination of conduct. This may or may not be so; it is certainly not a necessary deduction from the facts. The pyknic boy may indeed inherit his body and also a predisposition to

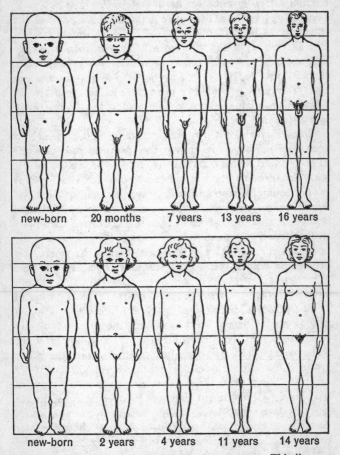

Figure 24. Bodily proportions change as a person grows up. This diagram shows the proportionately large head of the infant as compared with the small head of the adolescent (from K. Conrad, *Der Konstitutionstypus*).

criminal conduct, in the genes and chromosomes which he receives from his parents; it is also possible, however, that he is born with a body which enables him to carry out aggressive and other acts which the leptosomatic boy could not possibly imitate. Thus the possession of a certain bodily configuration might by itself determine conduct and personality. We would require a more direct proof of the influence of heredity on criminal conduct than that furnished by body build, and we will later on turn to a consideration of any such evidence which may be available. Before doing so, however, I would like to suggest another line of inquiry which has been opened up recently by Klaus Conrad in Germany, and which leads into many promising side ways.

Conrad starts out by considering a figure, which is reproduced above; it shows the proportional changes in body build which occur as the child grows up. It will be seen 'for instance that in the new-born the head is disproportionately large and gets proportionately smaller and smaller as the years go on. These changes are quite typical and occur in all races and in both sexes. Conrad then plots the relative size of head as a proportion of the length of the body against age. This is shown in Figure 24, where this proportion will be seen to decrease from about 27 per cent at birth to about 13 per cent at age twenty-four. In addition, Conrad studied the relative size of head in typical groups of adult pyknics and leptosomatics, and his results are shown in Figure 25, where it will be seen that the pyknics typically resemble, in this respect, children of a mean age of eight, whereas leptosomatics resemble, on the whole, the adult group. Conrad concludes that, with respect to this matter at least, the pyknics have remained at a lower level of ontogenetic development than the leptosomatics, and may be therefore considered to be relatively less mature. Another measure frequently used is the chest-shoulder index, i.e. the width of the shoulder as a percentage of the total chest diameter. This index, too, changes rapidly with the years, as is shown in Figure 26, and also given in the figure are results obtained from typical adult pyknic and leptosomatic groups. Again, it will be shown that the pyknics, on the whole, resemble the younger groups, whereas the leptosomatics resemble the more adult ones.

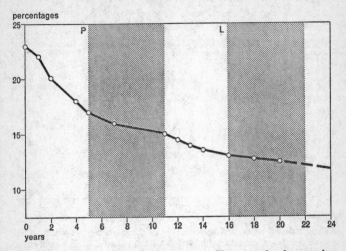

Figure 25. The curved line in this diagram illustrates the decrease in proportional size of head to body with advancing years. It will be seen that the new-born has a head which is about 23 per cent of the total size of the child, whereas the adult has a head which is only 13 or 14 per cent of the size of the body. It can be shown that adults with pyknic body build resemble the child rather than the grown-up with respect to this proportion, whereas adults with leptosomatic body build do not resemble children in this way. The column headed *P* shows the proportions observed in a group of pyknic subjects, whereas the column headed *L* shows the proportions observed in a group of leptosomatic adults. It will be seen that in this respect the adult pyknic resembles an eight-year-old child (from K. Conrad, *Der Konstitutionstypus*).

Conrad considers a large number of similar tables and figures, and comes to the general conclusion that, 'with respect to its morphological proportion, the pyknic body build is related to the leptosomatic body build as is an ontogenetically early compared with an ontogenetically later stage. In other words, those proportions in which there are marked differences between pyknics and leptosomatics

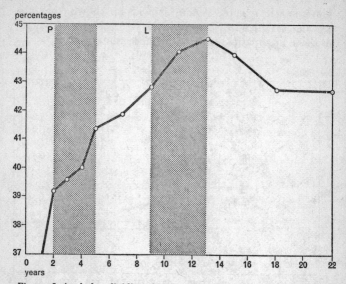

Figure 26. An index dividing the size of the chest by the width of the shoulder shows a considerable change with age, as indicated by the curve in this diagram. Here also grown-ups with pyknic body build resemble children, in this case the four-year old, whereas adults with leptosomatic body builds are displaced towards the values typical of older groups (from K. Conrad, *Der Konstitutionstypus*).

will also be different for young as compared with older children.' Conrad also went on to demonstrate the corollary of this; to wit, that where there were no changes with age in bodily proportions, there were also no differences between pyknics and leptosomatics.

He went on to demonstrate a similar principle in the physiological field, where he studied a variety of autonomic and other reactions, and in the psychological field, where he came to the conclusion that, here too, the pyknic, compared to the leptosomatic, is characterized by behaviour patterns which distinguish the child from the adult, or the younger from the older person. Altogether, the summary of his findings may be interpreted to mean that the pyknic tends to be more immature in personality, behaviour, and bodily functioning than is the leptosomatic. This conclusion, which has a good deal of empirical research to support it, could be of very great importance indeed, particularly when we remember that people of pyknic body build tend to be extraverted in personality, whereas people who are leptosomatic in body build tend to be introverted in personality. Now, one of the characteristics of the extravert, of course, is a certain immaturity of behaviour which, in our theory, is best accounted for by saying that he has failed to benefit as much as the introvert from the conditioning processes which society has imposed on him. To put it in a slightly exaggerated form, one might say that the ten-year-old introvert has formed as many conditioned responses as the fifteen-year-old extravert and is, therefore, more mature in his behaviour to that extent. This whole concept of maturity, of course, is very difficult to quantify, and a good deal of the discussion relating to it is perhaps of little scientific value. It is Conrad's great contribution that he has shown a way of quantifying this notion, and linking it up with testable, morphological, and physiological theories. We shall revert to this notion of maturity again later, in discussing the findings of Denis Hill and others, who showed that the electroencephalographic tracings from the brains of psychopathic individuals showed patterns characteristic of children rather than of adults, leading these workers to the notion of the 'immature E.E.G.' picture.

It is difficult to doubt, on the whole, that there is a true relationship between extraverted personality patterns and criminality. We must now ask ourselves what lies at the basis of this relationship. Is it due largely to environmental influences and factors such as differences in training, background, and so forth; or is it rather due to innate features of the personality, which are inherited from the parents? At the turn of the century, the hereditary view was very much in vogue, particularly due to the efforts of the Italian writer, C. Lombroso, who postulated the doctrine of *il reo nato*, i.e. the born criminal. He postulated that not only were all criminals possessed of an innate tendency to antisocial behaviour, but also that they were characterized by certain physical stigmata by means of which they could be recognized. When English and American workers failed to discover these stigmata in the majority of criminals studied, Lombroso's whole approach fell into disrepute, but this may have been a case of throwing out the baby with the bath water. It will be remembered that we have found considerable evidence, in an earlier chapter, of hereditary determination of both extraversion/introversion, on the one hand, and neuroticism, on the other. If, as we have also shown, criminals tend to be high on extraversion and high on neuroticism, then it would seem to follow that quite likely there is a considerable genetic component which may be responsible for their particular position in our descriptive personality framework. Is there any direct evidence for this?

The obvious method of attacking this problem is, of course, the twin method which we have already encountered. The first person to make use of it was a famous German investigator, J. Lange, who published his well-known book, *Crime as Destiny*, in 1928. He went through the Bavarian prison population, in an endeavour to find prisoners who had twins, and found thirty such, thirteen with identical, and seventeen with fraternal twins. Now, in line with the paradigm of twin research discussed in an earlier chapter, we would expect that if heredity played a powerful part in the causation of criminal conduct, then more of the identical twins would be concordant – that is to say, would also have committed crimes – than would be the case with the fraternal twins. Lange found that among the thirteen identical twins the second twin had also been imprisoned in ten cases and had remained clear of the law in three. Among the seventeen fraternal pairs, the second twin had also been imprisoned in two cases, whereas in fifteen cases he had remained clear of the law. 'This leads us to the following conclusion: as far as crime is concerned, monozygotic twins on the whole react in a definitely similar manner, dizygotic twins behave quite differently.'

Lange went on to compare the criminality of ordinary brothers and sisters with that of dizygotic twins. As he points out: 'If we found that among dizygotic twins both were punished more often than happened on an average among ordinary brothers and sisters, we should have to allow for the influence of environmental conditions more or less according to the degree of difference between expectations and the facts discovered.' In other words, ordinary brothers and sisters should both be criminal just about as frequently as dizygotic twins because in both cases the contribution of heredity is pretty much the same. If it were found that dizygotic twins were both criminal in a higher proportion of cases, then that might be due to the fact that being a little more similar, being born at the same time, and so forth, the twins were treated more alike by environment and, therefore, had a better chance of both being criminal or both being free of crime. In that case, we would have to allow environment certain contributory effects; but Lange's comparison shows that this is not so. He concludes that, 'In the case of crime in dizygotics a similar environment plays only a very small part.'

We may wonder why not all the identical twins were in fact concordant. If indeed crime is destiny, as Lange postulated, then why are there individual exceptions? There are, of course, several answers to this. In the first place, the other twin may have been criminal but may not have been found out. As we pointed out before, the efficacy of criminal investigation is by no means one hundred per cent, and we cannot expect that where chance plays such a large part concordance should be complete. Another answer is produced by Lange, who found that in the two undeniable cases of monozygotic pairs where only one was a criminal, in each case the criminal brother had suffered a severe head injury. In another discordant pair, one but not the other of the twins suffered from goitre, a disease which undoubtedly alters the character. Now it has often been found that brain damage has an effect on the normal person which essentially displaces that person's character in the direction of greater extraversion. Goitre, and the associated hormonal upsets in the nervous system, may work in a similar direction. We see, therefore, that in discordant cases there has been a definite interference with the intact nervous system of the twin, possibly leading to crime. These exceptions, then, may only be apparent and not real. In the concordant dizygotic pairs also there were some interesting features which should be mentioned. In the case of one pair, for instance, Lange suspected a common hereditary venereal infection. 'If this was a fact it might be that we were not dealing in this case so much with innate tendencies to crime as with the results of considerable brain lesions which, as we know, often predispose to antisocial behaviour.' On the whole, Lange's results were very impressive indeed, and no one who has read through the very detailed case histories which he gives, and which demonstrate not only a concordance between identical twins in criminality but also in many cases in the specific type of crime and in the specific way in which the crime was carried out, can doubt that heredity plays an important part in antisocial behaviour.

How have his conclusions fared at the hands of his successors? It was inevitable that so important a conclusion should be tested by many other people, and indeed, both in Germany and in the United States, numbers of similar studies have been carried out. On the whole, some investigators found even more impressive evidence for the influence of heredity, others – and that is perhaps the majority – found that the evidence supported the general conclusion, but at a rather less impressive level. In the Table below

	No. of Twin Pairs	Identical	Fraternal	Percentage concordant I	F
Adult crime	225	107	118	71	34
Juvenile delinquency	67	42	25	85	75
Childhood behaviour disorder	107	47	60	87	43
Homosexuality	63	37	26	100	12
Alcoholism	82	26	56	65	30

Proportion of concordant twins of criminals, homosexuals, and alcoholics; separate figures are given for identical and fraternal twins.

I have given the results of all studies which have

been published since his work (including his own), and the reader may draw his own conclusions. As far as adult crime is concerned, concordance rates are over double for the identical twins, as compared with the fraternal twins, and also in the case of childhood behaviour disorders for the two types of twins. The difference is considerably less for juvenile delinquents, but there, of course, the number of cases is rather small. Included in the Table are figures for homosexuality and alcoholism, although these may not be as relevant as the other figures given. Homosexuality is a crime in this country, but not on the Continent, and alcoholism may easily lead to crime and is very often associated with it. Consequently, the figures may be of some interest as they stand. On the whole, they do strongly support Lange's main point, which was that there is a powerful hereditary component to antisocial behaviour, although we may not be able to go all the way with him in considering it as overpoweringly important as he postulated, when he said 'crime is destiny'. The fact that he slightly exaggerated the position does not justify other writers, however, in completely disregarding the facts and treating crime as being exclusively a social phenomenon depending on environmental influences. Certainly we must admit that environmental influences are important, but also important is the precise structure and nature of the organism on which these influences impinge, and to neglect the biological nature of the organism and stress exclusively the social nature of the environment is to commit an error which is equally reprehensible. All behaviour, as we noted before, is the product of an interaction between heredity and environment, and to exaggerate the influence of one and denigrate the influence of the other is not the mark of a scientist.

One example of such interaction will, of course, be quite obvious to the reader. We have postulated that socialized behaviour is, in fact, a product of a process of conditioning which is very much interfered with, in some cases, by the constitutional nature of certain individuals which does not permit them to be conditioned as easily as the majority of people. It will be equally apparent, however, that even a very conditionable sort of person will not acquire the socialized responses which we consider so desirable if he is not in fact made to undergo the process of conditioning which we have regarded as essential. Thus, the son of a thief and a prostitute may never receive the type of conditioning which is required to make him into a law-abiding citizen; indeed, quite the opposite may happen. If he is easily conditionable, then it is quite possible that he may be put through a process of conditioning which in fact promotes as desirable those forms of conduct which society as a whole regards as undesirable. This possibility is perhaps not as serious as might be thought at first. Even in the most criminal of groups, certain patterns of behaviour are still required in order to make even such a small subsection capable of functioning; there must be 'honour among thieves'. Even the hypothetical prostitute mother and thief father of our example will find it essential to produce some kind of obedience among their offspring, at least to their own dictates, and even parents such as these will find it necessary to insist on the virtues of telling the truth and respecting property, at least as far as inter-family relations are concerned. Also, the children will receive a good deal of conditioning from their peers, from their teachers, and from other outside influences, so that, on the whole, they will not be entirely without some form of conditioning in socially desirable habits. It must nevertheless be stressed strongly that the outcome of a process of conditioning is due to two factors. One is the actual conditionability of the subject, the other is the number of pairings between the conditioned and the unconditioned stimuli. The former is a constitutional factor, the latter an environmental one, and both clearly cooperate in producing the final outcome.

Why have so many people tended to disregard the evidence about hereditary factors in criminality? One of the reasons undoubtedly is that those who advocated the importance of hereditary principles in this connexion failed to point to any recognizable mechanism through which these principles could express themselves. It is clear that behaviour as such cannot be inherited; to talk about the inheritance of criminality is, in a sense, meaningless. The theory we have been discussing supplies the missing link, because clearly the physiological basis on which conditioning and other learning mechanisms are dependent is precisely the kind of thing that can be inherited in the ordinary way, and this difficulty, therefore, can be overcome.

The other objection which is often made is that the acceptance of hereditary causes leads to therapeutic nihilism. If neurosis or criminality is due to a person's inheritance, then, so it is argued, nothing can be done about it. Consequently, it would be much better to investigate environmental causes, because these, so it is argued, can be altered and we can hope in this way to influence a person's behaviour. This argument, which is frequently put forward, is in fact quite erroneous. Let me take as an example the disease known as phenylketonuria. It affects about one child in forty thousand in this country and in Europe and North America. It can be tested in hospital by adding ferric chloride to a specimen of the patient's urine, making it appear green. Most patients with this condition are suffering from severe mental defect, although in a few cases intelligence quotients near the average have been found. Phenylketonuria is due to a recessive gene, and its mode of inheritance is exceptionally well-known. In view of the fact that heredity plays a completely decisive part in the causation of phenylketonuria, it might be thought that nothing could be done to save patients suffering from it. However, closer investigations show that children affected by phenylketonuria are characterized by an inability to convert phenylalanine into tyrosine, and can only break it down to a limited extent. It is believed that this causes mental defect, because of the poisonous character of some of the incomplete breakdown products of phenylalanine. Now phenylalanine is, fortunately, not an essential part of diet, provided that tyrosine is present and, consequently, it is possible to prescribe a diet to these children which is almost free of phenylalanine. In this way we can avoid the poisoning of the system, and it has been shown that if this procedure is adopted in the first few months of life, the degree of mental deficiency can be considerably reduced. In other words, a precise knowledge of the mode of inheritance and the specific way in which this disorder works is not only not antagonistic to therapeutic efforts, but provides the only possible basis for such efforts.

Is there any similarly dramatic suggestion we can make in relation to criminality? There is one notion which has been experimented with to some degree, and which may illustrate the kind of thing we are looking for. We have pointed out, in an earlier chapter, that the position of a person on the extraversion-introversion continuum can be changed by the administration of drugs, stimulant drugs, like caffeine, amphetamine, and benzedrine, pushing him over in the direction of greater introversion, whereas depressant drugs, like alcohol and the barbiturates, push him over in the direction of greater extraversion. Now we have also seen in this chapter that criminal and psychopathic behaviour tends to be found predominantly in extraverted persons, and we have tried to show how this is linked with certain inherited features of their nervous system. If all that is wrong with the criminal and the psychopath is his excessive extraversion, then would it not be feasible to shift him in the direction of greater introversion by the administration of some stimulant drug and, in that way, reduce his antisocial, criminal, psychopathic type of behaviour? Much of the early work in this connexion was done with the so-called behaviour-disordered children, and it was found, fairly uniformly, that the administration of stimulant drugs produced an immediate and, in some cases, almost miraculous effect. Children became much quieter, ceased to shout, became less excitable, more law-abiding, they took in their lessons much better, and altogether improved by something like fifty or more per cent. This work, carried out by many investigators in several different countries, left no doubt about the distinct improvement which can be produced by introverting drugs in behaviour-disordered children. They also found two facts which may be regarded as corollaries.

In the first place, they found that these children were much more tolerant of these drugs than were average children, or even adults. This is predictable on theoretical grounds; the extravert, being a long way away on the continuum from the extreme introvert position, can tolerate a lot of introverting drug before he reaches an extreme position; the introvert, being already quite near the extreme introvert position, can tolerate only a limited amount. The other fact which came out fairly clearly is that depressant drugs made these children very much worse, a point which is interesting, because in the neurotic type of person, barbiturates and other types of depressant drugs are used medicinally to produce a quietening down of excessive fears. This finding also, then, is in line with our hypothesis.

In more recent years, studies have been carried out with adults and adolescents. Professor D. Hill, for instance, found that personalities which responded best to stimulant drugs were those showing 'an aggressive, bad-tempered, and generally hostile tendency in inter-personal relationships, which is manifested whenever frustration is met ... The most satisfactory patients are those predominantly aggressive characters capable of warm inter-personal relationships but continually wrecking such relationships – in marriage, in employment, and in friendship – by impulsive irritability, minor acts of violence, and intolerance of others ... They quickly become intolerant of any treatment which does not materially help them. They are well-known for their fickleness, their irresponsibility, and their tendency for moral lapses.' Other characteristics of this group are their very deep sleep, a late cessation of nocturnal enuresis, an excessive or morbidly excitable sexual appetite, and often an immature E.E.G. pattern of brain rhythms. He also notes alcoholism, nail-biting into adult life, apparently motiveless petty pilfering, acts of arson and sabotage in the adolescent. All these fit in well with our theory. Thus, it will be remembered that we regard enuresis as a failure to establish the appropriate conditioned response, and, therefore, cannot be surprised to find such a failure so prominent in a group characterized by poor conditioning. Indeed, many people have remarked on the excessive predominance of enuresis in delinquent and criminal groups, where its occurrence may be as high as twenty-five or more per cent. Similarly, deep sleep may be expected in a group characterized by strong inhibitory potentials in the cortex.

Of particular interest is a recent experiment comparing the reactions to amphetamine of three matched groups of delinquents. (See also discussion in Chapter 2.) One group was used as a control and not given any form of drug; a second group was used as a placebo group – that is to say, they received dummy pills; and the third group received amphetamine. A composite rating for symptoms and behaviour was applied to these groups before and after the administration of the drug. The changes from *pre* to *post* were as follows: for the control group there was a slight improvement equal to two points; for the placebo group there was a slight improvement equal to two points; for the amphetamine group, however, there was a very marked improvement, amounting to twenty-two points. Taking this result with all the others, we must conclude that there is a remarkable and very quick shift from psychopathic behaviour-disordered and criminal types of conduct to more normal social and ethical types of conduct, due to the administration of relatively slight doses of an introverting drug.

How does this process work? It is possible, though doubtful, whether the increase in conditionability which is attendant upon the administration of stimulant drugs has very much to do with this effect. The times involved, which are usually of the nature of days and weeks rather than months, makes it unlikely that sufficient periods are allowed for conditioning to take place, and it is usually found that when the administration of the drug stops, the patient reverts more or less to his previous level of misconduct, although perhaps there is some evidence to suggest that the level may be a little lower than before. It seems very tempting to suggest an experiment in which a deliberate attempt is made at socialization conditioning while the patient or the criminal is under the influence of a drug of this type. It seems that in this way we might overcome the difficulties presented by his lack of conditionability, and achieve what, without these artificial aids, might be the impossible.

However, given that in the typical situation this is not the way in which the drug exerts its influence, we must consider alternatives. The most likely perhaps is a reduction in the 'stimulus hunger' which we noted in an earlier chapter as one of the consequences of cortical inhibition. Under the drug, the individual becomes less hungry for external stimulation and, therefore, temptation becomes weaker for him. As an example of this, we may take sexual activity. As Hill points out, in the group of psychopathic patients studied by him, the occasions of completed coitus were not always excessively frequent, but the continuous erotic titillation and preoccupation may be a source of great distress to the partner and to the patient himself when he is refused. This, he says, forms the basis of jealous accusations and marital disharmony. After administration of the stimulant drug, he found that the libido was greatly reduced and that sexual activity declined considerably, together with a reduction in the appetite of hunger and a diminished aggressive tendency. He concludes that, 'This effect would seem to be the significant operative factor in the treatment of the behaviour disorders by this drug.' Other causal chains, of course, can be postulated, and the reader might like to do so for himself, on the basis of what was said in earlier chapters about the relationship between Eysenck's demon and extraverted behaviour. Much remains to be discovered about the precise way in which these drugs work, but the fact can hardly be doubted that they have the postulated introverting and socializing effects.

There is one other objection which is sometimes made to this whole approach and even to the use of animals for carrying out experimental investigations supposedly relevant to criminal conduct. Do not human beings, so it is said, have freedom of will, which is disregarded by work of this kind? Rats and puppies, no doubt, have their place in the scheme of things, but a man is not a mouse, and what may be applicable to lowly creatures like those experimented with in the laboratory does not and need not apply to human conduct. It is unsafe to extrapolate from what is done by the rat to what is done by the human.

There is no doubt some truth in this general statement. Undoubtedly rats do not necessarily or always behave in a manner which is analogous to the behaviour of human beings. The essential point, however, is not to allege or deny that there are points of contact, but to carry out experiments to see to what degree there is or is not a certain degree of correspondence between the two. We have, in this chapter, drawn attention to some rather curious similarities between the behaviour of animals and the behaviour of human beings; whether these are mere analogies without any value, or whether they show the way to theories which may eventually help us to combat criminal and antisocial behaviour better, must be a question which had best be left to future research. It would be equally futile to assert that a relationship had, without doubt, been established, as it would be to assert that no such relationship was possible. Too many similarities in conditioning and learning behaviour have been shown to exist when animals and human beings are compared to deny a biological basis of considerable similarity for these various types of organisms, and if we maintain, as I think we must, that social behaviour is learned and conditioned very much as are other types of behaviour, then it is difficult to deny that a knowledge of these laws, whether derived from animal work or from human work, is an essential prerequisite for an understanding of such behaviour.

The question of free will is a philosophical one which need not really concern us very much. It is doubtful whether in fact the term 'free will' has any meaning. To the biologist, behaviour is a product of heredity and environment, the two combining to produce a particular state of motivation and a particular set of habits. The resulting behaviour is the outcome of this combination and, as such, must be supposed to be completely predetermined. It is difficult to see what, in this context, 'free will' could possibly mean. Does it mean that conduct is completely undetermined by motives, by habits, by past experience, or by anything else? Is it merely analogous to saying that blind chance may enter into human conduct, irrespective of inheritance or environmental pressure? It is not impossible, of course, that such an assertion may be true; Heisenberg's law of indeterminacy applies to the behaviour of the most minute, sub-atomic particles, and prevents us making exact predictions about the behaviour of these particles. In view of the fact that our bodies are made up of large numbers of atoms and molecules, which themselves are constituted of these sub-atomic particles, it is not unreasonable to imagine that chance may indeed enter into the determination of behaviour and, to that extent, reduce the determinism implicit in our stress on heredity and environment as efficient causes of conduct. But this is a far cry from the notion of 'free will' which, if it means anything at all, certainly means something very different from the interference of blind chance events at a sub-atomic level with the expression of human motives, desires, fears, and so on.

Whatever may be the philosophical status of free will, the scientist and the psychologist, and the biologist generally, no less than the physicist, must proceed in his investigations on the assumption that whatever he studies is determined and is subject to scientific law. It is only to the extent that he fails to establish such laws that his fundamental hypothesis can be defeated. It is very much too early in the history of psychology to ask to what extent the facts fail to bear out this fundamental hypothesis; in a thousand years, no doubt, we shall have more facts to base an opinion on.

Our discussion has some relevance to a topic which has been debated very fiercely ever since the formulation, in 1843, of the M'Naghten Rules. These rules were laid down by the judges in answers given to questions put to them by the House of Lords, and they relate to the question of whether a defendant should be exonerated on grounds of insanity when accused of murder. The original M'Naghten, labouring under the delusion that he was the victim of persecution, tried to assassinate Sir Robert Peel, whom he considered responsible for his misfortunes, and in mistake, killed the latter's secretary. He was acquitted, and the widespread dissatisfaction produced by this acquittal led to a debate in the House of Lords, which finally resulted in the formulation of these famous rules. These rules say, firstly, that everyone is presumed sane unless the contrary is proved. To be exonerated on the ground of insanity, the rules presume that the defendant must, at the time of the crime, have been suffering from a defect of reason due to a disease of the mind such that he either did not realize the nature and quality of his act, or did not realize that the act was wrong in the eyes of the law. If the defendant was suffering from a partial delusion, his responsibility must be assessed in the light of the facts as he imagined them to be.

These rules, emphasizing reason, as they do, and disregarding emotion, are a reflection of the times in which they were formulated, and much criticism has been directed at them. There has been a good deal of clamour to include among the grounds for exoneration 'irresistible impulses'. Some people have found even this to be insufficiently broad and have suggested that the law of insanity should be amended to provide for acts which are not impulsive in this sense, but which result from a continued state of emotional disorder.*

Whole books have been written on this topic, but it cannot be said that the outcome of all this discussion has been very positive. If it is true that a person's behaviour and conduct are the product of his heredity and his environment, then it is quite clear that no person is 'responsible' for his conduct, in the sense which the Law requires, and, therefore, any attempt to lay down arbitrary divisions as to responsibility must result in failure. That this is true is quite obvious from the fact that in almost every trial psychiatrists are ranged on both sides, giving their views, making contradictory claims for the responsibility or otherwise of the accused. To say that no one is 'responsible', in this philoso-

---

*A new way of applying Pascal's saying about 'Le cœur a ses raisons que la raison ne connaît pas.'

phical and jurisdictional sense, is not to say that no one should be punished; the purpose of the punishment, after all, is to protect society and to re-educate the criminal. It does not require the postulation of responsibility in him to permit society to re-educate him in ways which can be shown scientifically to be successful in altering his conduct. This is true both of those who are and those who are not legally insane under the M'Naghten Rules.

Discussion about the M'Naghten Rules, of course, is only kept alive because the death penalty is still in existence. In recent years, discussions about the death penalty have concentrated more and more on the one crucial point, which is whether or not it does in fact deter people from committing those crimes for which the death penalty is still in force. Statistically the evidence seems to be quite convincing that in fact the death penalty does not deter people from committing crimes. It has been shown quite frequently that when the death penalty is abolished there is no increase in the number of murders, and when it is re-introduced there is no diminution in their number. Further, since 1957 when the Homicide Act kept the death penalty for some offences and abolished it for others, it has been precisely in those offences for which the extreme penalty was retained that the murder figures have risen. There are still emotional arguments against the abolition of the death penalty, but the rational arguments seem to be very much in favour. One curious obstacle always seems to be the subjective feeling which many people have that they themselves would be prevented from indulging in murder and other types of activities punished by death, and that consequently other people, who are perhaps more likely to commit these crimes, would be equally deterred.

It is difficult enough to introspect when one is confronted with a decision of this type, but to imagine that one can introspect without even being in a situation like this is very optimistic indeed. Very little is in fact known about the mental processes of people who indulge in activities which are subject to the death penalty, but perhaps I can speak on this point with greater authority than most, because, unlike the great majority of my readers, I have several times indulged in conduct which was in fact subject to the death penalty, and have, therefore, some notion of the way in which at least one person feels about this deterrent. The first of these occasions arose when, after Hitler had come to power in Germany, he promulgated a law according to which no one was allowed to take more than a very limited amount of money or valuables out of the country. My mother and I decided that the time had come for the family fortunes to be transferred to a safer place, and accordingly we smuggled all our money and valuables from Germany to Denmark, knowing full well that if we were caught then not only would we be condemned to die but the death which we would suffer would be a particularly long-drawn-out and distressing one, as inmates of a concentration camp. But neither of us was deterred by the prospect or indeed gave it much of a thought. I have often heard it argued that a person who commits a murder or indulges in other conduct for which the death penalty is enforced must be insane, as in any rational calculus of pleasure and pain the punishment must be so very much greater than any reward he can hope to obtain from his 'crime'. This seems a curiously *a priori* and unrealistic definition of insanity, and all one can say is that the psychological problems involved in deterrents are much more complicated and subtle than is imagined by those who hold such a simple-minded belief.

Having now completed our rapid survey of some of the facts and theories in the field of criminality, we can see that just as the melancholic of Galen corresponds to the major group of neurotics in our society, with his combination of introversion and high emotional lability, so Galen's choleric corresponds to our modern criminal with his combination of extraversion and high emotionality. Note that it is, in both cases, the combination of extraversion or introversion with high emotionality which provides the danger. There are many introverts and extraverts who lack this emotional lability, and who lead perfectly normal lives without falling prey to neurotic disorders and without falling foul of the law. It is the strong driving force which is produced by an arousal of the emotions which must be held responsible for so much of the irrational and self-defeating conduct which characterizes our modern civilization. Even a few hundred years ago, strong emotions of this type might have had a useful outlet in hand-to-hand combat, in running away from enemies, in sailing the seven seas, and in other stressful and dangerous situations. In modern times such strong emotions are, in fact, an anachronism; they have no useful part to play and have no proper outlet in everyday activity. It is perhaps for this reason that they seek outlets in neurotic or criminal behaviour and that there has been such a marked increase in these types of behaviour. (I am assuming here that the alleged increases are, in fact, real ones; there is, unfortunately, very little evidence of a trustworthy nature to substantiate this hypothesis, but from a consideration of historical records, it is not impossible that such substantiation might in fact be found in due course.) However this may be, there is no doubt that the over-emotional arousal which characterizes the neurotic and the criminal is an essential part of his personality and one which would repay much closer study than it has received in the past. With criminals in particular, we tend to be suspicious of anyone wishing to study their personalities, because we feel that the criminal, through his acts, has lost the right to sympathy, and requires in some way to be punished instead. This, I am convinced, is an entirely wrong approach, if only because punishment has the effect of greatly exacerbating the strong emotional reactions already present in most criminals, thus making it much more difficult, rather than easier, to prevent such a person from carrying on with his particular set of criminal habits. This, of course, is also the reason why, as the evidence suggests, penalties such as flogging and other particularly cruel inflictions of pain, have such very poor and often contradictory results. If man were indeed *homo sapiens* acting entirely on rational calculation alone, then to make the punishment more severe should indeed ensure that fewer crimes would be committed. As, however, this hypothesis has received no confirmation from experimental work, and has so often been shown to be inapplicable to human or to animal conduct, we must, I think, throw it overboard and rely more on empirical investigations. Much as it may go counter to our grain, we must accept Samuel Butler's proposal in *Erewhon*, that criminals should be treated rather than punished. This, at least, is the conclusion one comes to if one wishes to stress rehabilitation and the reduction in criminal conduct; punishment may give greater satisfaction in a rather primitive sort of way, but it does not lead to an improvement in the general situation, and we should add perhaps that psychology also suggests one further point which is of particular importance. It is that we are not justified, on rational grounds, in treating all criminals alike and in imagining that the same treatment will benefit all of them. Quite clearly, treatment should be designed specifically for each person, depending upon his degree of extraversion or introversion, neuroticism or stability, and, particularly, the ease or difficulty with which he forms conditioned responses. Much the same, of course, is true of the upbringing of children. It is time we stopped the eternal swing of the pendulum from 'spare the rod and spoil the child' to *laissez faire*; we must realize that the extraverted child, who conditions only with difficulty, requires a fairly stern conditioning discipline in order to avoid seeing him grow up into a hooligan, delinquent, and a possible criminal, whereas the introvert who conditions all too easily requires a much more easygoing kind of discipline, in order that he, in turn, should not grow up into a neurotic. There are many books on the upbringing of children and on criminality which peddle panaceas. Before we suggest any ways of changing human behaviour and conduct, we should be aware of the fact that human beings are not an unending stream of uni-ovular twins, but differ profoundly one from the other, and that what is 'sauce for the goose' is by no means necessarily 'sauce for the gander'. To treat everybody alike signifies an ultimate abdication from the stand which the psychologist must take: that individuality is sacrosanct.

Suggested Readings

CHAPTER ONE: Eysenck, H. J. (Ed.) *Handbook of Abnormal Psychology*. London; Pitman, 1960.

CHAPTER TWO: Eysenck, H. J. *The Dynamics of Anxiety and Hysteria*. London; Routledge and Kegan Paul, 1957.

CHAPTER THREE: Rachman, S. (Ed.) *Critical essays on psychoanalysis*. Oxford; Pergamon Press, 1963.

CHAPTER FOUR: Wolpe, J. *Psychotherapy by reciprocal inhibition*. Stanford; Stanford University Press, 1958.

CHAPTER FIVE: Eysenck, H. J., and Rachman, S. *The Causes and Cures of Neurosis*, London; Routledge and Kegan Paul, 1964.

CHAPTER SIX: Welford, A. T. (Ed.) *Society; problems and methods of study*. London; Routledge and Kegan Paul, 1962.

CHAPTER SEVEN: Eysenck, H. J. *Crime and Personality*, London; Routledge and Kegan Paul, 1964.

Index

MORE ABOUT PENGUINS
AND PELICANS

Penguinews, which appears every month, contains
details of all the new books issued by Penguins as
they are published. From time to time it is
supplemented by *Penguins in Print*, which is a complete
list of all books published by Penguins which are in
print. (There are well over three thousand of these.)

A specimen copy of *Penguinews* will be sent to you
free on request, and you can become a subscriber
for the price of the postage – 30p for a year's issues
(including the complete lists), if you live in the United
Kingdom, or 60p if you live elsewhere. Just write to
Dept EP, Penguin Books Ltd, Harmondsworth,
Middlesex, enclosing a cheque or postal order, and
your name will be added to the mailing list.

Other Pelicans by H. J. Eysenck are described
overleaf.

Note: *Penguinews* and *Penguins in Print*
are not available in the U.S.A. or Canada

Other Pelicans by H. J. Eysenck

Sense and Nonsense in Psychology

There are many topics in modern psychology about which speculation has been rife for hundreds of years. Much has been written (and some of it amusing) on the powers and dangers of the hypnotic trance, the wonders of telepathy and clairvoyance, the possibility of the interpretation of dreams, the nature and assessment of personality, and the psychology of beauty. In recent years, however, much experimental evidence has been collected regarding all these topics, and the author has attempted to give a reliable account of it in this book, frankly acknowledging ignorance when the facts are still in dispute, and boldly putting forward a definite point of view where the evidence appears to justify it. Throughout the book emphasis is laid particularly on the detailed discussion of the facts, leaving to the reader the decision as to whether the conclusions drawn are justified.

Uses and Abuses of Psychology

In this book H. J. Eysenck indicates both to what extent the claims made for psychology are justified, and to what extent they fail to have any factual basis. The discussion is very fully documented by references to the most important and relevant researches carried out in this country and abroad. Topics dealt with are the testing of intelligence, selection procedures in schools and universities, vocational guidance and occupational selection, psychotherapy and its effects, national differences, racial intolerance, Gallup surveys, industrial productivity, and many others.

Also available

KNOW YOUR OWN I.Q.

CHECK YOUR OWN I.Q.